THE BUILDING OF
THE EIGHTEENTH-CENTURY CHURCH

Tetbury, Glos
Rebuilt by Francis Hiorne in 1777–81, "upon an elegant and regular Gothic plan"

THE BUILDING OF THE
Eighteenth-Century Church

BY

BASIL F. L. CLARKE

LONDON

S · P · C · K

1963

First published in 1963
by S. P. C. K.
Holy Trinity Church
Marylebone Road
London N.W.1

Printed and Bound in Great Britain
by Hazell Watson & Viney Ltd
Aylesbury, Bucks

BR
758
C5

CONTENTS

LIST OF ILLUSTRATIONS

The photograph reproduced on the jacket is of Gunton, Norfolk, rebuilt in 1765. The architect was Robert Adam.

INTRODUCTION

THE NINETEENTH-CENTURY attitude to the church building achievements of the eighteenth century is well known. The complete churches were pagan and un-churchlike, and ought to be rebuilt if possible: if not, they should be recast into a more Christian style and a more correct plan. Additions and alterations to medieval churches should certainly be removed: no one could tolerate a white-painted cupola, or an aisle raised in brickwork to make room for a gallery, or a classical porch. And all internal fittings must go— pews, galleries, organ case, three-decker, rails, altarpiece and ceiling; and the royal arms, benefactions boards and hatchments. There were, of course, some who objected to this kind of restoration, and there were architects who were prepared to spare a good deal; but that this was the ordinary attitude to the eighteenth century cannot be denied.

Pugin said that the adaptors of pagan architecture were "violating every principle that regulated the men whose works they profess to imitate . . . Vitruvius would spew if he beheld the works of those who glory in calling him master". There were, he admitted, some true principles in Classical architecture; but it was only the revivers of Gothic who understood them and carried them out. Ruskin would not even admit this: the Renaissance was the "foul torrent"; it was "base, unnatural, unenjoyable and impious". And of course neither Pugin nor Ruskin could say a good word for the frivolous Gothick of the eighteenth century.[1]

The Anglican ecclesiologists were very conscious of living in a new age. The Church of England was being marvellously revived, and, in many ways, recovering its rightful heritage. And of that heritage Gothic churches, correctly designed and correctly arranged, were certainly a part. The churches of the previous century seemed old-fashioned, musty, and rather grotesque—and they recalled the things

[1] I have tried to follow the common practice, and to use "Gothic" for the real thing, and "Gothick" for the eighteenth-century variety, which involved nothing more than pointed windows, battlements, and large quatrefoils. But it is difficult to be consistent. Some eighteenth-century buildings are serious enough to be called Gothic. And, in quotations from eighteenth-century writers, the real thing may be called Gothick.

that the Tractarians and their followers were trying to get rid of: Erastianism, the domination of the Church by the Whig party, pluralities, parish clerks, the metrical psalms of Tate and Brady, and so on. Of course they were not fair to the previous century: but there is no doubt that a real revival was going on, and most of the ecclesiologists were young men: they did not stop to find balanced words: like Hurrell Froude, they wanted to make a row in the world.

So they let fly at pagan architecture, with its shams and false construction, together with "outworn corruptions" such as pews and galleries; and made it quite clear that those who upheld them were out of date.

Altogether, the propaganda had considerable effect. It came to be taken for granted by most educated people that Georgian architecture, and Georgian churches in particular, were debased and contemptible.

This attitude was maintained by writers of guide books well into the twentieth century. Some of the Little Guides could hardly mention eighteenth-century work without making unpleasant remarks. "The church is a wretched building, showing much eighteenth-century rubbish, and was built in 1728." (Gayhurst, Bucks.) "The chancel was added in 1750, but the bad work of that period has been considerably improved in recent years." (Blurton, Staffs.) "The 18th cent., unfortunately, did its best to spoil the old work; it inserted a 'classical' S. doorway . . .". (Cannock, Staffs.) ". . . vandals, who erected a miserable brick edifice in 1745." (Fairwell, Staffs.) "The rest of the church was rebuilt in wretched fashion in 1721." (Forton, Staffs.) "The church (St. Peter) was terribly maltreated in 1732, when a new tower of blue and red bricks—surely the last word in hideousness—was erected." (Gayton, Staffs.)

"Classical" is nearly always put into inverted commas, and so even is "architect". "Semi-classical", "pseudo-classical", or "quasi-classical" are common. Dr J. C. Cox, who wrote so many guide books, is sometimes appreciative, but he takes dislikes to certain churches, and can be very abusive. Sir Robert Taylor's church at Long Ditton, Surrey, was "an eccentric absurdity", and many churches of this period are, to Cox, "singularly mean" structures.

Now everything is changed, and the eighteenth-century churches are treated with respect, studied, photographed, and written about. This is satisfactory: but a Churchman may feel that the architectural writers have had the field too much to themselves. It is interesting to be able to point out the sources of the designs, and the influences that the architects may have felt; but the architects themselves were not necessarily very interested: they borrowed what they liked, without having any very strong opinions. And the vestrymen who employed them were certainly not. They wanted something neat and handsome, of course, but their main concern was to provide accommodation for the parishioners.

Behind all the church building there is the life of the parish. The architectural writer is not much concerned with this, but to a Churchman it must be the most important thing. The church was built, or altered, or enlarged, for the parishioners to meet in for the worship of God. That is why they exist; and that is why they are—or were—like that.

Addleshaw and Etchells have made this clear in *The Architectural Setting of Anglican Worship*; but they have said little about the actual building of the church. This book is an attempt to see eighteenth-century church building from the parochial point of view.

In some ways the life of a parish is not what it was. The churchwardens and the vestry no longer have any civil duties, and can no longer levy church rates. The inhabitants of a parish, in spite of Crockford's estimate of the population, are no longer all regarded as members of the Church: the electoral roll and the P.C.C. have introduced a kind of congregationalism into the system of the Established Church. People who live in the country generally know to what parish they belong, and, if they go anywhere, they go to their parish church. But in the towns parish boundaries count for very little.

Nevertheless, when there is church building to be done, the procedure is still recognizably the same. The P.C.C. has taken the place of the vestry, but the kind of discussion that goes on there is much the same as the debates of the vestry in the eighteenth century.

There is always the problem of raising money. The appeal to every one in the place, the gift day, and the sale of work, have taken the place of the church rate; and the appeal in *The Times*, and even sometimes on the radio, is our attempt to reach the wider public that was formerly reached by the reading of briefs. But the process would be familiar to a revenant from the eighteenth century, though he would be shocked by the enormous size of the estimates.

The petition for the faculty, the citation, and the issue of the faculty, continue as they always did. And, at the end, there is the same satisfaction when the work has been successfully done and paid for.

I do not suggest that modern writers on eighteenth-century churches are necessarily outside all this; they may, for all I know, be members of their P.C.C.s, and very much concerned with it. But they do not show many signs of familiarity with it—and I suggest that it is impossible to understand eighteenth-century churches thoroughly without some knowledge of what went on behind the scenes, and some sympathy with the parish life that produced them.

It is not my purpose to write about architecture as such, nor to bring in the names of architects, except in so far as they come into the records. I will only say that, if one approaches church building from this point of view, it is obvious that the well-known men are not in the centre of the picture. The average parish could never dream of employing Hawksmoor or Gibbs. They relied on local men: working masons who had a thorough training in their trade, and who knew enough about the Orders to carry them out fairly correctly; and carpenters, plasterers, and smiths who were, in their own ways, equally competent. Occasionally, of course, the name of a famous man does appear; but if his eminence was recognized, there is no special acknowledgement of it in the records. Mr Gibbs, like anyone else, had to deal with the vestry, or with a committee; and his plans had to give satisfaction to them. It is interesting to see how the names of men that we all know come in almost casually—just as it is to see the signature of a bishop, whose name comes in all the church histories, attached to the application for a faculty.

The truth is, that there was a good deal going on, and that a great many people were concerned in it.

Where there is any quotation from parish or diocesan records, it can be assumed that I have seen them for myself, and made my own transcription. Sometimes a detailed reference number is given. This means, of course, that the book, or paper, is in some library or record office. No doubt many are left out that ought to be in; but I have been looking at such records, in a desultory way, for over twenty years, and during that time there has been great progress in the way of making records accessible to the public. I am sure that some of the books and papers which I took from vestry safes, or saw in diocesan registries, must now be in record offices, and properly catalogued; but I could hardly check up on all of them. I know that some of the parish books that I saw in record offices are now returned to their parishes, after having been catalogued. So it was difficult to be consistent in giving references. But I have said nothing without authority.

The trouble with such a book is, that it could go on for ever. A few examples are chosen; and then one asks, "But why only those? Why not some more, equally to the point?" And the temptation is to go on for far too long. I hope that I have resisted it—but suspect that I have not always succeeded. I can only advise readers who think that I have overdone the quotations to leave some of them out. For those with stronger digestions, I have given some more lists in the appendices.

The chapter on Nineteenth-Century Alterations has been added as a reminder that few of the buildings with which the book is concerned can be seen in their original state, and that many have disappeared altogether.

My thanks to all who have helped. Certain clergymen have allowed me to look through their parish records, and there have been many people, whose names I never knew, or have forgotten, in libraries, diocesan registries, and record offices. I am particularly grateful to those in the Berkshire Record Office at Reading, whom I have frequently troubled during many years. I should also like to mention the assistant at the Staffordshire Record Office who, in 1954, stood beside me during my hurried visit, undoing the bundles of Quarter Sessions records, sorting out the petitions for briefs, and pushing them in front of me, leaving me with nothing to do but to write, and saving a great deal of time and trouble. Many others have been helpful, but no one else has made it possible to take so many notes in so short a time.

In addition I must thank those who have read the manuscript at various stages of its development, and have given useful comments and advice.

It could be objected, with reason, that it is rather arbitrary to keep to the eighteenth century. Neither the beginning nor the ending of the century is of any significance in the matter of church building, and the account might just as well begin at the Restoration—or, indeed, a good deal earlier—and continue into the nineteenth century. All I can say, by way of excuse, is that the line must be drawn somewhere, and that more has already been written about the beginning and the end of the period. I hope that someone will soon produce a study of the whole subject of church building and repair from the time of the Reformation to the early nineteenth century.

B. F. L. C.

I

THE VESTRY

THE CHURCHWARDENS—the officers of the parish in ecclesiastical affairs, and formerly in civil affairs as well—are given by the Canons the duty of maintaining the fabric of the church in repair, guarding the things that belong to it, and providing such things as are necessary for the services in it.

The Churchwardens or Quest-men shall take care and provide that the churches be well and sufficiently repaired, and so from time to time kept and maintained, that the windows be well glazed, and that the floors be kept paved, plain, and even, and all things there in such an orderly and decent sort, without dust or any thing that may be either noisome or unseemly, as best becometh the House of God, and is prescribed in the Homily to that effect. The like care they shall take, that the church-yards be well and sufficiently repaired, fenced and maintained with walls, rails, or pales, as have been in each place accustomed, at their charges unto whom by law the same appertaineth . . .[1]

The Homily for Repairing, and Keeping Clean, and Comely Adorning, of Churches is Number XV. It proves from Scripture that "God is well pleased, that his people should have a convenient place to resort unto, and to come together, to praise and magnify God's holy name", and that he is "highly pleased with all those which diligently and zealously go about to amend and restore such places as are appointed for the congregation of God's people to resort unto", and sore displeased with people who adorn their own houses, and neglect his. So our parish churches must be kept in good order. "For like as men are well refreshed and comforted, when they find their houses having all things in good order, and all corners clean and sweet; so when God's house, the church, is well adorned, with places convenient to sit in, with the pulpit for the Preacher, with the Lord's table for the ministration of his holy supper, with the font to christen in, and also is kept clean, comely, and sweetly, the people are more desirous and the more comforted to resort thither, and to tarry there the whole

[1] Canon 85.

6

time appointed them." The churches of England had been purged of superstitious abuses, for which we should be thankful; but now that they have been "scoured and swept from the sinful and superstitious filthiness, wherewith they were defiled and disfigured", they must be kept in decent condition.

The duty of repairing the church did not extend to the chancel: indeed, the word "church" was normally used to mean the building apart from the chancel. That was the business of the rector—or the lay rector, in the case of an impropriate benefice; though in some places the custom prevailed of the parish undertaking it.

If the church should be out of repair, the churchwardens must have a survey made, and obtain estimates, and forthwith convene a meeting of the vestry. The vestry is, or was, the council of the parishioners. At the present time, it meets only for a few minutes each year to elect the churchwardens before the annual church meeting. By the Local Government Act of 1894, and subsequent Acts, the vestry lost all its powers, except those concerned with the administration of the church, and ecclesiastical charities. Its secular responsibilities have been taken over by the county council and parish council. In 1921, its ecclesiastical responsibilities were taken over by the parochial church council.

But in the eighteenth century the vestry had all its powers: it was responsible for keeping the parish church in repair, and for providing accommodation for the parishioners, and adequate ground for burials; it also had to repair the roads and bridges, maintain the poor, apprentice the poor children, and keep law and order. And for all these purposes it was entitled to levy rates, which were recoverable by law.

The vestry included all parishioners—that is, all persons rated for the relief of the poor—who were entitled to be present and to vote. Those who did not attend were bound by the decisions of those who did. The churchwardens attended as parishioners, with no right to preside: the president was the minister of the parish. If he were not there, a chairman could be elected. An Act[1] was passed in 1818 for the regulation of parish vestries, but Sir John Nicholl gave it as his opinion that it "neither altered the general authority under which, nor the persons by whom, vestries are to be called; it only added some further formalities in the mode of calling; such as, directing the notice to be put upon the church door, and that it shall be given a certain number of days before the vestry is to meet."

So the vestry met, and regularly voted the levying of rates for

[1] 58 George III, c. 69.

various purposes, including the repair of the church; and had surveys made, and considered estimates and plans, when repairs or alterations were necessary. It can probably be said that, on the whole, churches were kept fairly well. No one wants to worship in discomfort, and it is a mistake to imagine that the average church in the eighteenth century was in a more or less derelict condition. Some were. Secker's fourth charge, to the clergy of the diocese of Oxford in 1750, has often been quoted: "Water undermining and rotting the foundations; earth heaped up against the outside, weeds and shrubs growing against them or trees too near them. The floors are meanly paved, or the walls dirty or patched, or the windows ill-glazed, and it may be in part stopped up, or the roof not ceiled; or they are damp, offensive, and unwholesome for the want of a due circulation of air." And everyone who reads Church history knows the sentence which, with variations, comes in every later nineteenth-century text book: "The altar was a rickety table, covered with a moth-eaten baize cloth. The walls were green with damp . . .". That was certainly true of some churches in the eighteenth century.

At the beginning of the century, Bishop Nicolson found most of the churches in the diocese of Carlisle[1] in a bad state—the result of neglect during Elizabethan and Stuart times, and the troubles of the Civil War and Commonwealth.

John Throsby in his additions to Thoroton's *History of Nottinghamshire* (1797) sometimes mentions the condition of the churches. Sutton Bonington had a dirty chancel. At Kingston upon Soar the birds scattered their dung so plentifully that he could scarcely find room on the Communion table to lay his book; the floor, in some places, was intolerable. West Leake had some offensive lumber near the font. Staunton on the Wolds was "below description: it is, of all others, within and without, the most despicable place I ever beheld". At Stoke by Newark the chancel was sadly neglected. At Trowell the chancel was not kept clean; Radford was in disorder; Oxton was dirty within; Weston was a dirty place. In the north chapel of Laxton "the floor and old stones are completely covered with coal, coal-slack, cinders, fire-wood, straw, lime, broken bricks and stone, hassocks and floor-mats torn in pieces, ladders, an old sieve, broken scuttles, and brushes without handles, and handles without brushes, mortar boards and mortar, reeds, tiles, soot, broken glass, dog's dung and——".

But this kind of thing was not peculiar to the eighteenth century,

[1] *Miscellany Accounts of the Diocese of Carlisle*, ed. R. S. Ferguson, 1877.

and it is not fair to blame the Reformation or Protestantism for it. The churchwardens' presentments made at the visitation of the archdeaconry of Oxford in 1520, still in the Age of Faith, show that most of the churches were in a most unsatisfactory condition.

In the deanery of Aston: *Easington:* "The chancel is out of repair above the altar and also in the floor through the fault of the rector . . . the nave of the church is out of repair in the roof; the cure is neglected, for the parishioners have not had divine service from Easter up till today." *Brightwell Baldwin:* "The chancel is out of repair; the glass windows of the chancel have not been made." *Ibstone:* " . . . The seats of the church are broken." *Adwell:* ". . . The chancel is out of repair . . . The seats in the church are broken." *Shirburn:* "The chancel needs repair in the tiles of the roof; the seats in the chancel are broken . . . the glass windows in the chancel are out of repair." *Cuxham:* "The chancel needs repair . . ." *Stoke Talmage:* "The chancel needs repair. The glass windows are broken; there is no chancel door that can be closed; the walls of the church are out of repair." At Britwell Salome, Chalgrove, and Aston Rowant the chancel was out of repair.

In the deanery of Bicester, the chancel was out of repair at Finmere, Islip, Hampton Gay, Oddington, Chesterton, Noke, and Middleton Stoney.

At Yarnton, in the deanery of Woodstock, "the chancel is out of repair so much that rain falls on the high altar". And so on throughout the archdeaconry. In only a tiny number of parishes was all well.[1]

Churches were out of repair, and carelessly kept, before, during, and after the eighteenth century. Our forefathers' standards were lower than ours. But things were not always as bad as that, and the topographical writers of the eighteenth and early nineteenth centuries mention many churches that were neat and in good order. Throsby found that Gotham was kept very clean, and so was East Leake. Cotgrave was decent. Strelley was neat, particularly in the chancel. Greasley appeared to be kept in due order, and Hucknall Torkard was a neat and clean church. Beckingham, though rather gloomy, was kept clean.

It does not seem possible to come to any conclusion except the obvious one—that some churches were kept in good order, and some were not. But the evidence of parish records suggests that, on the whole, churchwardens and vestries did their duty, and raised, and spent, adequate money for church repairs.

[1] These presentments are printed in the Report of the Oxford Archaeological Society for 1925, from which the English translations are taken.

CHURCHWARDENS' ACCOUNTS

How was the money spent? The churchwardens' accounts mention the day-to-day repairs. Canon 89 directs that "all Churchwardens at the end of their year, or within a month after at the most, shall before the Minister and the Parishioners give up a just account of such money as they have received, and also what particularly they have bestowed in reparations, and otherwise, for the use of the church".

Very few churchwardens' accounts fail to mention some expenditure on the fabric of the church. In almost every year, there are payments for work by the mason, the plumber, the carpenter, or the glazier. The drawback of such accounts is that they so often fail to mention what the work was. The accounts of Newbury, Berks., for instance, begin well at the opening of the century:

1704. p^d William ffield for making iron Gates for the Chancell	03	16	00
p^d for Guilding & colouring the iron Gates & the new Seate	01	10	00
p^d Norcott for making the new Seate & for other work	02	10	00
1707. p^d for painting the Pillars & Cullums & Whiting the Walls & Gilding the Lyon	04	05	00
p^d John Clark for taking downe the Queens Armes	00	12	00
p^d Mr Jones for painting the Queenes Armes	02	00	00

Later, there are:

The Accompt of Saml Slocock And Wm Russell Church Wardens for ye Repairing of the Roof of ye Church in the Year 1720 [amounting to £43 3s 9d];
The Accompt of Saml Slocock and Wm Russell Church Wardens for the Gates and Rayles and paving the ways in the Church Yeard and mending the Wall in the year 1720–21 [£28 9s 9d];
and Mr Samuel Slocock and Mr William Russell Church Wardens for the Parish of Newbury in the County of Berks theire account for Erecting and build the New Gallarye in the sayd Church and for other Reparations in the sayd Parish Church to Ladye day 1720 [£220 3s 10¼d].

But for the rest of the century the entries give no details: they simply record the payments:

1730. p^d Bolton the Glazier his Bill	4	4	10
p^d Mr Nalder Junr his Bill for Timber	4	5	5
p^d Willm Flaggots Bill	5	1	6

[—and so on]

VESTRY MINUTES

What were they paid for? It is impossible to say. But sometimes the vestry minutes will come to our rescue, and help to fill the gaps. Vestry minutes vary from the many large and carefully written volumes of a big London parish to the scrawled and ill-spelt notes made by the village scribe in a book which contains the vestry minutes and a good deal more besides. But, whatever they are like, they seldom fail to contain something about the repairing, adorning, or enlarging of the church, and they are, generally speaking, far more informative than the churchwardens' accounts.

Mr Elliot the bricklayer was paid in 1800 for work at Newbury; the resolutions of the vestry make it clear what it was all about.

20 August 1794. Whereas it appears to the Inhabitants attending this Vestry that the Pinicles of the Tower are very much out of Repair It is recommended that the Churchwardens do procure Estimates of the necessary Expence for Repairing the said Pinicles in their present form, And also procure proper Estimates of the Expence necessary for taking down the said Pinicles and building new ones with Stone And that such Estimates be delivered in at a Vestry to be called for this day week at Eleven O'Clock in the forenoon for the Inspection of the Inhabitants to which time this Vestry is adjourned.

5 September. Whereas it appears to the Inhabitants present at this Vestry that a Sum of Money is likely to come into the Hands of the Churchwardens at a future period by a Lease of Lands belonging to the Church almost expired— It is recommended that the Repairations of the Tower be deferred until that Money be received by the Churchwardens And that a certain Plan agreable to the Estimate now delivered in by Francis Elliot Bricklayer which Estimate amounts to the sum of £56 be adopted . . . It is also recommended that the said Francis Elliott be the person employed to repair the same.

There is a great deal of this kind of thing in the vestry minutes of any reasonable-sized parish, and it is easy—with references from time to time to the churchwardens' accounts—to piece together a case history of the church during the century.

Here is a summary of the vestry's care for the church of a large village south of the Thames, St Mary Magdalene's, Bermondsey. The church was rebuilt in 1676–7 by Charley Stanton (who also rebuilt St Nicholas', Deptford), and the accounts were settled by 1679. On 22 June 1703 it was agreed that a gallery should be built, and that the pavements should be repaired. On 5 December 1705 it was stated that several gentlemen appointed by the vestry had agreed with the churchwarden for repairs to be done in and about the church, amounting to £70. In 1712 John Cordwell built a gallery for the charity children. 22 June 1715: the turret or lanthorn of the church steeple to be repaired. 28 November 1716: the gutters and tiling to be viewed by the upper churchwarden and the rector, together with John Cordwell and Joseph Heaton. 14 March: the leading to be repaired. 27 November 1717: "Ordered that the North and South East parts of the Church Ceiling shall be repaired." Thomas Steavens, John Cordwell and James Parker to view the ceiling and roof. 17 July 1718: the steeple to be plastered and the dial painted. 18 August: a new sun dial to be erected, and the lantern to be repaired. 4 March 1719: the church to be whitewashed, beautified, and repaired. 10 July 1723: the turret to be repaired. 12 August: the charity school galleries to be repaired. 23 May 1746: subscriptions to be asked for to repair the church. 9 April 1776: "Resolved, That the Church be repaired agreable to the Scheme and particulars delivered in by M.ʳ Jordan and the Alterations made therein by this Vestry That the Pews be repaired, but not new fronted, That All the Windows be Glazed with new Crown Glass . . . That the Vestry will Contract with One Person for performing the whole under the Inspection of M.ʳ Poultney Surveyor . . .". 17 July 1794: a gallery to be erected on the south side, and the church to be repaired under the direction of a committee. 21 July: the gallery to be extended; the pews in the gallery to range in the same manner as those in the gallery of St Anne's, Blackfriars; the whole church to be painted and whitewashed.

And so it continues through the early years of the nineteenth century.

Of course vestries might be tiresome, and try to avoid their responsibilities. In 1718, while the church of Chesham, Bucks., was being new pewed, the workmen discovered "a fracture in the peer, or southwest corner of the Tower". A vestry was called, and decided that a survey should be made by able and experienced workmen. Edward Strong made a report and suggested remedies. A second vestry was held, to obtain the agreement of the inhabitants, but only two votes were given in favour. The churchwardens were reduced to appealing to the bishop. "Wee are threatened my Lord that if wee proceed wee our selves shall bear the burthen. Wee are willing to doe our duty and faithfully execute the trust reposed in us. And hope wee shall not want your Lordship's direction and authority to guide and support us. Which is the end and scope of this representation." They sent Strong's report, to which a note has been added, "This is a True Copy of Strong's Judgmt: delivered in writing to Mr Newton the Undertaker."[1] The repairs were carried out a little later.

But the only vestry minutes of an important parish that I have seen which really tell a story of meanness, procrastination, and indecision in matters of church building are those of St Marylebone.[2] The church was reported to be dangerous early in 1740, and Mr Lane and Mr Lee were asked to survey it, "and make such Designs as they think Proper for the Effectual reparation thereof, & Advise with M: Gibbs or such others as they think fit thereupon". On 24 February Gibbs himself presented designs for a new church, and so did Lee; but the vestry rejected them, as there were no estimates, and no designs for repairing the church on the old foundations.

On 1 June they accepted Lane's proposal for rebuilding the church according to the plan delivered by him, for a sum not exceeding £800, exclusive of old materials, without putting the parish to further expense, on condition that the pews, and fees for burials and monuments, be assigned to him. The poor little brick church, that stood until recently, was accordingly built. The settlement of Lane's account dragged on for some time.

After this, the vestry seemed incapable of making progress. A committee was appointed in 1753 to consider the enlargement of the church, but nothing was done. On 6 February 1770 they agreed to apply to Parliament for a Bill to convert the church into a parochial chapel, and to build a parish church larger and more convenient. Trustees were appointed, and for a time it seemed as though something might happen. On 23 June elevations were delivered in by Gandon and Wolf, Charles Little, and John Johnson. John White of Marylebone sent a plan and elevations for "a neat roomy Church": "Sensible of my incapacity to give an eligant Drawing yet hoping that some useful hint may probably be taken from it I could not help offering my Mite as a young Parishioner who sincerely wishes prosperity to the Parish." A committee was appointed to consider the plans. On 2 July they reported that they had agreed to appoint William Chambers as surveyor, and on 12 February 1771, Chambers produced a design.

A piece of ground was obtained from Henry William Portman, but the scheme of building a church on it came to nothing, and in 1772

[1] Fac. 9/65.   [2] In the St Marylebone Public Library.

it was consecrated as a burial ground. In 1775 and 1778 the Duke of Portland made offers of ground, but the parish lost the opportunities. It was not until 1813 that a new chapel was begun, from designs by Thomas Hardwick. Then the committee decided that it was to be the parish church, and the architect had to alter the plans. It was not completed until 1818. The only pleasure in reading these minutes is the encountering of people whom one has always known as names of streets—Mr Baker, Mr Portman, and the Duke of Portland. But St Marylebone was exceptional: generally, in eighteenth-century parish records, one finds tales of successful achievement.

It is always interesting to read the vestry minutes of some well-known church, and to see how it assumed its present appearance.

The tower of St Clement Danes was rebuilt by Joshua Marshall in 1669–70, and left when the church was rebuilt in 1680–2. But the vestry soon wanted to improve it. They met on 26 May 1719. "The Quson now proposed is whether the Tower of the pish Church of St Clem^t Danes be raised higher . . . Resolved Nemine Contradicente that the tower shall be raised higher Resolved that the Bells be raised 25 ffoot higher than now they are & over the bells an ornamental Steeple not less than 50 ffoot The whole making 75 ffoot higher than the Tower now is & this worke to be finished by Xtmas next."

On 29 May the vestry agreed to Townesend's proposal to build the tower for £1650.[1] The design was made by James Gibbs[2], whose name is not mentioned in the minutes, except in connection with a repair of the roof. The argument from silence is certainly not applicable to parish records.

Occasionally, vestry minutes of one parish will contain something that has to do with another. On 3 November 1720 the vestry of St Clement's decided to get rid of their altarpiece, altar, and rails. "A Letter of Mr Geo: Cooke Rector of Warfield in Berks. relating to our old Alter Comunion Table & Railes to be putt up in their Church read: Ordered that the s^d Alter Comunion Table & Railes be sold to the Inhabitants of the s^d pish of Warfield for 12 Guineas." There is no mention of this in the parish records of Warfield, which mention only minor repairs, and the church was restored and refitted by G. E. Street in 1876.

Sometimes annotations have been added to the parish records by a later hand. The Newbury churchwardens' accounts record a collec-

[1] Vestry minutes in Westminster Public Library, B.1063.
[2] *Book of Architecture*, pl. 28.

tion amounting to £594 7s 4d for repairing the church in 1684. A note has been added: "This Sum was collected for repairing the damage done to the Church by the falling in of the Roof from the Chancel to the Pulpit on Sunday the 2ᵈ of February 1683-4 while the Revᵈ Isaac Mills Rector of Highclere Hants (who officiated that day) was administering the Sacrament, fortunately no lives were lost, as the congregation had just left the Church except those who communicated and who were in the Chancel—This Account is given in the Life of Mr Mills Published in the Year 1721 and taken therefrom by Samˡ Grigg Churchwarden in 1803."

But this note has itself been annotated: "Upon a close inspection there is great reason to suppose that the Pillar next the Vestry was knocked down and that it was the Roof of the North Aisle that fell the charges to the Stone Mason & for Stone is great and can no otherwise be accounted—there is now a crack in the wall close to the Pillar against which the Pulpit stands—Mr Griggs extract is correct but I doubt his authority which appears written by hearsay & not from ocular proof. Charles Bull 1808."

At Shottesbrooke, Berks., the spire was struck by lightning on 20 July 1757, and was so badly damaged that it was thought that it must be taken down. The lightning passed down to the north transept, destroyed the wainscot of the gallery, and broke the north window and the wainscot of the pews under it. The roof was shattered. The church was closed for more than a year, and was then repaired by Townsend of Oxford at the sole expense of Arthur Vansittart, and reopened on 24 September 1758. In the register is a note written in 1839 by William, the third son of Arthur. "My Father advertised the Steeple to be repaired. A Stone Mason from London engaged to repair it at 900 £. One from Bath at six hundred. Mr Townshend from Oxford at 300 £. His offer was accepted. I mentioned this Difference of Price to Mr Rickman the Architect employed by the Church Building Society, who replied that there are Traders in Warwickshire called Steeple Menders, which probably would account for the low price of the Oxford offer."

2

CHURCHWARDENS' PRESENTMENTS: VISITATIONS

THE CHURCHWARDENS were, and are, obliged, at the visitations of the bishop, archdeacon, or other ordinary, to make presentments according to the articles presented to them. Canon 86 is headed, *Churches to be surveyed, and the Decays certified to the high Commissioners*. "Every Dean, Dean and Chapter, Archdeacon, and others which have authority to hold Ecclesiastical Visitations by composition, law, or prescription, shall survey the churches of his or their jurisdiction once in every three years in his own person, or cause the same to be done; and shall from time to time within the said three years certify the high Commissioners for Causes Ecclesiastical, every year, of such defects in any the said churches, as he or they do find to remain faulty therein . . .".

Here are a few examples of presentments from Essex, taken more or less at random from the visitation papers in the muniment room at St Paul's.

1706. *Bradwell:* Our Church hath been downe some time but is now rebuilding—our Steeple is in good repaire.
Colchester, St Nicholas: Wee present our Parish Church to be demolished & fallen down.
Downham: Our Church & Chancell is now repaireing—& the Steeple is repaired.
Ingatestone [all in good repair], except ye Church porch which is now mending.
Little Laver: Our Steeple hath been newly repaired.
Great Oakley: Part of our Steeple dropt downe ab^t five or six Y^r since & hath not been since repaired.
Tolleshunt D'Arcy: The Church was out of repaire but is now mending.

1715. *Colchester, St Nicholas:* We have noe Church Steeple or Chancell, the whole being ruined by the fall of the Steeple several yeares since.

Debden: Wee present the steeple which is fallen by reason of whicht he Church & Chancell cannot be kept in that decent manner as it ought to be.

Ingatestone: I present all well Saving the Church out of repaire but the materialls are all ready for the repairing.

West Mersea: All well saving that the wall of the Church is crackt & wants six strong buttresses, & that the pillars of the Nave of the Church haveing given way the roofe is very much suncke in soe much that new rafters are wanting & the lead must bee new runn on yᵉ north side the charges of all which amount to neare one hundred pounds & saveing that a buttresse of yᵉ Steeple wants repaires.

Stondon Massey: Our Church was at the Arch-Deacon's last Visitation presented to want tiling and the Steeple repairing, which I was then order'd to repair, and I will take Care it shall be done before the Arch-Deacons next Visitation.

Little Warley: Whereas yᵉ Steeple of yᵉ Parish Church of Little Warley has been in a decaying Condition upwards of fourty years last past & by yᵉ Parishioners from time to time carefully supported & kept up with Buttresses, Cramps & ties of Iron & large Timber; & it notwithstanding all that has been done to it become very ruinous; Therefore It was by an Order of Vestrey viewed yesterday by a Master Carpenter & Mason, who agree yᵗ it is every day in danger of falling upon yᵉ Body of yᵉ Church, & breaking it down, yᵗ it must be taken down to yᵉ Foundation, & will cost at least 900l to pull down, & rebuild

The Parishioners being generally poor & yᵉ Parish very small, and not able of themselves to be at so great a Charge.

1724. *Alresford:* Our Church & Chancel are both in very good Repair, & were last year cieled, the One at the charge of the Rector, the other by the Parish, Our Pews & Reading Desk we are going to rebuild.

Birchanger: I have expended a considerable sum of money, and intend to perfect the Repairs, but the Parish being very poor I cannot do them at once.

Cold Norton: [the chancel was out of repair, but this was attended to afterwards]: I doe hereby Certifie that yᵉ Chancel of Cold Norton in yᵉ County of Essex which was presented at yᵉ Last Episcoll Visitation as ruineous has since been Rebuilt witness my hand

Janʸ yᵉ 3ᵈ: 1724/5   Henry Foster, Churchwarden.

Grays Thurrock: The Steeple was taken down aboute 2 or 3 years a goe it being an old decay'd Spear Steeple & now is made into a Tower Steeple.

Halstead: [a certificate was given on 20 January 1724/5]: These are to Certifie That the Parish Church of Halsted in the said County is in very good and sufficient Repair, the Pulpit & some part of the Roof only excepted. And that the Churchwardens have employed a Workman to cast the Lead wᶜʰ is decayed, and have this day agreed for a New Pulpit to be finished before

the next Visitation of the Arch-deacon. In Witness whereof I have hereunto
sett my hand the day & Year as above

M. Cooke.

Hatfield Peverell: [a certificate was given in January 1724/5 that the church
had been put into good repair. It is signed by the minister, the wardens, and
others, and by "Chris.ᵗ Shackleton", plumber and glazier].

Manningtree: [the church was being repaired].

Pentlow: All well save yᵉ Ch: wants Tileing and Beautifying but yᵉ workmen are now at work upon it, yᵉ Chancell wants paveing but our minʳ
will do it.

1727. *Alphamstone:* We have had a Grate Breech in the Steple and have Been
forcd to take downe yᵉ Bells . . . and wee doe intend to Repaire itt as soone
as we cane.

Debden: The Steeple hath been fallen down for several years and yᵉ Chancel
beat down by it which are not yet erected by reason yᵉ Parish is not able, &
yᵉ Gentlemen who have Estates in yᵉ Parish have not contributed to it.

High Easter: [the chancel was out of repair, but William Jolliffe, who had
purchased the estate, had promised to repair it forthwith].

Lambourne: He saith that the Chancel of the sᵈ Church hath been repair'd
& Beautifyed within these foure yeares, & the church both wᵗʰ in & without well repaired & Beautiyed & new pew'd in the yeare last past, & there
is a Handsome Communion table, Desk & Pew for the Minister.

Great Oakley: Our Steeple fell downe some yeares since & hath not since
been rebuilt.

Sible Hedingham: Our Church and Chancell are late Repaired.

Stansted Mountfitchett: The Steeple hath been rebuilt within 40 Years.

Takeley: We have lately been at considerable charges in repairing oʳ
Church & 'tis now in tolerable good condition: it only wants Beautifying,
wᶜʰ shall be done in a short time.

1731. *Great Braxted:* [was out of repair, but repairs were about to be done].

Lambourne: [The wardens presented that] The Chancel of the Parish Church
is in good Repair; that the church was within five years past repaired (as was
thought) Sufficiently & Beautifyed at the Expence of more than two Hundred pounds, but nevertheless a dangerous Crack is open'd in the wall on
one side of the body of the Church, and the present church warden cannot
undertake the repair thereof for that there is yet due to him from the Parish
upwards of one hundred & twenty pounds which he is in disburse for the
last repairing of the said Church.

Littlebury: The Spire of the Steeple of Littlebury was Taken Downe in
1726: and substantially repaired.

Takeley: We have lately been at great Expenses in Repairing oʳ Church:
there are still some ornaments wanting, but we hope in a short time to
pʳvaile with yᵉ parish, to set every thing in regular Order.

There is some glazing wanting in o^r Chancell wch belongs to ye Impropriator, & likewise some glazing & repairs wanting, in a little Chapell adjoining to the Church, belonging to John Rendell Esqr, but we doubt not, but y^t worthy Gentleman, in due time will set every thing in order.
Wethersfield: The Chancel and Body thereof are much out of repair and are now repairing by ye order of Mr Bate.

1735. *Salcott Wigborough:* The Church is much out of Repair, and thro ye Neglect of several my Predecessors has been decaying for several Years last past, however this last Year, vizt 1734 ye Parish have begun to put things in a little better Order, & I design to goe on therewith this Year current.
Shellow Bowells: Chancell is out of Repair but is shortly intended to be done.

Most of the churches in places near London, which were eventually to be absorbed into it, were approaching a condition which would make rebuilding necessary; and all of those in this list, except for Stepney, were afterwards rebuilt.

1711. *Clerkenwell:* Our Church hath lately been Beautify'd both within and without at the Charge of the Parishioners but is in a very weak & crazy condition not capable to be long supported by the inhabitants.
Islington: The said Parish Church is very ancient, and hath been lately certify'd by skilfull Surveyor as so much decayed or sunk in the foundation that It's not capable of being repair'd and that for the Present we are forc'd to support it with props in several places.

1715. *Hackney:* [the presentment refers to the annexed paper]
The Review Taken By the Persons Whose Nam's are und^r Written Of the Necessary Repair's Wanting in & about The Parrish Church of St John's Hackney in the County of Middlesex. [It is signed by]

Giles Dance Mayson	Nich^o North: Bricklay^r
Tho: King Glazer Plombr	Saml Passfield Carpent^r

Kensington: We present all well Saveing the Steeple of the s^d Church which is much out of repair concerning which we referr ourselves to the paper hereunto annexed. [The paper is a resolution of the vestry, 10 October 1715.] After some Debate held about the Steeple it was Unanimously Agreed by the Parishioners that the Church-wardens should give the Chancellor of Doct^{rs} Comons: A proper Answere (that is) that what is need full to be done as to the Repairs of the Steeple shall be performed at a proper reasonable time.
Edgware: Our Church is somewhat defective in the foundations wch will bee speedily done.

1727. *Edgware:* We present, that ye Church is old, & decay'd; but is propped up; & otherwise kept decent & clean.

Stepney: The Parish Church of S. Dun: Stepney afores^d is lately Beautified, both inside and out, as likewise the Chancel.

1730. *Ealing:* I do present the Church to be fall'n and to have laid in Ruins for near a year and half, and that no proper Methods have been taken as yet by Churchwardens and inhabitants towards rebuilding the same; That the Inhabitants are forc'd to assemble for Divine Service at a Tabernacle, which is very incommodious to the great dishonour of Religion.

Commissioners were appointed to make a visitation of the churches in the diocese of Chichester in 1724. Here are some of their reports. (The parishes are here put in alphabetical order for convenience.)

Albourne: The Church is in good Repair there is a handsome Gallery but not finisht being stopt by Sir Robt Fagg tho all the Materials ly ready (& a faculty granted out of the Ecclesiastical Court).

Arundel: The great Chancell repairable by the Duke of Norfolk who has given Orders to have it sufficiently done & t'is now accordingly in hand. Since our view it has been finish'd in the Outward Roof & Leadding but the Inside is quite indect & sordid.

Balcombe: The Church repaired & beautified lately at the Charge of above £200.

Beckley: North side of the Church & the whole roof new built.

Burwash: The Outside of the Church is in good repair. One side entirely new heal'd this last Summer. The Inside is also pretty well; but some of the pews want a little repairing. The Steeple wants new shingling which the Churchwardens have promis'd shall be done next spring.

Coombs: Tower & part of the Church lately fall'n to be contracted by Leave (as reported) from your Lordship, but when so lessened, sufficient to contain more than the Inhabitants, the remaining part in good repair.

Hamsey: The Chancel newly repaired; repaired by the Rector.

Lewes, St John, Southover: The Church has been newly repaired by a Breif The Seats all to be new made . . . The Steeple was built by the Brief as far as the first Floor & 4 good Bells put up in it; but not being finisht for want of a sufficient collection, the Timber is in a few Years so much Decayed, by being exposed to the Weather, that they have been obliged to take down three of the Bells which now lye in ye Church.

Nuthurst: Church & Chancell putting actually at this time in good repair.

Pett: [The chancel] In very good repair & very handsomely beautified at the charge of the Parish.

New Shoreham: The Church is in good Order & handsomely beautified of late by a Brief. The Chancell in good Order and handsomely beautified of late by A Brief otherwise to be done by the Parish also.

Singleton: Workmen are now repairing ye Church.

Walberton: The Church wants some amendment in the floor, the Pavem^t being uneven: one of the Cross beams is ready to fall . . .

N.B. That since our Visitation ye Beam abovemention'd is cramp'd with Iron and the Church new ceiled.

Woodmancote: The Chancell new ceiled & floored and Beautified, repaired by ye Rector.

And so it went on, year after year, in the various dioceses. Sometimes, no doubt, the repair work was put off too long, and sometimes it was done inadequately. But certainly a watch was being kept on the churches, and defects were faithfully reported.

3

ACCOMMODATION

THE ALLOTMENT OF PEWS

EVERY parishioner was, and is, entitled to a seat in the parish church, and the custom grew up of the churchwardens allotting the seats. As the vestry of Frieston, Lincs., put it when they decided to reseat the church in 1786, they were going to "place the Landowners Parishioners & Inhit^s of the s^d Parish in such new Seats or pews according to their respective Degrees, state quality & Interests". Faculties were very often granted assigning pews to particular people, though it is considered that there was never any real authority for this. There were many faculties, too, enabling gentlemen who had property in the parish to build an aisle which would be both a pew and also a burying place for themselves and their family.

Sometimes pews were assigned as a reward for financial help. In 1778 the parishioners of St Peter in Eastgate and St Margaret, Lincoln, decided to build a new church. St Peter's had been demolished in the Civil War, and St Margaret's was ruinous. The materials of the two old churches would be used to build a new church in the churchyard of St Peter's. A pew was to be assigned to every subscriber of ten guineas or upwards, belonging to the parish; and to every subscriber of twelve guineas and upwards belonging to another parish. Subscribers of five guineas would be entitled to half a seat, and two guineas would earn one place. The gallery and the rest of the church would be assigned in common for the use of the parishioners.[1]

The business of providing seating, and of dividing it up among the parishioners, was constantly engaging the attention of eighteenth-century churchwardens and vestries. Then, and for a long time afterwards, the matter caused many disputes.

In 1772 application was made to the court of the archdeacon at Leicester for a faculty to reseat Packington church. But difficulties

[1] Faculty Book 2, 1779–91, pp. 150–2.

22

arose about the workman to be employed, and the vicar's warden, John Hood, bought the boards and engaged a workman of his own. He succeeded in getting a faculty given, on 17 February 1773, to himself alone, contrary to the petition and the wishes of the parishioners; and he proceeded to repew the church and assign the seats. Litigation followed, and the vicar did not interfere; but when a new vicar was appointed, an effort was made to settle the dispute. Hood continued obstinate, and the parishioners made a petition to the bishop in 1787 asking him to appoint commissioners to settle the matter.[1]

The Reverend T. Mozley's *Reminiscences chiefly of Towns, Villages and Schools*[2] gives a long account of a dispute about pews which happened in the early years of the nineteenth century, but its roots went back into the century before. In 1815 his father came to Derby, found it impossible to obtain seats for himself and the family in St Werburgh's, his parish church, and secured a pew in All Saints'. In 1820 he had to give it up to a parishioner, and succeeded in getting a pew in one of the galleries of St Werburgh's. Early in 1828 he bought the Friary, and with it a pew of five sittings in a different gallery, but he allowed two ladies who lived in the house to continue using it. In 1830 another pew of five sittings came into the market, and he bought it; but the lawyer said that, though he would not be disturbed, "there is no title, and none can be made". The pew could not be detached from the house to which it belonged. Mozley senior, who was now churchwarden, decided to look into the matter, and sent to Lichfield for copies of the faculties. He found that they did not assign pews to persons, or to families, or to houses, but to persons and families residing in certain houses, for as long as they lived there, and no longer. The organ gallery had been erected in 1730, and the faculty had appropriated the seats to the builder and to his family, and to certain other inhabitants; but with that reservation. The north gallery had been built in 1778. Three proposals for a gallery on the south had been considered and rejected: then, in 1794, the vestry had agreed to build one, and decided who were to have the seats in it: they and their families should occupy them, "and not sell, or let, or make any pecuniary advantage from the same". The faculty restricted the pews to the first proprietors and their families. But by the time the Mozleys came into the picture, nearly all the original families had died out, or left the parish. The original and the subsequent owners had regarded the pews as private property, and had sold them, let them, and attached

[1] Fac. 4/23.   [2] 1885, pp. 67–102.

them to other houses: but Mozley had no doubt that they were wrong in doing this, and that practically all the pews in the church were at his disposal. He sent a statement of the case, with the faculties, to Dr Lushington, who replied that he was probably right, though caution was needed. Sir Herbert Jenner said the same. The vicar took no interest, so Mozley summoned a vestry, and said that he meant to re-appropriate the sittings. There was, at first, not much opposition, though many would be losing seats that they had paid for: but the Reverend Joseph Pickford (son of Joseph Pickford of Derby, architect), the vicar, and a lady, obtained a faculty, and bought the organ gallery for £600. A promise was made that occupants who had long possession of a seat, and who were fit persons to be placed there, would not be disturbed. But then trouble began, and one or two gentlemen said that they would defend their property by force. The bishop ordered Mozley to "suspend all future steps", and began to look into the matter himself. He came to Derby, and was captured by the aggrieved parishioners: when Mozley was admitted, it was only to be rebuked for assigning a seat to himself. The bishop proceeded to the church, and announced his decision, which was according to the wishes of the malcontents: but he did say that the purchase of the gallery was void.

Then Thomas Mozley took up the case for his father, and wrote a pamphlet, a copy of which was sent to the bishop. The bishop acknowledged it, and appointed a commission—which made an inquiry, and finally confirmed what Mozley senior had done.

They said that the parishioners had no power to let or to sell their pews: that persons with a faculty had an exclusive right of occupation—but that the faculty became vacated, and the pew must revert to the parishioners at large, if the person died or became non-resident: that mere possession of a pew gave no title to it, so as to exclude the authority of the ordinary, exercised through the churchwardens: that the churchwardens had power to remove a family from a non-faculty pew on the grounds of non-attendance, or a diminution of the size of the family, and to place the family in other seats: that when the demand for room became urgent, if several sittings in a pew were unoccupied, the churchwardens had the duty of filling the empty seats with "residents in the parish of equal station and respectability": and that pews could not be claimed as appurtenant to houses.

This kind of thing was the first round in the battle for Free and Open Churches, which has long ago been won.

THE INCREASE OF ACCOMMODATION

In the growing parishes, we can see the vestries making effort after effort to fit in more and more seats.

At Randwick, Glos., the congregation in 1724 was stated to be "generally about 800" (about twice the present total population), and the vestry asked for a faculty to build a new aisle.[1]

From St Giles's, Camberwell, at the beginning of the century, came a petition to new pew and beautify the church, and to build new galleries on the north, south, and west. The charity children's galleries were enlarged in 1724, and the other galleries in 1761. In 1786 the vestry decided to build a new aisle on the south, "to prevent the rising generation from assembling with Dissenting congregations":[2] the surveyor was John Robinson of Peckham. On 30 October 1817 the vestry decided that more accommodation must be provided: the pulpit and desk should be moved, and the space converted into pews. Still there was not enough room, and on 8 July 1825 the vestry agreed to accept Francis Bedford's plan for enlarging the church by extending the south-east angle.[3]

The picturesque, much patched old church was burned down on 7 February 1841, and the new Gothic revival church, by Scott and Moffatt, was built large enough to hold any congregation that there was likely to be.

Clapham church was enlarged in 1650. On 30 September 1653, Walter Frost was given leave to "erect & build a building or Chapell on the South side of the sayd Church": on 14 March 1694, John Frost, his son, conveyed it to the parish. On 12 June 1710, John Foltrop submitted proposals for building a south aisle, which were accepted. In 1716 Mr Hewer offered to rebuild the north aisle and to build a vestry room at the south end, at his own cost: a faculty was given on 30 April. On 11 April 1724, a committee reported that the church needed to be enlarged. Nothing more was done until 1753, when the vestry examined plans by Thomas Holden. A committee was appointed, which decided that it was no use doing anything to the church, but that an entirely new church was necessary. Kenton Couse made plans, and

---

[1] Gloucester diocesan records, 279A, p. 94.

[2] This does not seem to have been entirely successful. In 1796 a meeting of aggrieved parishioners agreed that the Gospel was not preached in the parish church, and decided to build a chapel where it would be. See p. 197.

[3] MS. vestry minutes.

eventually the new church of Holy Trinity was built on the edge of the Common.[1]

The old church was demolished, except for the north aisle: this was taken down when the new church of St Paul was built (1815).

Petersham, Surrey, was not a particularly large parish; but there were several big houses in it, and the church was very small. It is still there, and has escaped restoration or rebuilding in the nineteenth century, so that there is no need to look for an old water colour drawing in the reference room of a public library: the results of the vestry's resolutions can be seen to-day. This is a rather rare experience. A really seasoned ecclesiologist does not mind much if work has disappeared: but there are some who find it rather difficult to take an interest in what they cannot see. Petersham should be an encouragement to them, and help them to picture similar work elsewhere that can be seen no longer.

On 4 July 1703, the vestry agreed "That the said Church or Chapple of Petersham aforesaid be enlarged for the more convenient reception and seating of the inhabitants". A faculty was desired for building a new aisle on the north, "And alsoe for erecting a place or Room for a Vestry on the West end of the said intended Isle . . . And alsoe for the erection and building a Gallery over the entrance into the said Church, and alsoe another Gallery over the Row of pews on the North side of the said intended Isle." The faculty was issued on 10 November.

In 1769 the Reverend Daniel Bellamy issued an appeal: the church was extremely ancient and inconvenient, and the parish should consider the expediency of obtaining a brief for enlarging and rebuilding it. In 1773 he made a proposal for enlargement, but the nobility and gentry of the parish did not approve. Next year, at the Easter vestry, Bellamy read a memorial which he had prepared, addressed to the bishop, drawing attention to the urgent need to enlarge or rebuild the church. In 1777 the vestry agreed to try to find a site, and in 1778 Bellamy sent another memorial to the bishop, enclosing a plan for a new church. Next year, he made another appeal to the nobility, gentry, and inhabitants. In 1780 the vestry received the proposals, but did not agree to them. In 1788 Bellamy died.

In February 1796 it was "order'd that the Pews, Pulpit, Desks in the Church be executed according to the Plan given". The pulpit is signed "John Long fecit 1797". Finally, on 27 June 1839, the vestry approved of plans and estimates for enlargements. The faculty was

[1] See pp. 107-8.   [2] MS. vestry minutes.

granted on 25 June 1840. The south transept was widened and lengthened, and galleries were erected on its west and south sides. The work was done by John and Thomas Long, builders, to the design of Mr Meakin, architect. Some new pews were erected, and most of the old ones were rearranged.[1]

Lymington, Hants., is another church which keeps a more or less eighteenth-century appearance, in spite of some restoration. William Hedgman was paid for making a new gallery in 1682, and in 1703–4 a second new gallery was built. Hedgman was employed on this as well. On 14 May 1756 a faculty was given for an enlargment on the north side, 93 ft. in length and 23 ft. in width. This meant an addition of nineteen new pews, thirteen below, and six in the gallery.

10 August 1780: "At a Vestry held this Day . . . it was Agreed upon & Resolv'd that an Addition be made to the small North Gallery which is to be Rais'd & Extended in front to the two large Pillars: & that the Windows behind be enlarged for the benefit of the Light . . ."

19 October 1791: "At a Vestry meeting held this day . . . to take into consideration the most proper method to erect more pews in the Church—It is at this meeting unanimously agreed that the North Gallery shall be taken down and enlarged, and that Mr John Newell and Mr Tho[s] Coleborne be requested to convene the Master Carpenters and Masons (frequenting the Church) to form a plan and estimate of the same & produce it to the next Vestry which shall be summoned for that purpose." On 28 December it was agreed to adopt their plan.

On 19 January 1792, it was agreed that "the large Pillar opposite the Pulpit has always been found to be a very great Obstruction—not only to the Minister when officiating, but also to the Major part of the congregation in Hearing—as is likewise the party Wall adjoining to the Same". The meeting agreed to open a subscription towards the expense of removing the pillar, and the other alterations depending thereupon. Colborne and Newell made an estimate of £200. They intended to "erect four pair of Stone Columns to support the Roof instead of the present pillars, with Double breast summor for the front and returning to support old plates, a Beam for the front of the Gallery and binding Joists to the North wall to be all of the best Fir Timber, Including a New front to the Gallery Architrave and Cornice to correspond with the Gallery in a former Estimate, taking down the walls of the Above quite home to the Singing Gallery".

[1] The faculties are among the Surrey archdeaconry papers. The other facts are from C. D. Warren, *History of St Peter's Church, Petersham*, 1938.

3 May 1792: It was "Judged proper to continue the alterations quite
to the west end of the Church—by removing the Arch in the Singing
Gallery and by adding Columns to support the s$^{\underline{d}}$ Gallery to correspond
with the Others agreed to in the former Estimate." Colborne and
Newell were to do the work.[1]

The galleries, with their pairs of columns, remain. A proposal has
been made in this century for rebuilding the interior of the church in a
conventional Gothic style, but presumably this is not seriously intended.

PEWS AND GALLERIES BUILT BY INDIVIDUALS

It was always a relief when anyone would offer to build a pew, or
a gallery, for himself. There are hundreds of examples of this. What
was built has, of course, generally been removed by now. But Chaddleworth, Berks., for instance, has two built-out pews on the north of
the nave that have survived nineteenth-century restoration. They are
not quite unscathed, but, with their family monuments, they give a
good idea of what used to exist in so many other churches. A faculty
was given on 10 July 1706, for John Blandy to build out a pew on the
north side. In 1717 it was stated that Bartholomew Tipping of Woolley
had no seat room, and was willing and desirous to build an aisle 13 ft.
square, and to abut it against the north side of the church, as a pew
and burying place.

Among the family papers in the Berkshire Record Office is a resolution of the Chaddleworth vestry, passed on 3 May 1724, about the
erection of a gallery:

Whereas our parish church of Chaddleworth is Strait and hardly Capable of
affording Roome for the parishioners to attend divine Service And whereas
Bartholomew Tipping Esqr one of our principall Inhabitants is destitute of
Convenient Roome or pew for his Tennant and ffamily the said Bartholomew Tipping being willing and desirous at his owne proper Coste and Charge
to Erect a Gallery at the west end of our said Church for the use of such of
his Tennant and ffamily on the one side and the other side for the use of such
persons as the parish shall think proper . . .

The vestry approved of the proposal, and gave consent.

The pew for which the faculty had been given in 1717 had clearly
not been built. But on 20 April 1765, a similar faculty was given: to

[1] MS. vestry minutes.

build an aisle 13 ft. square, on the north side, etc. It must have been built at this time, though the *Victoria County History*, for some reason, gives the date as 1810.

At Upton Grey, Hants., a faculty of 17 June 1715, gave permission to John Limbrey to enlarge the church. He had an estate in the parish of the yearly value of £300, and a very considerable estate elsewhere in the county. He was desirous and willing to add another aisle on the north side, 36 ft. long and 25 ft. broad, for a vault and pew. Certain clergymen had viewed the church on 14 June, assisted by two able and skilful workmen, Henry Hore of Odiham, mason, and Thomas Marshall of Upton Grey, carpenter, who certified that the north wall might be taken down without danger to the tower or roof. The aisle was to be built of brick and timber, with a tiled roof as high as the roof of the church, and there would be two pillars set in the roof.

The gallery was taken down in 1941, but the front survives as a screen in the aisle.

At Titchfield on 14 September 1776, the vestry agreed that Mrs Renira Bentinck should have liberty to erect a gallery at the west end. Another gallery was erected by faculty dated 7 June 1793. Edward Otto Ives and James Anderson proposed to turn an arch from the present old arch nearest the porch, and erect a gallery under it, on a level with the other galleries, supported by an iron pillar.

Here are some typical examples from Sussex.[1]

A petition for a faculty came from Salehurst in 1702. Dame Elizabeth Harcourt wished to build a gallery, and John Cole and John Walker, carpenters, had certified that it might be built without harming the church. The faculty was granted on 14 July.

On 18 December 1721, Robert Burnett was given a faculty to make a pew at Dallington. It was alleged "that there is a void space on the North Side of the said Parish Church which by makeing a small Breach in the Wall for a Passage thereto to be made good and supported by an Arch may be Converted into a Convenient Seat Room . . .". Thomas York, carpenter, and Samuel Barker, bricklayer, had viewed the same, and decided that it could be built without any prejudice or damage to the church.

At Mountfield, John Oxley, carpenter, and Thomas Catt, mason, viewed the church, and stated that a gallery with "Stone Stepps or

---

[1] Faculties in the West Sussex Record Office, Chichester: Ep. I/40, Chichester archdeaconry; Ep. II/27, Lewes archdeaconry; Ep. V/18, S. Malling deanery; Ep. IV/13, Pagham and Terring.

Stairs on ye Out side for passage thereto by makeing a Small Breach in ye North Wall And to be made Good by a Substantiall Door and Case may (it being now void or unoccupied space) be built and Erected against ye said North Wall without any prejudice or Damage to ye said Church or ye Lights thereof". It was to be for James Nicholl, who at present had no seat. The faculty was given on 19 February 1722.

A petition came from Albourne in 1723 for a faculty to build a west gallery with a window on the north, and a door for a passage at the west. The cost was to be borne by John Stubbs. A certificate was given under the hands of Joseph Wood and John Gilham, carpenters, and of William King, bricklayer, who had carefully viewed the same, that the gallery could be erected without any damage to the church. The faculty was granted on 17 September.

Thomas Holles, Duke of Newcastle, built Bishopstone Place, and he was given a faculty on 28 June 1731 to pull down the seats in the south aisle of the parish church, and erect new seats or pews at his own charges and expenses.

William Milton, gentleman, was granted a faculty on 16 July 1756 to build a gallery at the west end of St Andrew's, Chichester, with a staircase leading to it, and a window on the south side.

In 1775 the Reverend and Honourable W. B. Cadogan became Vicar of St Giles's, Reading, and scattered the evangelical congregation. But after two years he was himself converted, and began to preach Calvinism.

Mr. C's ministry had now become so interesting at Reading, that his church could not contain the multitude which attended it. He, therefore, proposed at a Vestry the taking down, and that entirely at his own charge, an irregular and decayed part of the Church, and rebuilding it so as to correspond with the opposite aisle, and to afford much additional room. It was objected that after his death, the additional room might not be wanted (too sadly verified, as I hear) and that the addition would increase the expence of future repairs. He then nobly proposed that, he would not only clear the parish of all expence attending the alteration in the first instance, but secure an annual sum from his own property, adequate to keeping it in repair—: but all in vain . . . This want of room, however, was much remedied by his erecting a very large Gallery, which went nearly round the Church; for the whole expence of which he made himself accountable, though, afterwards, it was chiefly defrayed by voluntary subscription.[1]

[1] Richard Cecil, *Cadogan's Sermons and Life*, 1798, pp. lxiv–v.

The gallery was built in 1784–5 by Thomas Jones, carpenter; the surveyor was W. Latimer.[1]

SCHOOL GALLERIES

Galleries were often needed for school children. A faculty for a gallery at Battersea was given on 15 November 1705. Sir Walter St John, Bt., had founded a Free School. The boys had sat in the chancel about the Communion table, and he desired to build a gallery for the boys, and the master and his family, on the south side from the south-ward part of the front of the old west gallery (the dimensions of the new gallery are, as usual given); and to make two or three dormer lights in the southern roof, and a staircase out of the churchyard on the west side of the porch.[2]

On 19 February 1797, the vestry of Twyford, Hants., agreed that since George Hanington, schoolmaster, had no accommodation for himself, his family, and his scholars, he might erect at his own expense, as he was desirous of doing, a gallery in a convenient place at the west end, over the singing gallery. A faculty was applied for, and granted.

SINGING GALLERIES

Almost every church had a gallery, or a pew, for the singers. There is a note in the register of Welford, Berks.:

Memmorandum we the Churchwardens and other the Parishioners of Welford, whose hands are hereunto subscribed, have, on the Twenty fifth Day of January Anno Dom 17$\frac{18}{19}$, at the Request of Severall of the Inhabitants of the said Parish, who have no Distinct seats in any Part of y^e Church, Granted them leave, as farr as in us lyes, to Erect or Build a seat or seats in that Part of the Parish Church, which Adjoins to the Belfery, no Person, as we understand, laying any Claims to the old Decayed seats that now are there, and it being upon triall, the most advantageous Place for the singing of Psalmes, and the most commodious for Rendering the Congregation Regular and uniform; But upon the Condition that no Person shall have the Privilege of the said seat or seats, But he who Contributes towards the Building of it or them. And that they who do Contribute towards the Building of the s^d seat or seats, as often as they shall be there in Divine Service, shall sing or endeavour to sing at all Costomary times of singing of Psalms.

[1] For the opposition to a faculty, see p. 131.
[2] Surrey archdeaconry records.

On 10 February 1732 Pinchbeck, Lincs., made their petition. They needed "a Gallery or Loft for Young Persons to sitt in to sing Psalms", and George Brabins was willing and desirous to erect one at his own expense. It would not be "any ways incomodious to any of ye Parishioners a disornam^t to ye Church, or any part thereof, but an Ornam^t."[1]

Whaplode, in 1748, wanted to build a gallery at the east end of the church "for the more Comodious and orderly Seating Such of the parishioners and Inhabitants of the said Parish who attend Divine Service and more particularly skilled and experienced in Psalmody".[2]

PAYMENT FOR GALLERIES

A gallery at Coleshill, Berks., was built with money collected at the Communion. The rubric directs that "After the Divine Service ended, the money given at the Offertory shall be disposed of to such pious and charitable uses, as the Minister and Churchwardens shall think fit". This could no doubt include the erection of a gallery: the rubric as proposed by Bishop Cosin directed that half of the alms should be given to the priest, "the other half to be employed to some pious or charitable use for the decent furnishing of the Church, or the relief of the poor . . .". The Coleshill vestry passed a resolution on 1 March 1723 which emphasizes the responsibility of the vicar and church-wardens in the matter:

Whereas the little Gallery in the North corner of the Church was built with some of the Collections made at the Sacram^t with ye Consent of the Vicar and Church Warden; it is declard and agreed at this Vestry that for pre-venting all dispute, and all misbehaviour in the House of God, that the Vicar and Churchwardens for the time being shall, at the present, so at all time hereafter have full power to nominate and place every person to sit in the said gallery and to displace such as shall behave themselves irreverently there.

And also it is declard and agreed that the Vicar shall have two places in the front of the said Gallery for his Servants, they not having any certain place to sit in in the Body of ye Church.[3]

A gallery was provided at Bladon, Oxon., in 1723, for the modest sum of £8 14s. It was "erected by mony that was gained by witson sport".

---

[1] Fac. 2/9.   [2] Faculty bk I, 1739–71, pp. 69–70.
[3] Berkshire Record Office, D/P 40.8 81.

4

SURVEYS, PLANS, AND ESTIMATES

URING the Middle Ages, and for a long time after, the architect of a building was—as the name implies—a master crafts-
man, usually a mason, though a master carpenter would, of
course, design the roof. The architect in something like the modern
sense first appears in the seventeenth century, when it became necessary
to have someone who understood the Palladian rules. Even so, he
was not necessarily—or even usually—anyone with any experience of
building: he might be an artist, or simply an educated gentleman. But
the workmen soon learned the rules, and by the latter part of the century there were many who knew what was wanted; and in fact a great
deal of the detail might be designed by them, with the general approval
of the architect. And many craftsmen were able to make designs for
themselves. Changes in taste, and more exacting standards, might make
it difficult for them to provide what was required, but, even so, there
were many pattern-books of architecture which they could use to help
them to produce something that would pass muster.

In the later eighteenth century, the status of the workman was
declining, and he was coming to depend more and more on the plans
of the architect, which he had simply to execute.

Up to the end of the century, the vestries still made separate
contracts with the various trades. In the nineteenth century the big
contractors begin to appear, who employed workmen in all the
trades.

In parish records the word surveyor often appears. It certainly does
not always mean the same as architect. A committee of vestrymen
might act as surveyors; and the work might be measured by a surveyor
who, though he was an architect, did not necessarily make the design.
But it may be assumed that if a surveyor is mentioned in the earlier
stages of the work, he was probably the designer as well.

All plans for repairs and rebuildings had, of course, to come before
the vestry, or a committee appointed by it. There is seldom any reference in the minutes to matters of taste. Perhaps there were discussions

that did not find their way into the records; but the general impression is, that the vestrymen were ordinary people who did not concern themselves with the questions that interested the men of taste. They knew what they wanted: a neat, uniform, and regular building, not impossibly expensive, which would be large enough, or small enough, to hold the parishioners conveniently. They knew the correct names of the things that they wanted to have (almost every vestry must have included a builder or a carpenter); and they discussed them, and the vestry clerk took down their suggestions (though he seldom spelt them correctly: cornice almost invariably appears as cornish, aisle is usually isle, and cupola may appear as kupilo, kupalo, or almost anything else). But—unless, as sometimes happened, they decided that the design of some other church ought to be copied[1]—there is no evidence that they concerned themselves with the precedent for the design as a whole, or the authority for the details.

It is true that nineteenth-century vestry minutes are equally uninformative. In the 1850s and '60s the vestry clerks simply recorded that it had been agreed to rebuild, or restore the church, according to the plan of Mr Scott or Mr Street. But that does not mean that there had not been many learned ecclesiological discussions behind the scenes. The vicar, the squire, and the architect must have talked over the plans, and said many things about Style and Period. And their eighteenth-century predecessors may have said far more than ever found its way into the vestry minutes. But the farmers and shopkeepers who looked at the plans, and voted in favour of them, can hardly have had anything very important to say. They knew what they wanted, and their taste was sound enough. They were like the Duchess of Marlborough, who had the chapel at Blenheim "finish'd decently, substantially and very plain", and had no use for "Wonderful Figures and Whirligigs . . . that are no Manner of Use but to laugh at". Elaborate plaster work, or Gothick, might be welcomed if a private person would pay for them, but usually they could be dispensed with.

The following examples show eight vestries engaged in the preliminary stages of building a new church: the first two in country

---

[1] An interesting example of this, dating from the previous century, is the building of the tower at Crondall, Hants. In 1659 the churchwardens went to find a tower to copy, and decided on that of Battersea, which was measured and reproduced. The old church of Battersea was taken down in 1775, so that the copy has survived the original (C. D. Stooks, *A History of Crondall and Yateley*; J. G. Taylor, *Our Lady of Batersey*, pp. 71–2). For another example see p. 45.

towns; the next in a crowded town south of the Thames; the next two in the City of London; the next in a growing place on the edge of London; and the last two in villages.

The old church of St Mary at the Walls, Colchester, was ruined in the Civil War. A petition for a brief was made at midsummer 1709: the estimate for rebuilding was £6153 10s. A meeting of the trustees on 7 April 1713 agreed, "Item, that Mr Middleton doe inquire out a good Surveyor or Workman in London fitt for such a purpose & doe agree with him to take down and view y⁰ foundations of the said Church & for drawing a scheme or Model for rebuilding thereof". John Price (of Richmond) and Henry Hester came down, and each was reimbursed for his "trouble in making a Draft or plan for a New Church ffive Guineas". Price's plan and estimate were accepted. He proposed to build a new body, which could be finished in nine months: his estimate was £1250, "with the benefitt of thc old materials". "As to the Charges of the Steeple I have not so much as Considered, by Reason I am not acquainted with the Ornamen⁺ or what height you conclude to have it." On 14 May the trustees approved of the plan, and a parishioner, Jacob Johnson, a plumber, was deputed "to be Surveyor over the said Mr Price in y⁰ Building".[1]

The old church of Whitchurch, Salop, was destroyed by the fall of the tower on 31 July 1711. An estimate was made by William Smith:[2] "An Estimate for rebuilding the Church & Tower at Whitchurch according to a designe drawn by John Barker to be after the Doricke Order the Church to be 88 ft. long & 62 ft. wide within 38 ft. high from the floor to the Cieling of the North & South Isles." The total would amount to £3700. This was accepted, and there is an "Agreement between William Smith of the Weergs in the County of Stafford builder and the rector churchwardens and inhabitants of Whitchurch 23 Jan. 1711": "The said Mr Smith does agree to Erect and build a New Church and Steeple in Whitchurch aforesaid of the same largeness and extent exactly and also of the same hight." It is to be finished by 1 November 1713, as high as the roof; and the rest of the tower and the steeple are to be finished by 1 November 1714.

This is one of the cases in which the evidence is not as complete as one could wish. John Barker, who is said to have made the design, was a carpenter by trade, and subsequently worked on the church. There

[1] *Essex Arch. Soc. Transactions*, xxiii (2), 1945.
[2] In the County Record Office at Shrewsbury: it is not dated.

would be no reason to doubt his authorship, if it were not for the fact that the Smiths were far more important than he was. They built many later churches, which have a strong family likeness, and it would be natural to suppose that they made the designs themselves. It is hard to believe that the general idea came from Barker and that they never abandoned it. If Smith himself made a second design, the acceptance of which is not recorded, the mystery would be solved.

The vestry minutes of St Olave's, Southwark, contain a complete account of the rebuilding: they are in the London County Record Office, and the relevant parts were printed in the *Builder*.[1]
On 6 July 1737,

The said trustees took into consid^n the business of a surveyor to the intended new church, upon which Mr Fleetcraft [Flitcroft] and Mr Porter attended, and they were separately called in, and being asked sev^l questions ab^t the business of a surveyor, and what they intended to do under the character and denomination of a surveyor, Mr Fleetcraft informed the said trustees of his intention and design, and that he would perform his business as a surveyor for 4 l. per c^t. Mr Porter also informed the s^d trustees to the same purpose, and offered to pform the same at 2 l. per cent.; but the same being debated, as well in regard to the difference of price and the proposalls of the said surveyors as also of the prov^d ability of Mr Fleetcraft, a previous question was putt, whether the s^d trustees sho^d at this time proceed to the choice of a surveyor. Ordered, that the s^d trustees do proceed to a choice.

Flitcroft was chosen by a majority.

The said trustees, after the said choice was over, informed Mr Fleetcraft, that as they chose him their surveyor, they hoped he would abate somewhat of his proposall. He replied that he would contract for no less than 4 l. per c^t; but in regard to the parish he wo^d be obliged to make a deduction of an half p. ct. Ordered accordingly.

17 August: This day Mr Fleetcraft attended with a ground plan, and also a plan of the church and Steeple, and also a view of the inside and outside of the east end, but the said trustees came to no resolution.

14 September: Mr Fleetcraft's Clerk attended at this meeting with several drawings [which were approved].

1 February 1737/8: This day Mr Dunn for himself, and Mr Townsend the mason, Mr Devall and Mr Horsenaile, masons, and also Mr White,

---

[1] 1844, pp. 252–3 and 263–5.

Mr Cole and Mr Pratt, bricklayers, attended with their sev^l proposalls; and upon reading the masons proposalls in their sev^l turns,

Mr Dunn's   amounted to   £2513-0-0
Mr Horsenail's   ,,   to   2470-0-0
Mr Devall's   ,,   to   2450-0-0

But Mr Horsenail and Mr Devall's being the two lowest, and so near each other, they were severally called in, and ask'd if they would lessen their proposalls, and then they were desired to withdraw to consider thereof; upon which Mr Horsenail and Mr Devall withdrew, and signed a further proposall which amounted to 2425 l.; but even that was objected to as being too large a sum for the intended business, and they were then informed by Mr Fleetcroft that the masons work may be completed for the sum of 2271 l.; and if they thought proper to contract for that sum, they were at liberty to renew their proposall; and being again called in, Mr Devall and Mr Horsenail agreed to perform the business for the sum of 2271 l., and both signed their proposals accordingly.

After which Mr Cole, Mr Pratt, and Mr White, the bricklayers, proposalls were respectively read, and the amount of

Mr Cole's   Proposal was £1030
Mr Pratt's   ,,   ,,   940
Mr White's   ,,   ,,   905

Mr White being called in, acquainted the trustees that Mr Pratt was intended to be concerned with him, and they both agreed to perform the bricklayer's work for 905 l., and signed their proposalls accordingly.

On 15 February tenders were received for the carpenter's work. Marquand, whose estimate was £580, was declared to have the contract, and signed his proposal.

4 April 1739: Mr Boson, the carver, also attended with his proposall for performing the carved work of the church, and produced a specimen of a Cherub's head, &c; which proposall being read over, it was ordered that the said Mr Boson perform the said work for 50 £, according to his proposall, and that the same be entered in the book of the contracts.

Mr Batson was to be the plasterer.

Flitcroft presented his bill on 4 June 1740:

For Designing and Estimating the new church, with proposalls for the severall artificers, and assisting the Trustees to make their Contracts; making all the necessary drawings and conducting the Works, with measuring the extra Work, and Examining their accounts; ffor making models of the Roof and Ceiling, and the Alter End of the Church, patterns for the Steeple,

Consisting of Elevations, Plans and Sections, with the Estimate of the Charges of each, one of about £1050, the other £650, as the scaffolds were then up.

The trustees for rebuilding St Catherine Coleman, in the City of London, first met on 12 June 1739.[1] On 8 August the following were proposed as surveyors: Mr Joseph Stibbs, Mr Taylor Bates, Mr Horne, Mr James, Mr Dance, Mr Coley (Cooley), Mr Berry and Mr Allingham. "But it being agreed by the Major part of the Trustees then present that a Plan for Building of the said Church should be first fixed on and Approved, the Choice of a surveyor was deferred till the next Meeting."

On 5 September it was agreed that candidates for the post of surveyor might leave their plans with Mr Pond the chairman. On 26 September Mr Cooley and Mr Stibbs were separately called in. They were asked if they would take £2 in the hundred if chosen as surveyor. Cooley agreed, Stibbs refused. Mr Horne and Mr Berry were proposed, but did not attend. On 10 October Horne, Cooley, and Bates attended and offered themselves as candidates: the choice fell on Horne. It was agreed that Mr James, Mr Flitcroft and Mr Cooper, who had surveyed the church for the petition presented to the House of Commons in 1732, should be written to and asked to bring in their bills for work done in and about the church.

This was done, and they were paid off.

On 17 October the site of the new church was settled: it was to be rebuilt to the south wall of the churchyard, and close to the East India warehouse. On the 31st Horne produced a plan of the intended church, and on 3 January he produced proposals for building it, which were approved.

The security of Stibbs and Cooley was considered sufficient, and their proposal was accepted. The draft of the agreement between the trustees and Thomas Stibbs and William Cooley was approved on 12 February. Cooley was the mason and Stibbs the carpenter.

It is hard to read the accounts of the building of such churches as St Olave's and St Catherine's without a feeling of sadness: so much trouble was taken to build, in one case a really handsome church, and in the other a decent, plain, solid one. But within a couple of centuries both had become useless, and both disappeared. The final state of St Olave's is mentioned on p. 212. St Catherine's was one of the least

[1] Minute book in the Guildhall Library, MSS. 1133.

regarded of the City churches, and no one wanted it. The last service was held in 1921, and the church was demolished in 1925. A man said to me, "Yes, and I had the pleasure of helping to pull it down". But it was appreciated in its day. Holy Trinity, Guildford, is said to have been built on the model of it. It is not particularly like it, but it was also designed by Horne; and the Guildford parishioners must have thought that St Catherine's was well done, and that the fact that Horne had built such a church was good reason for their choosing him as the architect for theirs.

The committee for rebuilding All Hallows', London Wall, met on 1 May 1765, and plans were presented to them.[1] They were those of (1) Mr Holden: estimate £3000, (2) Mr Robinson: estimate £3150, (3) Mr Gibson: estimate £2500, (4) Mr Dance: estimate £3000, (5) Mr "Dublican" (Dowbiggin): estimate £3000. On 8 May it was "Moved and Seconded that the several Serveyors attending with Plans of the Intended New Church be called in and that they do produce the same separately". Robinson declared that his estimate was now £2942. "Mr Gibson's Plan was next called for but no Person attended to produce the same." Then Dance said that his estimate was £3000, and Dowbiggin said that his was £2980. "It was then Moved by Mr Cox and seconded by —— that the said Mr Dance be appointed the surveyor for Building the Intended New Church and that his plan be carried into Execution and the Question being put the said Mr Dance was appointed accordingly and his Plan Ordered to be carried into Execution." The other surveyors were given five guineas each.

On Thursday 9 May: "Ordered that M\.r Dances Plans Sections & Elevations be left at the House of M\.r George Dance in Chiswell Street for the Inspection of any Person who shall be willing to Contract for building the Inte\.d New Church." Advertisements were to be inserted in the papers. The old church was to be closed on the Thursday in Whitsun week. "Moved and seconded that no Sounding Board be put over the Pulpit which was Agreed to."

On 23 May the proposals of the workmen were read, and Joseph Taylor's estimate—£2941—was to be taken into consideration as the lowest. Taylor was called in to know if he could do it for less. "He desired to have a little time to consider thereof and then he was desired to withdraw." When he was called in again, he said that he could not do it for a less sum.

[1] Minute book in the Guildhall Library, MSS. 5344.

18 June: Dance's particulars of piling and planking were produced; Taylor was to execute them. 25 June: Taylor had found that the foundations were wet. The contract for piling and planking was made with him. 29 August: Dance delivered in a certificate that the brick-layer's work already performed amounted to £350, and mason's work £151; Taylor's bill for piling and planking was £166 18s 10¼d. It was resolved that Taylor be paid in full, and £330 paid for the other work.

On 19 April 1779 a committee was appointed to consider the best way of accommodating the inhabitants of Hackney. In July, William Jupp made a plan for rebuilding the body of the church at a cost of £5798 16s. It was decided to defer the matter.

On 5 May 1788 another committee was appointed, who made a report on 23 March 1789. William Blackburn had surveyed the church: if it were rebuilt on the old foundations, it could be made to hold 1700; but accommodation was needed for 3000, and it seemed to Blackburn and to them that nothing would be adequate except to build a new church on a new site. A ballot of ratepayers was taken: 313 agreed with the report, 70 did not.

The committee for rebuilding first met on 26 June 1790. On 16 August a letter from Blackburn was read. He hoped that he would be appointed surveyor. He was sorry that his state of health prevented him from making personal application, but he hoped to recover speedily. On 6 September he wrote again, saying that he would have been happy to attend a meeting on Monday next, but that he had to attend an engagement to survey the cathedral at Exeter, and a consider-able piece of business under his direction at Dorchester. At the meet-ing, a surveyor was voted for. Blackburn obtained 46 votes and Gibson 23.

On 4 October Blackburn attended, and was asked to make an esti-mate, which he gave on the 18th. But he died suddenly during this month.

On 15 November the chairman reported the vacancy. There were six candidates for the post, Messrs Spiller, Gibson, Wooding, Robinson, Fellows, and Carter. On 6 December three were balloted for: Spiller was given 51 votes, Gibson 44, and Robinson 5. On 24 January 1791 Spiller laid three plans before the trustees, and "the plan upon the Principle of an Octagon" was accepted. However, another plan was produced on 4 April and accepted—with certain alterations, which were made. On 26 November Spiller reported the tenders of the various tradesmen.

On 16 January 1792 a committee was appointed to wait on the bishop: on 6 February it was stated that he had approved the specifications, estimates, contracts, and sureties, and the workmen were authorized to begin.

The vestry of West Malling, Kent, on 12 October 1778 agreed to write to Mr Wyatt, who had surveyed one of the pillars, to know if he could send down a foreman to superintend the repair or rebuilding of it. On the 20th the churchwardens were to apply to Wyatt to come as soon as possible, and give his opinion as to the best method of removing materials and preventing further damage. On the 25th it was agreed that the dangerous parts should be taken down at once.

28 December: able and experienced workmen to make a survey and estimate so as to make a report in order to obtain a brief.

14 August 1779: Mr Shakespear had declined to give a plan and estimate. The churchwardens "desired to write to Mr Wyatt for a plan of a church 36 ft. clear in width, to extend from tower to chancel, 74 ft. in length".

29 May 1780: Whereas Mr Wyatt, having declined attending the survey of re-building the church, it is become necessary that some person be appointed in his room; and Whereas at the several vestry meetings held the parishioners have been divided in the manner of re-building and carrying on the works, causing delay and prejudice, that a new surveyor be appointed and the works speedily and with spirit carried through, a committee be appointed for this purpose, and that Mr Francis Brooke be appointed treasurer . . . Mr George Gwilt to be the surveyor.

On 10 June 1780 the committee agreed "That there be a Portland stone fascia between the upper and lower windows; that the jambs be quite plain, and that there be dripping eaves to project 2 feet 6 inches."

On the 19th Gwilt attended with plans, elevations, and sections. James Martin was appointed foreman of the masons. The new nave was completed in 1782.[1]

At Dagenham, Essex, a vestry was held on 27 November 1797, "to Receive particulars or proposals from Mr Cockran Respecting the State

[1] A. W. Lawson and G. W. Stockley, *A History of the Parish Church of St Mary the Virgin, West Malling, Kent*, 1904, pp. 72–5.

of the Church Steple". Samuel Cleare was requested to make estimates for rebuilding the tower either with brick or with stone quoins. On 1 January 1798 he produced plans and estimates, and the plan with stone quoins was accepted: it was resolved to apply for a brief. On 5 March it was resolved that the tower be pulled down by William Bentley according to his agreement with Cleare.

> 8 April: Resolv'd that Mr Sam! Cleare be directed to bring a plan and estimate of a Church a foot and an half narrower in the Body and a foot and a half narrower in each of the side ailes making in the whole four feet and an half narrower than the old Church, the pews to be laid out on a modern plan like some of the new built Churches. The length of the Church to be reduced to the gallery to join on at the length of the north-west pillar now standing and the tower to be reduced to a size sufficient to hold the six bells.
>
> 6 May: Ordered that Mr Cleare bring a model of a Church according to the plans produced and an estimate of the Expence.

> 28 April 1800: Mr Cleare to advertise for contracts to take down and rebuild the Church.

On 8 December it was resolved that Mr Mason be appointed surveyor. No reason is given for Cleare's dismissal. "Mr Mason the Surveyor having Attended & Viewed the Church & deliv'd it as his oppinione that the wall particular the Arch between the church & Chancel were in danger of falling he was Desired to bring in a plan & Estimate of a Church at the Next Vestry the 5th of Jany. next." He attended on the 5th with plan and estimates for a church, tower, and spire. He was asked to propose some competent person to contract for the building. The first stone was laid on 13 April 1801.[1]

In the case of an entirely new church, there was, of course, no vestry in existence, and a committee had to be appointed to collect money, decide on the plan, accept estimates, and see that the work was carried out.

The Act of Parliament under which St Philip's, Birmingham, was built[2] empowered the Bishop of Lichfield and Coventry to appoint a certain number of persons, not exceeding twenty, to carry out the scheme. Their powers were to come to an end within twelve months after the completion of the church. One of them was Thomas Archer,

---

[1] Vestry minutes in the Essex County Record Office.
[2] 7 Anne, c. 34: 1708.

who was chosen as the architect of the church. They met for the first time on 23 May 1709; their first minute is about the conveyance of the site. By 9 September they were discussing stone: Mr Pedley (Joseph Pedley, the mason) undertook to go to Mr Archer's quarry, and to Rowington quarry, to inquire about the price of stone, and the carriage of it to Birmingham. The contract was made with William Shakespear of Rowington, who agreed to deliver at Rowington quarry 200 loads of stone ready for loading.

The church was finished by the middle of 1715, and was consecrated on 4 October.[1]

St George's, Liverpool, was erected by the Corporation. On 15 April 1725,

An Estimate and sev[ll] plans of a New Church to be erected in the late Castle upon the ground where the old large square stone Tower and the stone buildings adjoining to the same Northward now stand, being now laid before this Council by Mr Tho Steers and Mr James Shaw,

And this Councill haveing taken the same into consideration, and being very desirous to promote so pious a work w[ch] is now much wanted, and with all possible speed to erect a convenient church, with a proper spire steeple, doe agree that a new church be there built and a spire steeple att the West side or end and an alcove for a chancell on the east side or end; and in order to perfect the same

It is now order'd that a Committee be appointed to agree with workmen and contract for building the same, and a Comittee is now appointed viz[t] Mr Mayor and Bayl[s] and all Mr Aldermen, Mr Tho Steers and Mr James Shaw or any five of them ...

5 Nov. 1725 William Marsden Mayor
It being propounded to this Councill that a proper Modell of the New intended Church sho'd be settled, ascertain'd and fix'd upon, It is now order'd that the Walls thereof shall be plain without pillars or pillasters, and the windows after the same forme as in Mr Shaw's Modell.

2 Nov. 1726 Thomas Bootle Mayor
Mr Sephton haveing drawn some draughts or models of a Church, It is order'd that the Comittee settle his demands, and that the Treasurer doe pay him not exceeding tenn guineas.

That the Comittee consider of vaulting the Church

The Comittee appointed for building the New Church representing to this Councill, that they have agreed with Mr Thos Steers and Mr Edw[d] Litherland for building the walls and part of the steeple; this Council doth approve

[1] The Commissioners' minutes are in the vestry of St Philip's.

thereof, and order that a contract be entered into, and a bond for performance, and that they begin imediatly.

That the old Castle wall att the top of Lord Street be imediatly pull'd
down and the ground clear'd for the contractors to begin.

1729: Order'd . . . That the new church in Derby Square be vaulted and
arched with brick.

18 Dec. 1732: Ordered, that the Treasurer do pay to Mr Ed Litherland
sixty pounds tow^ds his work in the steeple to the new church in Derby
Square.[1]

The committee for building St Mary's, Birmingham, first met on
15 October 1771. By 4 November 1772, they had reached the point of
discussing the building. It was resolved

that the chapel of St Mary's shall be vaulted round the inside of the said
chapel and that the form of the said chapel be an octagon if approved of in
regard to the expence, to be galleryed round and to be covered with slate
and be finished with a tower, in proportion to the building, the whole to
be built with brick (except stone Cornish stone scills battlement walls stone
frontispieces and the floor laid with stone). The Pillars to be left to the judgment of the architect and to contain one thousand sittings and the said
sittings to be twenty-two inches each. The seats to be wainscoted with oak.
The whole expence to be estimated at between three and four thousand
pounds.

The committee resolved to find persons to level the ground. Abraham Stephens was to make all the bricks at 14s 6d per thousand: the
dimensions of the bricks were decided. Then a plan was "exhibited by
Mr Joseph Pickford of Derby", and was accepted. Thomas Saul was
appointed to inspect the building in regard to materials and workmanship, and was to be allowed ten guineas for his trouble. Pickford's
estimate was £3666 18s 6d.[2]

Contracts were often advertised in the papers. The following
advertisement appeared in the *Northampton Mercury* on 17 September
1753:

The Parish Church of Great Houghton, in the County of Northampton,
being greatly decayed, and intended to be pulled down and re-built, the
Steeple whereof is already taken down: This is to give Notice to all Carpenters, Bricklayers, and Builders who are willing to contract for Re-building
the said Church and Steeple, that they may deliver Plans, Particulars, and

[1] J. A. Picton, *Municipal Records of Liverpool*, Vol. II, 1886, pp. 70–1.
[2] Minute book at the Birmingham Reference Library.

Proposals for doing the same, on Wednesday the 26 of September Instant, between the Hours of Nine and Ten in the Forenoon, at the Red-Lion Inn in Northampton; in which Proposals they are required to set forth what they will give for the several Materials of the old Church, such as Lead, Stones, Timbers, Glass, Iron, Bells, &c. In the mean Time they may be further inform'd, by applying to Mr John Archbold, of Great Houghton aforesaid; or to Peter Roberts, Esq; at his Chambers in the Old South-Sea House, London. NB. It is intended that the said Church shall be built in a plain, decent, and commodious Manner, without unnecessary Ornaments, and shall not exceed forty-five Feet in Length, and thiry-five Feet in Breadth, and the Steeple to hold only two Bells.

The Warden and Fellows of the Collegiate Church, Manchester, advertised on 24 April 1753 for tenders for building a new church (St Mary's, Deansgate). It was to be "according to the plan and dimensions of the Parish Church of Knotsford, in the County of Chester, except that it will be cased with stone".

Stepney Church was surveyed early in 1767 by William Smith, and the vestry agreed, on 2 March, on the work to be done. Advertisements were to be inserted in the *Daily Advertiser*.

5

INDIVIDUAL BENEFACTIONS

THE RESPONSIBILITY of keeping the church in repair (apart from the chancel) is the parishioners', and they also have to provide the necessities of worship. The Canons mention the Bible and the Book of Common Prayer (Canon 80), the Communion table, covered with a carpet of silk or other decent stuff, and with a fair linen cloth at the time of the ministration; the Ten Commandments, and a seat for the minister (82), a comely and decent pulpit (83), an alms chest (84), the bread and wine and "a clean and sweet standing pot or stoop of pewter, if not of purer metal" (20), register and chest (70), surplice (58), table of prohibited degrees (99)—and presumably the font, though Canon 81 does not explicitly say that it is to be provided "at the charge of the parish".

But there is, of course, no reason why anyone who wishes to do so should not make a present of any of these things; and many people in the eighteenth century gave generously towards the fitting up and adorning of their churches.

Gifts were usually recorded on benefactions boards, painted with gold lettering on a black ground (in the humbler churches, black on white). These, when they survive, are most informative, and no doubt the writers who compiled the earlier county histories, or wrote descriptions of churches in the *Gentleman's Magazine*, made use of them. We do the same when we can. There is, for instance, an excellent series at the west end of St James's, Poole, which has been continued to the present day. At Kirkby Overblow in Yorkshire is a board recording the work done in the time of the Reverend Charles Cooper. The church was repaired in 1780, and the tower rebuilt in the next year. The builder was John Muschamp. In 1799 Cooper adorned and beautified the chancel. These are the kinds of things that we want to know, but which it is not usually easy to find out.

Bucklebury, Berks., had its benefactions painted on the gallery front in 1824. The earlier ones are gifts of sacramental plate. In 1809 the Reverend W. H. H. Hartley gave the organ (£210); in 1812 more plate, two prayer books for the altar, a kneeling cushion, and chairs covered with crimson cloth; also a marble font (£18 11s), and £60-worth of bricks and timber for building the churchyard wall.

Such records are most useful: when they are there, it is an easy matter to copy them into a notebook. But the nineteenth-century restorers did not like benefactions boards, and generally threw them away. They thought that if a Churchman gave anything to God, he ought to be content to do it anonymously, and not advertise the gift. This is no doubt true in theory, but it makes things more difficult for those who come after, and would like to know about it.

Nor did the ecclesiologists like the appearance of the boards: their shape, and their style of lettering, did not fit in with the church as they would like it to be. So most of them were thrown out, and the direct evidence, on which the older writers relied, has been taken away. If we want to check their statements, we must look through the vestry minutes, and hope to find a vote of thanks to the benefactor. There is much to be said for reviving the benefactions board as part of the furniture of our churches. It is certainly much better to look at, and easier to read, than the separate small tablets of stone or brass that are put up nowadays to record gifts of electric light, organ blowers, sanctuary mats, and so on.

But there must have been many pieces of work that were not recorded—not necessarily of special importance, but of interest as part of the history of the church. Mention of repairs and alterations will be found in many collections of family papers. I give two examples, both from collections in the Berkshire Record Office.

Among the Radnor papers from Coleshill are several about the alterations to the chancel of Great Coxwell church in 1795.[1]

First, a memorandum of the Earl of Radnor.

THINGS TO BE DONE AT COXWELL CHANCELL

The *four* side Windows to be stopt up—flush on the Inside—The little Arch now in S.E. angle to be introduced in the stoping up of the Window next to it. to leave on the outside the Appearance of the Windows—also the Door Way on the South Side the same. Buttresses of Stone to be put against the Angles of the Chancell—not angular-wise, but in Addition to the Eastern Work as—[rough drawing] the Buttresses to reach to the Ramps at the Foot of the Eaves. Cut off the stone Rib on the north Side in the Inside—& the Seat thro' the Arch. Cut off the Ledge of the Window on the South Side of the inside—

[1] Berkshire Record Office, D/EMt A.21.

Insert a plain Rib in Plaister (like that in Stone ordered to be taken off) at the Spring of the Cieling Cove the whole Length on each Side—The Crack in the S.E. angle to be made up as firm as possible—

The arch between the Church & Chancell to be pointed neatly, and white washed

All the Wood Work From between the Church, & Chancel to be removed—

The Eastern Window to be lengthened three Feet, and the mullions lengthened likewise—

The Bottom internally to be sloped down—thus— [drawing]

The Glazing of the Window I will order when the Work is in forwardness

R——

There follows, "Coxwell Chancell—Design for the Glass of the Window"—a rough drawing with notes. George Foxton, the incumbent, writes on 22 May:

My Lord,

I received yr Lordship's Favor of yesterday and have given Directions to the plaisterer in Writing (as the Mason was not at work) to slope down the seats between the Church and Chancel according to your Lordship's Instructions, whenever the Alterations are begun; tho' I confess myself rather at a loss to know, whether you mean that the Slope should be continued as far as the Seat extends round the Chancel, or only thro' the Arch-Way.

Upon taking down the plaistering in the Chancel yesterday, several stone Niches or Recesses were discovered in the Eastern Wall just above the Communion Table which I have attempted a sketch of on the paper herewith sent . . . I thought it my Duty to apprize your Lordship of these Circumstances as they may suggest to you some Alterations which you may wish to have made. The central Niche is only about 18 Inches below the Window, so that it must necessarily be taken down in making the proposed Alterations . . .

His drawing, with the measurements, is in pencil. There is a note at the bottom: "The plaisterer thinks to serve the Chancel as your Lordship's seat at Coleshill is will be neater and the Expence the same— The wall over the Arch into the Chancel very much craked indeed."

His lordship makes a rough drawing of the east end, based on Foxton's, with notes on the alterations to be made. The recess under the east window is to be lowered, the recess on the south is to be shortened to correspond with that on the north, and the rest are to be stopped up.

Then there is a more careful drawing (not by the Earl of Radnor) endorsed "The Drawing of Coxwell Chancel Window". Then another scribble by his lordship, then seven drawings of the coats of arms for the glass (possibly by Eginton). Foxton writes on 5 November:

My Lord,
I confess myself much pleased and much obliged by everything that has been done in the Church and the Chancel, as both are rendred peculiarly neat and comfortable, and have only to lament that more was not attempted: the pulpit which was before not ornamental, is by the Improvement rendred more unsightly—nor do I find that there is the least Intention on the part of the Parish of putting up a new one, as all the scaffolding has (tho' not till within these ten days) been entirely removed: I have to hope, however, my Lord, that you have not abandoned the Idea of obtaining a Majority [sic] at Vestry and voting it, as I consider that Mode more preferable, than an Appeal to the Archdeacon, which would probably give offence to my Parishioners, and subject me to their Displeasure. The Singing-Gallery is not painted, but probably I may be able to get that done, as the Expence will be but trifling The Chancel is very much improved indeed by restoring the Arch, lengthening the Eastern Window and stopping up the side ones; but would it not be rendred still more neat and decent by the Addition of a light Railing across a few Yards from the Altar? Is it your Lordship's wish too that nothing more be done to the Niche's in the wall?
Mr. Capel a Brother in Law of Farmer Morse's has given a plain neat mahogany Table for the Communion Service, which I found already placed at the Altar, and which makes a very good Appearance . . .

The Mount papers contain some mention of repairs to Wasing church.[1] There is a bill for a painted window by T. Palmer, for John Mount, Esq., dated 11 December 1760:

	£	s	d
To a painted Window sett & Compleated	7	7	0
To a strong Gothick frame Oke sill & Eight Iron Bars	1	8	—

Wasing House was remodelled in 1770–3 by John Hobcraft. The work was supervised by John Uzzell, who kept continually in touch with Hobcraft, and sent regular reports and accounts to John Mount. The church is mentioned in three of his letters.

9 November 1773: ". . . the plaisterers are now working at the Church . . ."

The next letter is torn, and there is no date, but it is endorsed "Mr. Uzzells Acct settled to 20 Novr 1773":

This will inform you we have quite finished the Plaistering of Church begin the Painting in [page torn] . . . it looks exceeding neat considering

[1] Berkshire Record Office, D/EPb83.

what a Job it has been have taken down the Shores on the outside every part I hope is safe therefore needs no Buttresse.

7 December 1773: the Church will be quite finish'd painting the middle of the Next week, shall have compleated the terrat and fix'd the Clock the Middle of next Week.

There must be hundreds of such references to be found in family papers; but how many have perished?

Alterations such as Lord Radnor's at Coxwell must often have puzzled, or misled, conscientious antiquaries. It is often difficult to be sure about the date of a particular feature, and it is certain that some, which we accept as medieval, are really seventeenth or eighteenth-century repairs. But who is to say which are, and which are not? The study of documentary records is absolutely necessary—though, when everything has been read, there may still be doubt.

The following lists give a few examples of eighteenth-century generosity. Some are taken from inscriptions in the churches, some from the local historians, and some from parish records. It must be understood that they are manifestly incomplete, and that hundreds more examples could be given without difficulty.

There are two lists for each county: the first is of new churches and more or less complete rebuildings; the second is of partial rebuildings, adornments, and beautifications. No mention is made of the erection of pews or of galleries, though these were sometimes of some architectural importance; nor of the very frequent gifts of Communion plate, linen, or branches.[1] It must not be assumed, of course, that work mentioned here still exists; in very many cases it does not.

BEDFORDSHIRE

I. *Markyate Street* chapel was built and endowed by John Coppin, to whom a faculty was granted on 17 June 1734: he, "being Desirous to promote the Exercise of Our most Holy Religion", had proposed to "erect at his own costs a Chapel containing about 48 ft. in length and 18 in breadth, and to endow it with £10 a year from certain lands to be charged with the payment thereof".

Souldrop was rebuilt in 1800 at the cost of John sixth Duke of Bedford.

[1] I.e., chandeliers; but the word branch is normally used in the eighteenth century.

II. *Biggleswade:* a painting of the Last Supper was given in 1765 by Charles Barnett of Stratton Park to serve as an altarpiece.

Dunstable: Jane Cart and Frances Ashton gave an altarpiece, nearly 30 ft. high, by Sir James Thornhill: the Last Supper, with architecture and draperies, and the heavens opened in the centre.

Woburn: John Duke of Bedford, about 1750, decorated the chancel with an elliptical arched roof ornamented with flowers and cross ribs supported by Roman corbels in plaster of Paris. Altarpiece in the Roman style, and pavement of freestone and black marble.

BERKSHIRE

I. *Kingston Bagpuize* was rebuilt by John Blandy in 1799–1800. He left £2000 for the purpose.

Midgham was rebuilt by John Hillersdon (1714)

Pusey was rebuilt by John Allen Pusey, whose epitaph (1753) includes the words: "This Church, rebuilt at his own Expence, will be a lasting Monument of his Zeal for the Worship of God, in the Beauty of Holiness. He, who paid this Attention to the *External* Part of Religion was equally exact in a due Observance of the *Internal*, and more *Essential* Duties."

Twyford chapel was founded by Edward Polehampton, citizen of London and painter-stainer. It was opened on 16 September 1728.

West Woodhay church was out of repair in 1716, and William Sloper, lord of the manor and patron, offered to rebuild it, "in the place and as near as may be to the same Dimensions it is now of, as may be done with solidity and ornament, and so finish the inside thereof according to the best methods that are now used in Buildings of that nature both for Decency and Worship".

II. *Arborfield* chancel was beautified in 1744 by John Waterman, the rector. The glass in the east window (of which only a fragment remains in the new church) was by John Rowell of High Wycombe, and had two compartments with half-length figures of Moses and Aaron.

Basildon: the Reverend George Bellas (died 1802) wrote a few notes at the beginning of one of the registers "for the amusement of his successors". "The Font was given by me Geo: Bellas Vicar 1774. The Design was mine own—the *Marble Cross* & Bason were executed by the ingenious Mr Hill of Reading, and cost £1 16 0d."

Buckland: "Sir Robert Throckmorton, near his 100th year, now quite blind, but in health, has done great things to preserve and restore Buckland (his parish church). An excellent example to Roman Catholick gentry."[1]

Bucklebury chancel was mostly rebuilt by Sir Henry Winchcombe at the beginning of the eighteenth century.

Coleshill was repaired and decorated by the Earl of Radnor in 1782. A painted window from Angers was erected in the chancel.

Newbury: the altarpiece, of the Corinthian order, was given by William and Barbara Cundell in 1719.

Peasemore tower was built in 1737: a stone is inscribed

WILL: COWARD
GENT:
built ye TOWER
1737

Coward is buried under a stone in the nave: out of an income of £110 he built the tower, and gave the great bell and the Communion plate.

Shrivenham: the Coleshill papers contain the correspondence between the Earl of Radnor and Francis Eginton, in 1791, and 1793, about the heraldic glass which the earl erected in the church.[2]

Wargrave chancel was paved by Henry Frinsham, the vicar. In 1757 Mrs Pritchard had it handsomely wainscoted in oak.

Winterbourne: Philip Weston of Bussock Court built the brick north chapel as a pew and burying place (faculty 18 July 1712); and in his will (26 June 1727) bequeathed money to adorn the altar and font, to erect a steeple, and to add three more bells; to build a wall round the churchyard; and to erect a convenient house for the schoolmaster, and a handsome school house. It was stated in 1759 that this had been carried out, except for the steeple. A faculty was given on 7 June, and the tower was built. There is an inscription on the leads: "Iohn Slyhope bild this tower Nov ye 1, 1759."

BUCKINGHAMSHIRE

I. *Biddlesden* church was taken down by Henry Sayer, and a new church built about 1730.

Buckingham: the tower of the old church fell on 26 March 1776. The new church was built on a different site. Richard Grenville Temple, Earl Temple, offered to build it, if the inhabitants would

---

[1] Nichols, *Literary Anecdotes*, Vol. III, p. 698.   [2] See pp. 172–3 above.

pay £2000, and allow the use of the old materials. The new church was begun in 1777 and finished in 1781. It cost about £7000.

Eton: the Reverend William Hetherington built a chapel, which was consecrated on 8 September 1769.

Fenny Stratford: The story of Browne Willis's work for churches in Buckinghamshire is fairly well known.[1] The old chapel at Fenny Stratford had disappeared, and Willis bought the site, and had a new chapel designed; he laid the foundation stone on 11 November 1724. During the next six years he collected funds, and the chapel was consecrated on 27 May 1730.

Gayhurst was rebuilt at the expense of George Wright. The faculty, given on 23 March 1724/5, said that he was willing and desirous to rebuild the church "in a more Beautiful and Handsome Manner", and to fit it up "very Decently and Handsomely".

Hartwell was rebuilt by Sir William Lee, fourth baronet. His uncle, Sir William Lee, Lord Chief Justice of the King's Bench, gave £1000, and Sir George gave £500. It was begun in 1753 and finished in 1755; the architect was Henry Keene. This interesting piece of Gothick is now a ruin.

Loudwater was built in 1788–90 by William Davis.

West Wycombe was rebuilt in 1760–3 by Sir Francis Dashwood.

II. *Addington:* the chancel was repaired about 1710 at the cost of Dr Busby, the patron and rector. He ceiled the roof with a coved ceiling, wainscoted around the altar, and paved it with Warwick-shire stone.

Bledlow: in 1777 the chancel floor was lowered and the sanctuary paved with stone and black marble. Johnshall Cross gave the altar-piece, with a picture by Samuel Wale, R.A.[2]

Bletchley was repaired and adorned by Browne Willis in memory of his parents in 1704–7. The accounts of his expenditure are printed in *Records of Bucks.*,[3] and in *The Dragon of Whaddon.*[4] A writer in the *Gentleman's Magazine*[5] gives some notes on various Buckingham-

---

[1] See J. G. Jenkins, *The Dragon of Whaddon*, 1953.

[2] The inventory of this church in 1783 is printed in J. Wickham Legg, *English Church Life from the Restoration to the Tractarian Movement*, 1914, pp. 160–3. It includes "A Paste-Board with the Consecration Prayer, bordered with Purple Ribbon", and an alb.

[3] Vol. XII, 1931, No. 5, 239–56.   [4] pp. 234–9.

[5] 1849, Part I, pp. 156–8.

shire churches, beginning with this. "The fine works of Browne Willis, which cost £1500 in the aggregate, are still rich, though faded. The chancel ceiling, with the Twelve Apostles and the Glory at the end, will yield to none of its immediate class in England; the chancel, altar, and gallery screens, Ionic and Corinthian, and pewing of excellent wainscot, may see centuries yet: the careful marbled painting of the pillars and arches is in surprising preservation." But it is all gone now.

Brickhill, Little: Browne Willis repaired the chancel, which had fallen in 1703.

Brickhill, Bow: this was also repaired by Browne Willis.

Buckingham: in 1737 Browne Willis began to raise money for the building of a new steeple: the spire had fallen in 1699. He made a design himself, but finally the tower was simply raised, and crowned with "small irregular mean pinnacles, pediments and balustrades". The tower was not strengthened to bear the extra weight, and it fell on 26 March 1778.

Chicheley chancel was rebuilt in 1708 by the fourth baronet of the Chester family.

Clifton Reynes had its chancel repaired by the rector, the Reverend H. A. Small, at the beginning of the century, and the windows were profusely adorned with the coats of arms of the Reynes family and its alliances.

Fawley chancel was rebuilt in 1748 by John Freeman, and the church was beautified; woodwork and font came from Canons.

Hambleden was adorned with windows made by John Rowell of High Wycombe in 1732, at the expense of Dr Scawen Kendrick, the rector.

Langley Marish: the Gothick arcade on the south was erected by Sir Robert Bateson Harvey.

Latimer was repaired and altered in accordance with the will of Benjamin Hynmers, who died in 1743.

Great Linford was repaired in 1708 by Sarah, widow of Sir William Pritchard, and two nephews.

Marsh Gibbon was completely repaired and liberally decorated by Dr Robert Clavering, rector, and Bishop of Peterborough (1729–47).

Olney altarpiece was erected by Thomas Nichol, 1727.

Penn chancel was wainscoted and railed, and a new altar was given, by Roger Penn in 1714. When the Curzon family came to Penn, the chancel and south chapel were mainly rebuilt, the roof of the aisle was raised, the porch was rebuilt, and a vestry was added. This work was done at the expense of Sir Nathanael Curzon.

Soulbury had an east window inserted about 1710 at the cost and under the direction of Robert Lovett. Each compartment had stained-glass rims, and in the centre were the arms of Lovett, and the initial letters of the donor and of the artist—Richard Staniford, a mason. The ceiling was coved; above the altar it was painted to represent the sky, with a dove in the centre surrounded by clouds.

Winslow: about 1700 Mr Secretary Lowndes repaved the chancel with Bicester stone and new leaded the roof, sank a vault in the chancel, raised the altar on two steps, and paved the space within the rails with Danish marble. His eldest son Robert set up the Creed, etc., behind the altar in gold.

CAMBRIDGESHIRE

I. *Wimpole* was rebuilt by the Rt Hon. Philip Earl of Hardwicke, Lord Chancellor in, 1759. The architect was Henry Flitcroft.

II. *Graveley:* a faculty was granted on 11 September 1733 to rebuild the chancel to "the size chancels usually bear to the body of the church". It was rebuilt and beautified by the Reverend Henry Trotter.

Newton was decorated in 1718 by John Lumpkin, who was church-warden for fifty-one years, and died in 1762. The church was painted and adorned with figures and sentences, and the pillars were painted like marble.

West Wratting was altered and beautified by Sir John Jacob.

CHESHIRE

I. *Alsager* was built by Mary, Margaret, and Judith Alsager of Congleton. On 16 February 1789 the House of Commons heard their petition: they were building at their own expense a church or chapel on Alsager Heath, and were desirous of building a school and a master's residence: they asked for a Bill to enable them to complete the church and establish the school.

Little Budworth was rebuilt in consequence of the bequest in 1798 of £1000 by Ralph Kirkham, who died in 1803. His monument is in the church. The cost exceeded the amount of the bequest, and the widow of Kirkham's brother came to the rescue.

Capesthorne: 1722, by John Ward. Bishop Gastrell visited the chapel in 1723, and wrote: "This is a new chapell lately built by John Ward, Esq., who has given all the tithes of this township towards its augmentation."

Carrington was built by Isaac Shaw in 1757–9 at the expense of Mary Countess of Stamford.

Chelford: 1776 at the expense of Samuel Brooke and Catherine his sister, John Glegg, and the Reverend John Parker.

Latchford was built in 1777 as a chapel of ease to Grappenhall by Roger Rogerson. It was consecrated in 1781.

Christchurch, Macclesfield, was the gift of Charles Roe, silk manufacturer of the town in 1775–6. An Act was passed in 1778 "for making the Church or Chapel erected by *Charles Roe* Esquire, in the Town of *Macclesfield,* in the County Palatine of *Chester,* a perpetual Cure and Benefice, and for endowing the same, and vesting the Right of Nomination or Presentation thereof in the said *Charles Roe,* his Heirs and Assigns".

Rode was built by Mr Dobbs, paper manufacturer.

St Peter's, Stockport, consecrated on 31 May 1768, was erected at the sole expense of William Wright, who also endowed it.

Woodhey chapel was built and partly endowed by Lady Wilbraham c. 1700.

II. *Burton* was beautified in 1729–30 by Bishop Wilson of Sodor and Man, who was born there.

Davenham chancel was rebuilt c. 1795 by Dr Cotton.

CORNWALL

I. *Helston* was rebuilt by Lord Godolphin at a cost of about £6000. the foundation stone was laid on 8 May 1756. It was opened on 18 October 1761. The work was done under Mr Edwards, "reckoned a very skilfull architect".

II. *Camborne:* the altarpiece of Siena marble was given by S. Percival, Esq., in 1761.

CUMBERLAND

I. *Allonby:* in 1743 the Reverend Dr Thomlinson, Vicar of Newcastle on Tyne and Canon of St Paul's, proposed to build a chapel on

1. Berkswich, Staffs
   One of the gallery pews in the chancel

2. St Catherine Coleman, City of London
   Rebuilt by James Horne in 1739–40

by kind permission of John Piper

4. Cherry Willingham, Lincs. Rebuilt by Thomas Becke in 1753

3. Avington, Hants. Rebuilt in 1770 by the Marchioness of Carnarvon

some waste ground, but the Quakers opposed the scheme. Next year, he built a chapel on ground which he had purchased, and furnished it. In a letter to the Bishop of London he spoke of "the communion table and pulpit enriched with such ornaments as no country church I know of can excel or equal them".

II. *Dacre:* Bishop Nicolson (1704) wrote, "Feb. 28. S? *Edward Hasell*, who has the Impropriation of this parish, has lately repair'd and adorned the Quire in a very exemplary and honourable manner; having rais'd the Altar part, floor'd the whole anew and Rail'd in the Communion Table most decently. He has likewise put a new Roof (of Slate and Timber) above the old one . . .[1]

DERBYSHIRE

I. *Birchover* (Jesus Church, Row Tor) was built and endowed by Thomas Eyre (d. 1717) on condition that prayers were said twice daily, and Holy Communion celebrated on Sundays.

Cromford was built by Sir Richard Arkwright (1732–92). His son Richard completed it after his death, and it was consecrated on 20 September 1797. Joseph Farington went to church here on 23 August 1801: "We went to Church at Cromford where is a Chapel built abt. 3 years & ½ ago by Mr Arkwright. On each side the Organ a gallery in which about 50 Boys were seated. These children are employed in Mr Arkwright's work in the week-days, and on Sundays attend a school where they receive education. They came to Chapel in regular order and looked healthy & well & were decently cloathed and clean."[2]

Intake chapel was founded by Francis Brown in 1723.

Trusley was rebuilt in 1713 by William Coke (1679–1718).

II. *Alvaston:* Charles Benskin (d. 1739) gave a reredos of ironwork.

Barlborough: the windows on the south of the nave, and the ceilings of nave and chancel, were the gift of Margaret Pole and Mary Pole, who both died in 1755.

Brimington tower was rebuilt in 1796 at the expense of Joshua Jebb.

Matlock: the north aisle was rebuilt at the cost of Richard Arkwright in 1783.

Peak Forest was enlarged towards the east in 1780 by Mary Bower,

---

[1] *Miscellany Accounts*, p. 127.
[2] *The Farington Diary*, ed. James Greig, Vol. I, p. 314.

who left her harpsichord to the chapel, with an endowment for a player.

Ravenstone was altered and adorned early in the century by John and Rebecca Wilkins.

DEVONSHIRE

I. *Filleigh* was rebuilt by Earl Fortescue in 1732.

Teigngrace, a Gothick church, was rebuilt in 1787 by three brothers of the Templer family.

Werrington: on 1 February 1739 Sir William Morice said before the Commons that the church was decayed and ruinous, and that he was desirous of rebuilding it in a larger, more commodious and beautiful manner, and in a more convenient situation. The new church was built in 1740. It was remodelled in 1891 by Messrs St Aubyn, but its extraordinary Gothick front has been left alone.

II. *Tiverton:* in 1709 the Reverend John Newte set up the battlements of the chancel and glazed the windows.

Widworthy: the altarpiece was given by James Marwood.

DORSET

I. *Charlton Marshall* was rebuilt at the cost of nearly £1000 by the Reverend Dr Sloper. There is a vestry minute of 12 May 1713:

> We whose names are hereunder written, considering ye danger our church is in of falling in some little time, and having at this present juncture ye fav^ble opportunity of a general bounty from Dr Sloper our Revd. Minister and chancellor of ye Diocese bestowed in raising ye walls of ye church, adding 3 new Pillars of Purbeck stone, plaistering ye whole roof, and in paying for all ye materials and workmens' wages (excepting ye Carriage) have thought it fit to thank our generous Benefactor, and agree to ye raising of so many rates, as shall be necessary to ye rebuilding ye two Roofs, ye tiling ye same, and for ye payment of ye carriage of all ye materials belonging to ye church.

East Lulworth was rebuilt but for the tower in 1788 by Mr Weld.

Mapperton was rebuilt in 1704: there is an inscription: *Sumptibus Ri: Brodrepp Armig. Anno Dom. 1704.*

Melbury Osmond was rebuilt in 1745 by Mrs Susannah Strangways Horner.

Milton Abbas new church, consecrated on 15 October 1786, was built at the expense of Lord Milton. The architect may have been

Lancelot Brown. "It is admired for its elegant simplicity, and is an exact model of Gothic architecture."[1]

Moreton: the south aisle was rebuilt and beautified by James Frampton in 1733, and the whole church rebuilt in 1777.

Toller Fratrum was rebuilt by George Brown, Esq.

Wimborne St Giles was rebuilt in 1732 by the fourth Earl of Shaftesbury. Some alterations were made in 1785 by the fifth earl, who gave the font.

Winterbourne Thomson was partly rebuilt and neatly pewed by William Wake, Archbishop of Canterbury 1716–37.

II. *Abbotsbury:* the altarpiece was erected in 1751 at the expense of Mrs Strangways Horner.

Almer: the south side of the nave, and the porch, were rebuilt early in the century for General Erle, who died in 1720.

Beaminster: the north chapel was beautified by Mary Mills of Meerhay in 1767, and repaired by William Clark of Beaminster in 1794.

Bridport: the north transept was repaired and beautified in 1778 at the cost of Mr Jullantigh.

Over Compton: an aisle was built in 1776 by Robert Godden, Esq.

Okeford Fitzpaine: the chancel was rebuilt in 1772 by the Reverend Duke Butler.

Sherborne had an altarpiece of Norway oak 32 ft. broad and of a proportionable height, with a pediment supported by four fluted Corinthian pillars. It was the gift of William Lord Digby.

DURHAM

I. *Castle Eden* was rebuilt in 1764 by Rowland Burdon, Esq.

Gibside chapel: George Bowes in 1756 made a will directing his trustees to apply £1000 to building a chapel. James Paine made the design, and a beginning was made in 1760. Bowes died in that year. The chapel was not completed until 1812—by the tenth Earl of Strathmore, who spent nearly £12,000 on it.

St John's chapel was rebuilt by Sir Walter Blackett. A legacy of £50 was also given by Dr Hartwell.

II. *Bishop Wearmouth* chancel was repaired and altered by the Reverend Mr Smith, who was appointed rector in 1704.

[1] *Reading Mercury,* 13 Nov. 1786

ESSEX

I. *Ingrave* tower is inscribed

DOM

ET DIVO NICOLAO SACRUM

ROBERTUS JACOBUS PETRE BARO DE WRITTLE

AMBABUS AEDIBUS PAROECIIS

THORNDON OCCIDENTALI ET INGRAVE

IN UNAM EX S.C. COALESCENTIBUS

POSUIT MDCCXXXIV

Mistley was built by Richard Rigby, and consecrated on 6 June 1735. Robert Adam made the designs for its remodelling in 1776.

II. *Barking* was repaired and beautified in 1771 by Sir Bamber Gascoyne.

Debden: chancel built in 1793 by Muilman Trench Chiswell, Esq.

Halstead: a new spire was built in 1717 at the cost of Samuel Fiske, apothecary. Prior wrote some verses for the occasion.

Harlow was largely burned in 1708, and rebuilt by the direction of the Reverend Mr Taylor. Much of the ornamental work was at his expense, and he also gave the organ.

Pentlow: a certificate was given on 18 February 1724/5 that the rector "has lately pav'd ye Chancel of the Parish Church of Pentlow, in a very handsome manner; & repair'd the said Chancel so substantially, that nothing further will be requir'd to be done to it, for many years to come."

Pleshey was largely rebuilt in 1708 by Henry Compton, Bishop of London 1675–86.

Wanstead old church was renovated and enlarged by Earl Tylney early in the eighteenth century.

Witham church and chancel were beautified from 1701 to 1706. A board states: "The whole was Projected carryed on and Finished by the care of the Present Vicar, who besides Erected the Organ at his own Expence . . .".

GLOUCESTERSHIRE

I. *Adlestrop* was rebuilt in 1764, chiefly at the expense of James Leigh, Esq., who died in 1774, and whose monument is here.

Great Badminton was rebuilt by the Duke of Beaufort in 1785, from designs by Charles Evans of London.

Bourton on the Water: the rebuilding was begun in 1784 from designs by William Marshall; £1500 was bequeathed by Sarah Yates.

Chalford was rebuilt in 1724, and endowed by Mrs Hester Tayloe and others.

Driffield was rebuilt in 1734 by the first Lord Coleraine: "of great Symmetry and neatness: especially in the internal Decorations".

Flaxley was rebuilt in pursuance of the bequest of Catherine Boevey, who died in 1726, by Mary Pope, her executrix.

St Aldate's, Gloucester: Mrs Elizabeth Aram, who died in 1741, left £500 towards rebuilding the church.

Matson was rebuilt in 1739 by direction of the will of Albinia, widow of General Selwyn, formerly Governor of Jamaica.

Redland Chapel, Bristol, was built and endowed by John Cossins of Redland Court. The foundation stone was laid on 1 July 1740, and the first service was held on 5 October 1743.

Preston on Stour was rebuilt in 1752-7 by James West, who was president of the Society of Antiquaries, and died in 1772 aged 69. It is Gothic, designed by Edward Woodward of Chipping Campden.

Sapperton was mostly rebuilt by Earl Bathurst early in the century.

Tetbury: John Wight, the vicar, offered £1000 if the parishioners raised the rest of the money needed for rebuilding. They formed a subscription society in 1754, and with the sale of some church property, succeeded in raising the money. In 1764 they resolved that the church should be rebuilt "upon an elegant and regular Gothic plan"—which was supplied by Francis Hiorne.

Toddington: THE BODY OF THIS CHURCH WAS REBUILT IN THE YEAR OF OUR LORD ONE THOUSAND SEVEN HUNDRED & TWENTY THREE BY THE RIGHT HONOURABLE THOMAS CHARLES LORD VISCOUNT TRACY WHO DIED ON THE 4TH OF JUNE 1756 IN THE SIXTY SIXTH YEAR OF HIS AGE.[1]

II. *Bromsberrow* was adorned by the Yate family. The mortuary chapel was built in 1725; in the same year Walter Yate provided the altarpiece. In 1781 Dr Yate the rector had a new arch struck in the chancel, paved the floor, and repaired the monuments.

Cirencester: the organ loft was built by Sir Anthony Hungerford. The organ was purchased by the inhabitants, and the font was given by the female inhabitants. About 1790 Mrs Catherine Cripps

[1] Inscription on monument in the church.

left £50, which was used in collecting glass from various windows, and arranging it in a window at the west. Samuel Lysons the antiquary made the design, and it was carried out by James Miles, a plumber of the town. Glass was similarly arranged in the east window at the cost of Mrs Williams of Ponthowell, Carmarthen. The battlements of the nave were rebuilt in 1793 at the sole cost of Susan Rawes.

Doynton chancel was rebuilt by Thomas Coker, the rector, in 1767.

Painswick: altarpiece, 1743, given by Charles Hyatt.

Sherborne: the chancel rebuilt by James Lennox Dutton, who died in 1776.

Temple Guiting: work done at the cost of the Reverend George Talbot, D.D., whose monument is here:

> . . . This FABRICK Substantially Repaired and Beautified at his
> sole Expence
> And the HOSPITAL of this County which his Liberality and Exertions greatly
> contributed to found and Establish
> Will be lasting Monuments of his Piety and Humility
> But his GOOD NAME will survive both.

Great Witcombe tower and south porch were built in 1750 for Sir Howe Hickes.

HAMPSHIRE

I. *Abbots Ann* was rebuilt in 1716 by Thomas Pitt ("Governor Pitt", of Fort St George, Madras).

Avington: James Bridges, Marquess of Carnarvon, was granted a faculty on 23 February 1770 to build the church. It was, in fact, rebuilt at the cost of Margaret Marchioness of Carnarvon. She died in 1768, and her epitaph says: "Amongst Many other Acts of Piety this Church was built from the Ground, by her order, and at her Expence, tho' it pleased God to remove her to a better World, a few months before it was begun."

South Baddesley was rebuilt by Sir James Worsley in the latter part of the century.

Farleigh Wallop was rebuilt at the cost of Viscount Lymington, who died in 1762, and whose monument is here.

Hale was enlarged by Thomas Archer, who bought the manor in 1715. The register notes: "In 1717 That the Church was begun building, that is the addition that Mr Archer builded."

Hinton Admiral: the act of consecration says that Joseph Jarvis Clarke had erected a chapel in 1774. In his will (14 March 1778) he had left most of his possessions to his cousin George Ivison Tapps, who had finished the chapel, and adorned it with Communion table, rails, pulpit, desk, and other things requisite and necessary for the worship of Almighty God.

Hursley was rebuilt in 1752–3 by Sir Thomas Heathcote, second baronet.

Stratfieldsaye: on 17 January 1753 the vestry agreed to George Pitt's proposal to take down the church, and build a new one on another site. A petition was presented to the Commons on 19 February: a new church was proposed to be built on a field called the Further Down, and a churchyard to be formed. Consecration, 1 September 1758.

South Tidworth: 1784. The petition for consecration stated that Thomas Asshicton Smith had taken down the old church, and rebuilt it on a certain piece of glebe called the upper Piece of Hitching Furlong, and "put up a Pulpit Seats and other Furniture and Ornaments and completely finished the said Church in a decent fit and proper Manner". The act of consecration is dated 29 September 1785.

Ryde, Isle of Wight: Thomas Player built a chapel (St Thomas's) in 1719.

II. *Crofton:* A faculty of 11 October 1728 says that Thomas Missing of Stubbington had "already erected and built entirely from the ground an addition to the south side of the s^d Chappell of Crofton consisting of one whole Isle".

Gosport: the Reverend Richard Bingham proposed to build a new vestry in 1795.

HEREFORDSHIRE

I. *Shobdon:* this well-known Gothick church was built by John second Viscount Bateman.

Stoke Edith was rebuilt by Thomas Foley in 1740–2. Mrs Foley to Mrs Dewes, 14 July 1741: "Our church is almost finished, but by the blunders of the workmen, and obstinacy of Mr Wickins, it will not be so handsome as the draught, which vexes me extremely; I wish Mr Foley had not so much complaisance in the affair."[1]

[1] *Life and Correspondence of Mrs Delany*, Vol. II, 1861, p. 163.

Tyberton was rebuilt in 1720 by William Brydges. The apse, ceiling, and woodwork of the sanctuary were designed by John Wood of Bath in 1728.

HERTFORDSHIRE

I. *Ayot St Lawrence* new church, designed by Nicholas Revett, was built in 1778–9 by Sir Lionel Lyde and Mary Lyde. The steeple and walls of the old church were to go to Sir Lionel, "and be by him suffered to remain in its present ruinous State or be repaired or taken down at his own Expence and for his own Use as he shall think fit". The old church was, in fact, left as a ruin.

Ayot St Peter was rebuilt by the rector, Dr Ralph Freeman, in 1751.

II. *Essendon* chancel was rebuilt by the rector in 1777.

St Paul's Walden chancel was rebuilt in 1727 by Edward Gilbert.

Tring: the altarpiece and wainscot of the chancel were the gift of Sir Richard Anderson. About 1710 the church was repaired at the cost of the Hon. William Gore: it was new pewed in oak, and the columns were painted to resemble marble. The confirmatory faculty says that he "did lately out of a Religious disposition & zeal for the Honour of God & the Decency of his house & his publick worship" beautify and adorn the church, and had since new seated and pewed it.

HUNTINGDONSHIRE

I. *Little Gidding* was rebuilt in 1714 by Mr Ferrar.

II. *Folksworth* chancel was rebuilt by the Reverend Robert Pupplett in 1702–6.

Haddon: "1745, Church repd. and beautified at Expense of Rob. Pigott."[1]

KENT

I. *Mereworth* was rebuilt in 1744–6 by the seventh Earl of Westmorland.

Otterden was rebuilt under the direction of the Reverend Granville Wheler. Lady Elizabeth Hastings gave £400. It was completed in 1759 at an additional expense of £500 given by Wheler.

[1] Note in the church register.

Shipbourne was rebuilt in 1722 by Christopher first Lord Barnard. The design was by Gibbs.

Teston: the faculty was given on 8 May 1736, to rebuild the church according to the plan proposed by Sir Philip Boteler, who paid for it.

II. *Ash:* the altarpiece was given by the Reverend Samuel Attwood, incumbent 1701–35.

Bexley: the altarpiece was given by the Reverend Benjamin Huntington, just before his death in 1706.[1]

Chatham, St Bartholomew's: repaired by Dean Pratt.

Lullingstone was repaired and beautified by Percyvall Hart, Esq., who died in 1738.

Otham: William Stevens laid out about £600 in repairing and adorning the church.[2]

Rochester, St Nicholas': a handsome wainscot altarpiece was given by Edward Bartholomew in 1706.

St Peter in Thanet: the chancel was beautified in 1735 at the expense of Mrs Elizabeth Lovejoy. The font was given by John Deweker in 1749.

Westerham: Sir John Crisp gave the marble pavement of the altar in 1702, and the Right Honble Edward Earle the cedar altarpiece in 1709.

Wickambreux: a tablet to Mary Young (died 8 May 1767), says:

She left
To the wainscoting & ornamenting
this Chancel;
To the Small Pox & Foundling Hospitals
100 £ each.

Wrotham: the chancel was paved and beautified by Dr John Potter, son of Archbishop Potter, incumbent, and afterwards Dean of Canterbury.

LANCASHIRE

I. *Burtonwood* was rebuilt by Sir Peter Bold in 1716.

Dendron: 1795, by Robert Green, Esq., of Gray's Inn.

Liverpool, St Anne's: 1770–2 at the cost of Thomas Dobb, Richard Dobb, and Henry North.

[1] Epitaph in the church.
[2] *Memoirs of William Stevens, Esq.,* 2nd ed., 1814, p. 183.

Christchurch: 1797–8, built by John Houghton, a wealthy distiller. (It is true that it was built for the use of an amended version of the Book of Common Prayer; but the experiment failed, and it was put on the Establishment, and consecrated in 1800. Houghton spent a good deal on it.)

Holy Trinity: begun 1790 by Isaac Hodgson, John Brown, and Henry Holt.

Manchester, St Clement's, opened in 1793, was built by the Reverend E. Smyth.

St James's: 1788, by the Reverend Cornelius Bayley.

St John's, Deansgate: 1768–9 at the expense of Edward Byrom.

St Mark's, Cheetham Hill, 1794, was founded by the Reverend E. Ethelston.

St Michael's, 1789, by the Reverend Humphrey Owen.

Poulton le Fylde was rebuilt in 1752–3 by Roger and Margaret Hesketh of Rossall.

II. *Broughton in Furness:* north aisle 1738, and south 1758—"at the private expense of several persons, who completed them in a handsome manner".

Lancaster, St John's: the tower and spire were built in 1784 by the benefaction of Richard Bowes of Lancaster.

Manchester collegiate church: Samuel Brooke gave the tapestry to cover the altar screen in 1700, and Nathanael Edmundson of Manchester, woollen draper, gave the marble pavement, to be equal in beauty to the new altar.

LEICESTERSHIRE

I. *Carlton Curlieu* was rebuilt by Sir John Palmer in 1767.

Galby was rebuilt by William Fortrey in 1741. The architect was Wing, "the father of the present Mr Wing of Leicester".

King's Norton was also rebuilt by Fortrey, from designs by Wing the younger. One of the best of eighteenth-century Gothic churches.

Saxby: 1788 by the fourth Earl of Harborough.

Stapleford: 1783, by the same. The architect was George Richardson, who was probably responsible for Saxby as well.

II. *Barkby:* William Pochin was a benefactor to this church. In 1753 he re-roofed the chancel and gave it new glass: the altar rails and table were his gift. He died in 1798.

Bitteswell chancel was improved by Mrs Elizabeth Walker, who gave an altarpiece, table, and rails.

Coleorton was beautified in 1800. Sir George Beaumont gave an altarpiece of St Peter's deliverance from prison.

Dalby on the Wolds: the chancel was built in 1729 by Charles Duncombe, Esq.

Langton was adorned by the Reverend William Hanbury, incumbent from 1753. He proposed an organ in the west gallery, and the gallery enlarged on both sides, new pewing, a handsome corona before the pulpit, a pavement of black and white stone before the altar, rails, and a marble altarpiece. The organ was completed in 1757. Emblems of corn and wine were painted on the east wall, and a text.

Hanbury also proposed to build a collegiate church, "truly Gothic", with a lantern tower, and east and west steeples 399 ft. high. The floor and pillars to be of marble, and the high altar of the finest marble, porphyry, and jasper. The windows to be the grandest that could be devised. He made an enormous list of saints who were to have statues. The most able architects were to exhibit models for the church: the estimate was £19,307 8s. He marked out the site before his death in 1778.

Long Clawson was given a stone altar by the Reverend William Turville in 1738.

Market Harborough: the rails were given in 1701 by Henry Coleman. In 1757 the chancel was repaired, repewed, and wainscoted by the Reverend Richard Parry, D.D. New pavement of Ketton stone.

Ragdale: the chancel and porch were rebuilt in 1787 by Earl Ferrers, who repaired, new paved, and refitted the church.

Rolleston was repaired and fitted up by Richard Greene, Esq., about 1740.

Scraptoft was pewed and paved, and the font given, by the bounty of Mr Wigley. The faculty was given on 20 April 1765.

Swithland: the chapel at the east of the south aisle was built by Sir Joseph Danvers in 1727—and another part as big to the west of it.

LINCOLNSHIRE

I. *Baumber:* a faculty was given on 24 December 1760 to the Earl of Lincoln to repair the church and chancel at his own expense, "and to make additional new works and alterations". It was mostly rebuilt in red brick in a Gothick style, and is very attractive.

Castle Carlton: a faculty was given on 30 June 1707, to Sir Edward Smith, Bt., "at his own proper costs and charges to take down the present ruinous Fabrick and in Lieu thereof to Erect a New Church and Chancell, which as is suggested will in all respects be convenient and sufficient for the Reception of the Congregation . . .".

Cherry Willingham was rebuilt by Thomas Becke of Lincoln, and opened on Trinity Sunday 1753. Becke died in 1757; his monument is here.

Doddington was mostly rebuilt by Lord Delaval in 1770–5. The work was done by Thomas and William Lumby.

Gate Burton was rebuilt in 1784 by the rector and William Hutton.

Gunby: a new church was built, near the site of the old one, in 1788, "by the benevolent assistance of the Rt. Honble the Earl of Yarborough".

Harmston: 1717, by Sir George Thorold, Bt.

Humberston was rebuilt in 1710 by Matthew Humberston, who left £300 for his monument, £1000 to rebuild the church, £1000 to erect a grammar school and almshouses, and an annuity of £40 towards the vicar's income.

Humby (in the parish of Somersby): the chapel was rebuilt by Thomas Hotchkin, lord of the manor, in 1754.

Moulton chapel was rebuilt in 1722 by Maurice Johnson.

Owersby: the petition for a faculty states that the Right Hon. Lord Monson, owner of the rectory, had largely contributed towards the erection of the new church. The faculty was issued on 12 May 1762.

Nocton: a faculty was granted on 28 October 1769 to the Hon. George Hobart to rebuild at his own expense the church and vicarage on a more convenient site.

Revesby was rebuilt in 1730 by Joseph Banks, who is buried here (1741).

Stainton by Langworth was rebuilt by the Pierrepoint family in 1792–3.

Stubton: faculty given on 21 March 1790 to Robert Heron to rebuild the church at his own expense on a new site.

Woolsthorpe: the Reverend M. W. Peters, R.A., became incumbent in 1788, and his first care was to provide a suitable church. The demolition of the old one began in 1791, and the new church was first used for worship on 18 April 1792.

II. *Alkborough* chancel was rebuilt in 1771 by Christopher Goulton, Esq., who is commemorated here.

Glentworth: the nave was rebuilt by Archdeacon Illingworth in 1782.

West Torrington was repaired in 1770 by George Harrison.

LONDON

The City churches were completed and fitted up by the beginning of the eighteenth century. Some, that had escaped the Fire, were rebuilt later in the century, but the work was done by the parishes. At *St. Andrew Undershaft:* "Mr Henry Tombes, 1725, a worthy inhabitant, did, at his own cost and charge, guild the organ 1725; gave the centre piece of painting over the altar, 1726; painted the pillars and arches in oyle, with the figures of the apostles, and Scripture pieces under them; besides having given formerly the Book of Martyrs, and been a liberal subscriber to the building the organ and the altarpiece."

LONDON NORTH OF THE THAMES

I. *Chelsea:* In 1775 the Reverend and Honourable W. B. Cadogan was appointed vicar. "Finding the church at Chelsea small and inconvenient for so large a parish, and in a decayed state, he made, as he informed me, a very advantageous proposal for rebuilding it . . . He could not, however, awaken the same zeal in his parish, and accordingly his proposal was rejected."[1]

II. *Clerkenwell, St John's,* became a Presbyterian chapel, and was burned in the Sacheverell riots. In 1716 it was advertised for sale, and was bought by Simon Michel, who was erecting many houses in the neighbourhood. He enlarged and repaired the chapel, roofed the whole, and built the west front. In 1723 he sold the building, all fit for service, to the Commissioners for the Fifty New Churches.

But most of the work was done by the parishes—except in the case of the New Churches: and the buildings erected by private individuals were proprietary chapels.

LONDON SOUTH OF THE THAMES

I. *Christchurch, Southwark,* consecrated on 17 December 1671, was built at the expense of John Marshall. It became ruinous, and was

[1] Richard Cecil, *Cadogan's Sermons and Life*, p. xxii.

rebuilt in 1738–41 by his trustees, with £2500 that had accumulated from the trust.

II. *Camberwell:* the rails, wainscot, and altarpiece, 1715, were the gift of Mrs Katherine Bowyer.

Southwark, St John's, Horsleydown: the altarpiece, with painting of St John writing the Apocalypse, by the Reverend Mr Peters, is said to have been erected by the executors of Richard Russell, who died in 1784, in place of a monument in the church.

Wandsworth: on 1 March 1715, the vicar offered to enlarge the church at his own charge. A faculty was granted on 30 April 1716: Samuel Edgley, vicar, intended to pull down the north wall of the church and chancel and build a new aisle.

MIDDLESEX

I. *Ashford* was rebuilt in 1796 at the expense of the principal inhabitants, but the chancel by the lord of the manor.

Brentford, St George's, was built in 1762 at the expense of Messrs Trimmer, Clark, Newton, Fisher, and others. They engaged Joshua Kirby as architect.

Cranford was rebuilt in 1716 "by the pious benefaction of the R^{t} Honble Elizabeth Countess Dowager of Berkley".[1]

Whitchurch was rebuilt in 1715–16 by James Duke of Chandos: the building was designed by John James.

II. *Shepperton* tower was built *c.* 1710, solely at the expense of the Reverend Lewis Atterbury, save for £27 from the sale of a broken bell.

Teddington tower was built in 1754 by Dr Hales, who invented the ventilator. He paid the cost, and superintended the work.

NORFOLK

I. *Gunton* was rebuilt by Sir William Harbord of Gunton: faculty 19 April 1765. The architect was Robert Adam.

Thorpe Market is inscribed, "This Church was rebuilt fitted up and Finished by HARBORD Lord Suffield at his own Expence in the year 1796." It is Gothic. "In it Mr Wood, the architect, has combined simplicity with elegance . . . the interior displays a consider-

[1] Note in the register.

able degree of taste, consisting of a single aisle. The windows ornamented with painted glass."[1]

II. *Baconsthorpe* was thoroughly repaired and beautified in 1779 at the
cost of £600, chiefly provided by the Reverend William Hewitt.
Mary Ann Stuart gave the font.

Fersfield: the church and chancel were new paved about 1708 at the
charge of the Reverend John Barker, the rector, and Elizabeth.
The chancel was new roofed.

Holkham was repaired in 1767 by the Countess of Leicester, at a
cost of about £1000.

Houghton: the tower was rebuilt, and the church fitted up, by Sir
Robert Walpole.

King's Lynn, St Margaret's: the library at the west of the south aisle
was built in 1714–17 by John Fellows.

Kirby Cane: the vestry was built in 1753 by Sir Charles Turner, Bt.
"out of a pious and pure regard for the memory of his second
wife".

NORTHAMPTONSHIRE

I. *Aynho* was rebuilt by Thomas Cartwright, lord of the manor and
patron, in 1723–5.[2]

East Carlton was rebuilt by Sir John Palmer: faculty 8 April 1785.

Stoke Doyle was rebuilt by Edward Ward, lord of the manor and
patron, in 1722–5.[3]

Wicken is inscribed, "This Church was designed and built by
THOMAS PROWSE Esq[r] in the year 1758 and finished after his
Death".[4]

II. *Abington:* Thomas Rocke (died 1715) was a great benefactor. The
space in the altar rails was wainscoted by him, and a handsomely
carved pulpit given.

Canons' Ashby was in a dilapidated state until Edward Dryden
repaired it, rebuilt the south wall, and embellished the interior with
new seats, a pulpit, and a beautiful but plain altarpiece.

Cosgrave was substantially repaired in 1774 by Dr Pulter Forester,
who died in 1778, and is buried here. "The established Church
(whose Temples, especially This and others near him, he was ever

---

[1] J.P. Neal, *Views of the Seats of Noblemen and Gentlemen*, Vol. III.
[2] See p. 134.   [3] See pp. 133–4.   [4] See p. 136.

solicitous to improve and adorn) lost in him a constant and steady friend."

Haselbeech: the monument to Sir William Wykes, erected in 1721, speaks of

> *... Hoc Sacrarium*
> *Tabulato Opere pulchre Vestitum,*
> *Cancellis Ferreis affabre distinctum,*
> *Suggestum Reparatum*
> *Libri ad Sacrorum Solemnia Comparati,*
> *Totiusq Ecclesiae Navis tam*
> *Pavimento quam Parietibus*
> *Renovata & Exculta ...*

Horton was repaired early in the century by the Earl of Halifax. A chancel screen was erected.

Lamport: Sir Justinian Isham, who died in 1737, left a legacy of £500 towards rebuilding and beautifying the church. His brother and successor Sir Edmund, his brother Euseby, the rector, his widow, and her mother Mrs Dorothy Hacket, carried out the work. The church was remodelled, except for the arcades and the tower, by Francis Smith of Warwick.

Stanwick was restored by Bishop Denison Cumberland, a former incumbent. His son Richard wrote:

> The spire of Stanwick church is esteemed one of the most beautiful models in that style of architecture, in the kingdom; my father added a very handsome clock; and ornamented the chancel with a railing, screen and entablature, upon three-quarter columns, with a singing gallery at the west end, and spared no expense to keep his church not only in that neatness and decorum which befits the house of prayer, but also in a perfect state of good and permanent repair.

Steane chapel was given a marble altar, and furniture for the altar, desk, and pulpit, by Nathanael Lord Crewe, Bishop of Durham, 1720.

Whilton was adorned by the Reverend William Lucas Rose:

> This gentleman ... has laid out about 300 *l* in making this church elegantly neat ; which is a greater sum than is often raised throughout the kingdom, by brief, for building a new one. The pews are regularly placed, and accommodated with books, hassocks, etc, that the congregation may readily kneel and join in the responses of the service ... The furniture of the desk and pulpit is rich and becoming; that of the

5. Wheatfield, Oxon. A georgianized medieval church which has escaped alteration

6. Honiley, Warws. Rebuilt in 1723 by John Sanders

by kind permission of John Piper

8. Adderley, Salop. This church was rebuilt with the help of briefs issued in 1709, 1793, 1795, 1799, 1802, and 1809

by kind permission of Gordon Barnes

7. St John's, Wapping. Rebuilt by Act of Parliament in 1756

altar splendid, but without the smallest mark of ostentatious finery. A beautiful organ has been lately erected, of sweet tone and full power, which leads a well-instructed choir . . .[1]

NORTHUMBERLAND

I. *Howick* was rebuilt at the expense of Sir Henry Grey, Bt., 1746.
Kirkheaton was rebuilt by Mrs Dorothy Windsor in 1753.

II. *Kirkharle:* the west porch and the bellcote were built by Sir William Loraine.
Newcastle, St John's: in 1710 Robert Percival beautified the altar at his own expense. In 1712 Robert Crow, merchant, gave a new altar.
St Nicholas': the library was built in 1736 by Sir Walter Blackett.
Norham: Thomas Kidd in 1790 left £100 for repairs.

NOTTINGHAMSHIRE

I. *Awsworth:* 1746, by Harry fourth Earl of Stamford.
Kinoulton: the old church was taken down in 1793, and a new one was built by Henry Earl of Gainsborough.
Ossington: the estate was bought in 1780 by William Denison, who rebuilt the church in 1782–3. The architect was probably Carr of York.
Papplewick was rebuilt, but for the tower, in 1795, "in a very elegant Gothic style", by the Hon. Frederick Montagu.
West Stockwith: 1722, by the trustees of William Huntington, shipbuilder of the parish, who died in 1722, and whose monument is here.

II. *Bingham* chancel was handsomely ceiled, with devices of stucco work over the altar, and an altar of marble, and other plaster work —done at the cost of the Reverend Henry Stanhope, who died in 1773.
Gotham chancel was rebuilt in 1789 at the expense of the widow of the late rector, the Reverend John Lightfoot.
Hoveringham: the spire was built by Sir Richard Sutton, Bt.
Kirkby in Ashfield: Sir Richard Kaye, afterwards Dean of Lincoln, was rector from 1765. He began at once to improve the church. It was reseated in 1765–6: the Duke of Portland gave £50. Kaye

[1] *Gentleman's Magazine,* 1797, Pt. II, pp. 931–2.

presented the pulpit. In 1768 he raised the chancel, put in an ornamental ceiling, inserted a painted east window by Peckitt, and some painted glass in the side windows, built a vestry, and made some other improvements.

Nottingham, St Nicholas', was refitted in 1783. Mr Elliot gave two paintings for the altar.

Wilford: Mr Carter, the rector, who died in 1732, gave the Communion plate and beautified the chancel. He also left a sum of money for the embellishment of the church.

OXFORDSHIRE

I. *Ardley:* the nave was rebuilt by the Duchess of Marlborough in 1791–2.

Bladon was rebuilt in 1802–4 by the fourth Duke of Marlborough in a similar style.

Chislehampton: the new church was built about 200 yards to the west of the old one by Charles Peers. The consecration was on 27 August 1763. The register records that all things were done decently and in order.

Glympton: "The Church and Chancell have both been lately Rebuilt, the Former at yᵉ Sole Expence of my much honored and Generous Patron above mentioned [Sir Thomas Wheate]

and yᵉ Latter at the Cost of
My Lord
Your Lordship's Most Dutyfull Son and Servant
Sam: Jones Rector.[1]

Godington old church was dilapidated, and had to be taken down in 1792. All the property except the glebe land belonged to Mr Fermor, who was a Roman Catholic. He rebuilt the church very plainly, employing an architect of the same obedience.

Hailey: Thomas Howell of Whitechapel, who held certain lands in Hailey, "mov'd with a pious Zeal for the Honor of God the advancement of Religion, the ease and Convenience of the Inhabitants", surrendered in 1760 the said land on condition that his trustees should build on part of them a chapel for Hailey and Crawley. It was consecrated on 4 August 1761.

[1] *Bishop Secker's Visitation Returns* 1738, Oxfordshire Record Society, 1957, p. 67.

Hampton Gay was rebuilt by the Reverend Thomas Hindes in 1767.

Mongewell: Bishop Shute Barrington lived here, and in 1791 applied for a faculty to enlarge the west end of the church, pull down and rebuild the walls of the chancel, new pew the whole, build a gallery, and erect buttresses on the outside, and battlements round the roof. Wyatt was doing work at Salisbury for the bishop at the time. There seems no evidence that he rebuilt Mongewell, but it may be assumed that he did.

Nuneham Courtenay new church was built by Simon first Lord Harcourt: faculty 1762. The design was made by himself.

Oxford, All Saints', was rebuilt with the aid of a brief. But there were also several personal gifts. Strong, mason, gave the stone for the columns of the south porch, valued at £30 15s. Lord Crewe gave £100 for the church, 100 guineas for the altarpiece, and £200 for the tower. The Queen gave 100 tons of timber and £225. Sir John Walter gave the glazing (value £41 12s), and the Duke of Marlborough gave £200.

Weston on the Green was rebuilt by Norreys Bertie, whose tomb is in the church, in 1743.

Wheatfield was rebuilt by Edward Rudge *c.* 1740.

II. *North Aston:* Lady Howard repaired, whitewashed, and wainscoted the chancel, paved it, and gave the rails and a new pulpit and desk.

Baldon Marsh: Sir Christopher Willoughby at the end of the century gave a picture of the Annunciation, formerly in Corpus Christi College chapel, as an altarpiece,

Garsington: in 1782 Richard Turrill presented a new font.

Kirtlington made a petition in 1761 for a confirmatory faculty. Sir James Dashwood, Bt., had been asked to repair, new pew, and decorate the church, "with which request the said Sr James Dashwood benevolently comply'd and hath with great munificence repair'd new pewd and decorated the same at his own Cost and Charge".

North Leigh: the additional north aisle was built by James Perrott, who died in 1724. His monument is here: the epitaph mentions *Haec sumptibus suis decorata Aedes,* and says that his arrival *exhilarabit civitatem Dei.*

South Leigh: William Gore gave the pulpit, ceiling of the chancel, and royal arms in 1716.

Spelsbury: the Earl of Lichfield offered £1000 and timber from

Ditchley to rebuild the church. It was partly reconstructed. Rainwater heads are dated 1774.

Standlake: Mr Chambers wainscoted the east end. It was ornamented with a cross, IHS, and texts.

Thame: in the east window were Lord Weymouth's arms, and inscription: "Thomas Viscount Weymouth patron of this church repaired this chancell totally decayed & ruined anno dom. 1707."

Wroxton tower was rebuilt by Lord North and Guilford: the foundation stone was laid on 13 April 1748. Sanderson Miller was the architect. The tower fell down and had to be rebuilt.[1]

RUTLAND

I. *Normanton* was rebuilt by Sir Gilbert Heathcote in 1764.

Teigh was rebuilt by the fourth Earl of Harborough in 1782. A remarkable Gothick church, with unusual internal arrangements, probably designed by George Richardson.

Tickencote was rebuilt in the Norman style, from designs by S. P. Cockerell, by Mrs Sarah Wingfield in 1792.[2]

SHROPSHIRE

I. *Jackfield* was built in 1759 by Francis Turner Blithe.

Welsh Hampton was rebuilt in 1788 at the expense of Mary, widow of Edward Kinaston.

Whitchurch was rebuilt with the help of a brief, but £977 19s 3d came from benefactions: the Earl of Bridgwater subscribed, and so did Dean Swift.

II. *Shrewsbury, St Mary's:* the altarpiece was given in 1706 by the Reverend Richard Tiesdale. Marble altar given by Archdeacon Owen in 1789.

Upton Parva: a tablet says that John Wase desired in his will of 1715 to be buried in the chancel, which he rebuilt.

SOMERSET

I. *Babington:* rebuilt in 1750 by Mrs Long, lady of the manor.

Bath, Christchurch, Walcot, was built by Archdeacon Daubeny as a

---

[1] See *An Eighteenth-Century Correspondence,* ed. Lilian Dickins and Mary Stanton, 1910.
[2] See p. 127.

free church for the poor: only the seats in the gallery were to be let. The S.P.C.K granted £500.

Bathampton: nave and south transept rebuilt in 1754 by Ralph Allen.

Foxcote was rebuilt in 1721. There is a monument to Robert Smith. Either he or his wife Dorothy rebuilt the church.

Godney was rebuilt by Peter Davis in 1737.

Wincanton was mainly rebuilt in 1748 by Nathanael Ireson, and at his expense.

Woodlands: 1712, by Thomas Viscount Weymouth.

Woolley, by Wood of Bath the younger, was rebuilt by Mrs Parkins. In the nineteenth century a piece of parchment was found with the inscription:

> DELAPSURA ANTIQUA CAPELLA
> HANC SPLENDIDIOREM, SOLA IMPENSA,
> ELIZABETHA PARKINS DE RAVENFIELD
> AGRO EBORACENSI ET HUJUS MANERII
> WOOLLEI DOMINA AEDIFICARI JUSSIT
> ANNO XTO 1761

II. *Bath Abbey:* in 1725 Marshall Wade presented a costly marble altarpiece with a picture of the Wise Men's offering, and wrought-iron rails, recently replaced in the abbey.

Binegar: the chancel was rebuilt by the rector, the Reverend Thomas Collins, 1749.

Brushford: the top of the tower was rebuilt by the Reverend John Norris (died 1746).

Bruton chancel was rebuilt in 1743 in memory of William Berkeley, Lord Stratton, who died in 1741; to the order of Charles, second surviving son of William Earl of Berkeley.

Claverton was repaired by Ralph Allen.

Farmborough: According to William Stevens, "The excellent Doctor G. [the Reverend Dr Gunning] employed the first fruits of the wealth which had been bequeathed to him in adorning the house of God, and in works of charity and benevolence."[1] Stevens wrote: "The building of a new chancel, and the improvements to be made in that quarter, are worthy of Peter, who loves to have 'every thing done decently and in order'."[2] ". . . The good man

[1] *Memoirs of William Stevens, Esq.,* p. 81.
[2] Ibid., p. 84. The date of the letter is 4 March 1794.

has not only the satisfaction to find the great work carried on with zeal and alacrity, none weakening the hands of the people, or troubling them, as in the re-building of the temple; but he has the pleasure to reflect, that when the work is finished, none of those who knew the church in its former state, will have reason on recollection, to weep and lament, but all may shout aloud with joy."[1]

Marksbury tower was rebuilt by John Butler, "as a testimony of his regard and affection for the church and place of his nativity".

Mells: a marble altarpiece was erected, and the chancel fitted up, in 1785 by the Reverend John Bishop, D.D.[2]

Road: the church was repaired throughout, and the east end rebuilt, by Archdeacon Daubeny in 1778, according to an inscription in Road Hill church, which he built in 1824.

St Michaelchurch: a note in the register: "note this chancel was thoroughly repaired, bills being paid by the generosity of John Hale Esq. 1794."

Stratton on the Fosse: inscription in the chancel:

THIS CHANCEL
was rebuilt
all but the East Wall
at the expence of the
Rev.d *RICHARD HUGHES* Rector
1765

STAFFORDSHIRE

I. *Great Barr:* founded by Mrs Bromwich: bells the gift of Mrs Whitby. The steeple was converted into a spire on the plan of Wolverhampton at the expense of Mr Scott, who also gave the organ.

Cotton was built in 1790 by Thomas Gilbert, Esq., who endowed it, and left the payment of repairs a perpetual charge on his property.

Hanley, St John's: founded in 1737 by John Bourne of Newcastle, who offered £500 for building, if the inhabitants would raise the rest; and 54 acres of land for endowment. The site was given by John Adams and Mabel his wife. The chapel was afterwards enlarged by Bourne.

[1] Ibid., p. 87: 4 July 1794.
[2] See illustration in Markland's *Remarks on English Churches,* 1842 ed., p. 48.

Himley was built in 1764 by John Lord Dudley and Ward.

Lane End was built by John Bourne, and consecrated in 1764.

Patshull was rebuilt by Sir John Astley, from designs by Gibbs. It was consecrated in 1743.

Smethwick was built in 1732 by direction of the will of Dorothy Parkes of Harborne, who died in 1727. It was to be "a neat, Convenient Chapel", not to cost more than £800, and to be furnished with "convenient and proper ornaments".

II. *Adbaston* chancel was beautified in 1721 by J. Downes at the expense of Henry Jervis.

Arley, Upper: in 1793 Lord Valentia raised and enlarged the chancel, adding a window by Eginton.

Cauldon: the chancel was partly rebuilt in 1784 by Sampson Whieldon, the lay rector.

Shenstone: the chancel was built by Samuel Hill, Esq., of Shenstone Park, in Venetian taste.

SUFFOLK

I. *Saxham Magna* was mainly rebuilt in 1798 by Thomas Mills, the patron. His epitaph says: "His first care was to rebuild this church then in a most dilapidated state/And to render it meet for divine service."

II. *Chevington:* the tower was heightened by the fourth Earl of Bristol, who died in 1803.

Grundisburgh: a new tower was built in 1756. An estate was left by Robert Thinge to be sold for that purpose.

Ickworth: Augustus John Earl of Bristol in 1778 built a tower, and a plain brick cemetery against the east wall. The church was beautified, and a pavement of grey marble laid.

Lowestoft: "The chancel is remarkably neat and elegant, being repaired and beautified by the Rev. John Tanner and the Rev. John Arrow, two late vicars, who died in 1760 and 1789. The latter erected a new altarpiece, enclosed the communion table with handsome iron railing, and opened out the lower part of the east window, which had been bricked up."[1]

[1] W. White, *History, Gazetteer, and Directory of Suffolk*, 1844, p. 50. Extracts from Tanner's account book are given in *The Chronicles of a Suffolk Parish Church*, by H. D. W. Lees, 1949.

Mendham: the chancel was rebuilt by William Freston, Esq. (d. 1746).

Pakefield was repaired and beautified at the expense of the rector, the Reverend Dr Leman, who new laid the floor, erected a new pulpit and desk, placed over the font a handsome model of the tower and spire of Norwich cathedral, and embellished the church with other useful ornaments.

Rendlesham: John Spencer, by his will dated 1 August 1706, gave £20 towards repairing the body of the church and bells, and £10 towards repairing the chancel. He also paved the nave with Newcastle stone. In 1783 the chancel roof was put up by the rector, and an east window "in the florid Gothic". Also an altarpiece of the Corinthian order, painted as Siena marble.

Shotley: the chancel was rebuilt in 1745 by the Hon. Hervey Aston, D.D.

SURREY

I. *Felbridge* was built by James Evelyn, owner of Felbridge Park, in 1787.

Kew: the inhabitants decided to build a chapel in 1710. Queen Anne, as lady of the manor, was approached. She gave £100, and, on 28 June 1712 a grant of land on which to build. At a vestry meeting on 19 July 1766 "Mr Kirby communicated to the Inhabitants now present a Most Gracious Offer from His Majesty to enlarge this Chapel according to a plan now laid before them for that purpose at his Majesties Expence". The plan was made by Kirby. Other members of the Royal family made gifts.

A vestry meeting on 17 December 1804 "Resolved Unanimously that leave be given to His Majesty to make such Alterations in the Church as may be deemed requisite for the Accommodation of the Royal Family". The plans were made by Robert Browne.

Shalford was rebuilt at the expense of Robert Austen in 1788–90.

Titsey: in 1775 Sir John Gresham conveyed a piece of land for building a new church. A vestry meeting was held in June. The Reverend Mr Bodicoate reported that the church was ruinous. Dame Henrietta Maria Gresham, wife of Sir John, was willing and desirous at her own costs to pull it down, and to build a new church on a new site in a more convenient situation. The vestry accepted the offer. There is an elevation of the new church among the papers of the archdeaconry of Surrey, unfortunately unsigned. It was consecrated on 19 July 1776.

II. *Addington:* the tower and nave were partly rebuilt in brick by Alderman Trecothick about 1773.

Beddington: altarpiece, Communion table, rails, and pavement were the benefaction of Sir John Leake (1710).

Carshalton: the south aisle was raised in 1723, and the church was beautified, mainly at the expense of Sir John Fellowes and Sir William Scawen. In 1725 the vestry agreed that Edward Fellowes should build the north aisle to resemble the south.

Cheam: in 1750 Lady Stourton rebuilt the Fromond chapel.

Esher: a faculty was granted on 6 August 1724, to the Most Hon. Thomas Holles, Duke of Newcastle, to build a gallery pew and porch on the south. The vestry, on 20 April 1725, decided that "his Grace the Duke of Newcastle may beautify the Church according to his Grace's pleasure".

SUSSEX

I. *Brighton, The Chapel Royal,* was erected at the expense of Thomas Hudson, the vicar, as a chapel of ease to the parish church.

Chichester, St Pancras: the old church was destroyed in the siege of the city during the Civil War, and it was not rebuilt until 1750. The chief subscribers were Mary Countess of Derby, £400; the Duke of Richmond, £105; Elizabeth Powlett, £100; John Page, £31 10s; and the Dean and Chapter of Chichester, £25.

Crowborough: Sir H. Fermor left £9000 by will in 1732: £1500 was to be laid out in building a chapel and school house; £500 was to be invested, and the interest used for the repair of them.

Glynde was rebuilt in 1764–5 at the expense of Sir Richard Trevor, Bishop of Durham. The architect was Sir Thomas Robinson.

Shermanbury: there is an inscription, *Sancti Aegidii Labentem refecit & restituit Joannes Gratwick Armiger; Liberaliter opus promovente* IOANNES STONE A. M. *Rectore,* A.D. MDCCX.

II. *Bramber* was repaired by the Reverend Dr Green, with £25 from the Duke of Rutland and Lord Calthorpe, £50 from Magdalen College, Oxford, and about £20 from Mr Lidbetter.

Buxted: the Reverend Dr Saunders, rector in the reign of Queen Anne, gave a plaster ceiling with an ornamented cornice.

Clapham: the chancel "is now finely adorn'd and beautified at the charges of Sr John Shelley". (Visitation of 1724.)

Hastings, St Clement's: altarpiece painted by Roger Mortimer in 1721. The chancel ceiling was painted by Mortimer with Faith, Hope, Charity, and Fortitude for 30 guineas. The walls were painted at the same time. The Hon. Archibald Hutcheson gave £100 to the repair of the church, and £125 to paving, wainscoting, and ceiling the chancel, and making and railing the altarpiece.

Hunston: the chancel was rebuilt in the earlier part of the century by the Reverend Charles Randel Covert, vicar.

Itchingfield: "Chancell better in repair than ordinary at the Expence of Mr Hay. Chancell rebuilt."[1]

Lurgashall has an inscription: "This Chancel was first cield ye South window rebuilt. ye wall strengthened, & ye Inside beautifȳd at ye sole Expence of James Bramston A.M. in ye year of our Lord 1731 . . .".

Warminghurst: the commissioners who visited the church in 1724 reported, "Church in extraordinarily good repair by the Expence of James Butler Esqr".

Westbourne: the spire was built in 1770 by Lord Lumley of Stanstead. It was designed by Henry Keene. The chancel was remodelled in 1774 at the expence of the rector, the Reverend John Frankland, who gave the altarpiece.

Woolbeding: in 1727 the parish made an agreement with Sir Richard Mills that he should take down the "stipple", and build a tower at the cost of £742.

Yapton: the report of the visitation held in 1724 stated, "The Repairs of the Chancell belong to Lawrence Elliott Esqr & is now by him beautifully adorn'd".

WARWICKSHIRE

I. *Binley* was rebuilt in 1771–3 at the expense of the sixth Lord Craven. The architect was probably Robert Adam.

Birdingbury was rebuilt with money left by Charles Biddulph, 1752.

Birmingham, St Philip's: "His Most Excellent Majesty, King George, upon the kind application of Sir Richard Gough to the Right Honourable Sir Robert Walpole, gave £600 towards finishing this church A.D. 1725." (Inscription)

[1] Visitation of 1724.

St James's, Ashted: in 1777 Dr Ash built "a sumptuous house".
Then his fortunes declined: "it hurts his spirits, and he told me
he had built a house too much" (Hutton). The lease was purchased
by Mr Brooke, and the house was converted into a church (1791).
"A cupola arose from its roof; a pulpit and pews were within."

Castle Bromwich was rebuilt in 1726–31 by Sir John Bridgeman.

Elmdon was rebuilt in 1780–1 by Abraham Spooner, who purchased
the manor in 1760, and died in 1788. His monument is here.

Hall Green was consecrated on 25 May 1704. Job Marston gave
£1000 for the building, and £1200 to be laid out in lands to repair
and endow it.

Honiley is inscribed: AD GLORIAM DEI JOHANNES SANDERS: ARM:
PROPRIIS SUMPTIBUS HANC ECCLESIAM AEDIFICAVIT AN^O SALUTIS
MDCCXXIII.

Kineton was visited by Dr Richard Pococke on 29 September 1756:
"A new Gothic church, built to a good old tower by the care of
the worthy minister, Mr Talbot, nephew to the late Lord Chancellor, with the help of some subscriptions, but chiefly . . . at his own
expence."

Leek Wootton was rebuilt in Gothic, mainly at the cost of the Honble
Mrs Leigh of Stoneleigh Abbey.

Lighthorne was rebuilt in 1773–4 at the sole expense of the Rt
Honble Lord Willoughby de Broke.

Great Packington: by Joseph Bonomi, 1790, for Heneage fourth
Earl of Aylesford.

Sherbourne: nave and tower were rebuilt in 1747 at the cost of
Thomas Webb. The chancel was rebuilt in 1802 by the Reverend
Elias Webb and Thomas Webb Edge.

II. *Arrow:* tower 1767, at the expense of the Right Hon. the Earl of
Hertford.

Baginton: William Bromley beautified the chancel in 1723.

Birmingham, St Bartholomew: "At the annual meeting of the Bean
Club at the Swan, a proposal being made for beginning a subscription to erect an altarpiece in the New Chapel, Lord Fielding
generously gave the whole sum, being £120, the estimate of a
design given in by Messrs W. and D. Hiorn, which is to be executed
with all expedition." (1753)

Bulkington: marble altar and font were the gift and workmanship
of Richard Hayward (1789).

Cubbington: the chancel was repaired by Lord Leigh in 1780.

Edgbaston: about 1725 Sir Richard Gough, lord of the manor, had it put into very good repair, mostly at his own expense.

Hatton: Dr Parr was incumbent from 1783–1825. Field's *Life of Parr* says that he was "a strenuous advocate not only for decency and solemnity, but for pomp and splendour, in the construction of religious edifices". He improved the church, built a vestry (in which he was accustomed to take a pipe before, after, or during the service), and made "a plan for improving and adorning the chancel, ultimately with a view of forming it into a mausoleum for himself and his family". Eginton of Birmingham directed the improvements. There was a painted window of the Crucifixion and St Peter and St Paul, 1794; this was destroyed by a storm a few years later, and replaced by Eginton's son. In the side windows were the Agony and the Ascension. On the walls, oil paintings of Moses and Aaron. In the body of the church were painted windows, with "Cranmer and the Holy Lamb: Tillotson and a Dove". Parr also gave "the splendid decorations of the pulpit", the altar service, and organ (1818). "My parishioners", he wrote, "hear from me no mystical or controversial, but plain, earnest, practical discourses. They hear them with greater pleasure, because the house of worship is endeared to them by the improvements I have made in it."

WESTMORLAND

I. *Helsington* was founded by John Jackson, 1726.

Kendal, St George: 1754; Dr Stratford in his will gave £600.

Temple Sowerby was rebuilt in 1754, and enlarged in 1770 "in a very handsome manner" by Sir William Dalston.

II. *Lowther:* Bishop Nicolson visited the church in 1703, and wrote: "The whole church here, having been lately put into a new Form by *John L*$\underline{d}$ Viscount *Lonsdale*, is in the fairest condition of any parish-Church in the Diocese."[1]

Warcop: Bishop Nicolson noted in 1703: "The Quire a little Ruinous; but far too large. Agreed, with Mr *Brathwait* the Patron and Impropriator, that it be presently rebuilt in a handsome manner, the East Window as large as at present, and shortened about three yards. This will be an Ease both to him and the Vicar."[2]

---

[1] *Miscellany Accounts*, p. 69.   [2] Ibid., p. 45.

WILTSHIRE

I. *Fonthill Gifford:* a new church was built by William Beckford in 1748.
Hardenhuish: a new church was built by Joseph Colbourne in 1777–9.[1]

II. *East Coulston:* a faculty was given on 3 March 1728. The Hon. Elizabeth Godolphin had left £200 to beautify the chancel. It was to be wainscoted, new paved with marble, and given new rails, new Communion table, and a new covering for the same, and new plate.
Foxley: a tablet in the chancel is inscribed:

> This Chancel was
> Pav'd by John Stump
> Rector here June
> the 20th 1708. never
> done before.

West Knoyle: ceiling painted, and chancel new paved and beautified in 1739 by Richard Willoughby.
Salisbury, St Thomas': a faculty was given on 24 April 1711 to Mrs Katherine Gough, widow, to erect a monument to her husband, "and also to beautify and adorn the said Chancell by placing a Screen of beautifull Iron Worke across the west end of the said Chancell, and making two handsome and commodious Iron doors in the same screen . . .".
Stourton: a faculty was given on 3 February 1721, to Henry Hoare to beautify and adorn the church and chancel. A "bad old Skreen" was to be removed, "that so the Beauty of the Said Altar piece may be seen in the body of the Said Church".
Stratford sub Castle: in 1711 Thomas Pitt, Governor of Fort St George, gave the panelling at the east end, and the royal arms and Communion plate. He also rebuilt the tower, which is inscribed THO. PITT ESQR. BENEFACTOR; [and] ERECTED ANNO 1711.

WORCESTERSHIRE

I. *Croome d'Abitot:* a new church, on a different site from the old, consecrated on 29 June 1763. It was built for the Earl of Coventry

[1] See p. 184.

by Lancelot Brown, but there are drawings by Robert Adam, who was responsible for the Gothick detail.

Dudley, St Edmund's: the old church was destroyed in the Civil War. It was rebuilt in 1722-4. A monument to George Bradley, "whose Piety and Munificence erected this Temple to THE ALMIGHTY".

Finstall was rebuilt in 1773, chiefly through the exertions of Thomas Brettell (d. 1792), to whom there is a memorial.

Stanford on Teme: new church built by Sir Edward Winnington, Bt., consecrated in 1769.

Stourbridge: the nucleus of the subscriptions was a bequest made in 1726 by Mr Biggs, a clothier, who left £300 towards the building of a church.

Great Witley, opened in 1735, was built at the cost of the first Lord Foley.

Wolverley was rebuilt through the liberality of Edward Knight: opened 20 September 1772.

II. *Frankley* was ceiled and beautified in 1750. Sir Thomas Lyttelton contributed.

Hagley chancel was rebuilt by Sir George Lyttelton from designs by Sanderson Miller.[1]

YORKSHIRE, NORTH RIDING

I. *Cleasby* was rebuilt by Dr John Robinson, Bishop of London 1714-23, who was a native of the place.

Eskdaleside: 1767 at the cost of Robert Bower, Esq., Tabitha his wife, and Mrs Gertrude Burdett her sister. "A new and very elegant chapel", on a different site from the old. The benefactors also built a parsonage and endowed the living.

Hunton was rebuilt in 1794 by Gregory Elsley, who endowed it with £200.

Rokeby: in 1761 it was to be rebuilt by the Hon. Sir Thomas Robinson, M.P., who made the design. In 1775 an exchange was made with John Sawrey Morritt, who bought the Rokeby estate in 1769. The old church, vicarage, and glebe were handed over to him, and he gave a field opposite to the new church, and undertook to complete it and build a vicarage. John Carr completed the church, and it was consecrated on 30 May 1776.

Thirkleby was rebuilt about 1722 by Sir Thomas Frankland, Bt.

[1] See *An Eighteenth-Century Correspondence.*

Thornton le Beans was rebuilt by Mrs Heber in 1770.
Warthill was rebuilt in 1787 by Robert Bowes.

II. *Coxwold* chancel was rebuilt in 1774 for Henry Earl of Fauconberg.
Deighton was new roofed and repaired by George Brown, Esq.
Kirkby Misperton: the chancel was rebuilt by Dr Conyers.

YORKSHIRE, EAST RIDING

I. *Boynton* was rebuilt in 1768–70 by Sir George Strickland.[1] The architect was probably John Carr.
Escrick: a petition to the Commons on 27 January 1781: Beilby Thompson was willing to take down the old church, and build a new one, and a new rectory, at his own expense.
Seaton Ross was rebuilt in 1788 by Mr Constable, the impropriator.

II. *Beverley minster:* the altar was given by John Moyser about 1717. It was a marble slab on a Gothic base.
Bubwith: the chancel was repaired at the expense of Mrs Ann Barnes of Spaldington in 1781.

YORKSHIRE, WEST RIDING

I. *Allerton Mauleverer* was rebuilt about 1745 by Richard Arundel.
Bierley: 1766, built by Dr Richard Richardson.
Bishopsthorpe was rebuilt in 1766 by Archbishop Drummond.
Drighlington was a Moravian chapel, built about 1783 by James Sykes. He joined the Church of England, and in 1813 handed the chapel over to the Church. It was consecrated in 1815.
Gildersome: consecrated on 29 August 1787. It was built through the agency of Mr Turton, who lived at the New Hall, and Mr Sharp.
Harrogate: a chapel was built in 1749. Subscriptions began to be raised in 1743. The principal subscriber was Lady Elizabeth Hastings of Ledstone, but other visitors, local gentry, and inhabitants, gave money.
Horbury was the native town of John Carr, the architect, who bought a house there in 1789, and offered to build a new church at his own expense. It was opened on 17 May 1794. The cost was about £8000. The south front is inscribed:

[1] But the faculty (7 Sept. 1767) says that the chancel is to be rebuilt by Sir George, and the church by the parishioners.

HANC AEDEM SACRAM
PIETATIS IN DEUM ET AMORIS
IN SOLUM NATALE MONIMENTUM
PROPRIIS SUMPTIBUS EXTRUXIT IOANNES CARR, ARCHITECTUS,
ANNO CHRISTI MDCCXCI
GLORIA DEO IN EXCELSIS

Carr's monument is in the church: the epitaph bids the reader, *Sacrosanctam hanc aedem aspice laudatissimâ ejus munificentiâ extructam.* *Horsforth* was rebuilt in 1757–8. There is a tablet to the Stanhope family, including John Stanhope, barrister-at-law and attorney-general of the County Palatine of Lancaster, who died in 1769, aged 68.

This Chapel itself may be reckoned a Monument of him
Much at whose Expence and more by whose Exertions
In the Years 1757, and 1758
It was rebuilt and greatly enlarged

Leeds, Holy Trinity: 1721–7, built mainly through the instrumentality of Lady Elizabeth Hastings. Henry Robinson, minister of St John's, promised to endow it, and Lady Elizabeth promised to pay half the cost, if it were not over £1000. At the consecration, on 21 August 1727, she was first led with great ceremony into the church, as the principal benefactress.

St James's was opened in 1794 for the Countess of Huntingdon's Connection, but was "purchased by a clergyman of the Established Church", and consecrated in 1801.

Ravenfield: Mrs Parkin, "a pious and benevolent lady", took down the old chapel and erected a new. The date was 1756.

Sheffield, St Paul's, was built through the benefaction of Robert Downes, goldsmith, with the help of subscriptions from other gentlemen of the town and neighbourhood, In 1718 Downes offered £1000 towards the building, and £30 a year for the minister. The foundation stone of the church was laid on 28 May 1720. Because of a dispute about the patronage, it was not consecrated until 1740.

Slaithwaite was rebuilt and enlarged in 1719 by the exertions of the Reverend Robert Meeke. A faculty to rebuild was granted on 27 August 1787: the site of the new church and graveyard was given by the Right Hon. William second Earl of Dartmouth.

Tong was rebuilt in 1727 by Sir George Tempest.

II. *Kirkby Overblow* was repaired in 1778: Mrs Cooper gave the Communion table. The tower was rebuilt in 1781: the Earl of Egremont gave £50, the Reverend D. R. Cooper £50, Francis Fawkes £50, the Duke of Devonshire £21, etc. Mr Hodgson "gave a great part of the same". In 1799 Dr Cooper gave a new roof for the chancel, and a new door and battlements, and repaired the east window. *Pro salute restaurata post febrem periculosam Deo Omnipotenti gratias agens, cancellum hujusce Eccelsiae refecit atque ornavit* C.C.S.T.P. A.D. 1799. The south front of the church was raised and beautified, and a new porch was built, in 1802. In 1803 Cooper gave a painted-glass window for the chancel. He died in 1804.

Pontefract, St Giles': the tower was taken down in 1707 and rebuilt by Sir John Bland, Bt., of Kippax Park.

Tinsley: the chapel, which was in decay, was restored in 1710 by Thomas Watson Wentworth, who gave the books and necessary ornaments.

6

THE RAISING OF MONEY: RATES

WHEN the churchwardens had brought before the vestry the specifications and estimates for church repairs, and the vestry had accepted them, it was open to the churchwardens, or to anyone else who was present, to move that the necessary amount should be raised by a rate on the rateable property of the parishioners. The vestry were not bound by the estimate of the churchwardens, and it was their own duty to make a decision about it; but if the church was in need of repair, they were bound to grant a rate.

The next step was to assess the parishioners. The rate was to be laid upon every occupier of land in the parish. He was liable even if he lived in another parish, but he could not be charged in the parish in which he lived for land in another parish. The rectory or vicarage was not chargeable for the repair of the body of the church, or the steeple; but the impropriator, even though he was bound to repair the chancel, was bound also to contribute to the repair of the church if he had lands in the parish that were not part of the rectory. The parson also had to contribute if he had any other estate in the parish.

If a parishioner refused to pay, it was the duty of the churchwardens to begin proceedings to enforce payment. One or two Acts were passed for furnishing easy and summary methods for recovering church rates from Quakers.

The Church Building Act of 1818[1] laid down that the formation of a new parish, or district parish, was not to affect the poor rate or other parochial rates, except as regarded church rates, in so far as they were regulated by the provisions of the Act. Rates for church repairs could be made in the districts: but a district would for twenty years be rateable for the original parish church as well.

Church rates were not always popular, and in the early part of the nineteenth century they were not infrequently refused. The Reverend W. Gresley's *Portrait of an English Churchman* (1842) has a chapter

[1] 58 George III, c. 45(2).

entitled "The Vestry Meeting". The Reverend Mr Herbert, incumbent of Welbourne, gives notice that a vestry is to be held to levy a church rate. The people of Ashdale—a new and ungodly township in the parish—decide to oppose it, and a body of them marches to the meeting with a banner inscribed "Civil and religious liberty". The churchwarden reads an estimate for church repairs: then Mr Stubbs, a shopkeeper in Ashdale, gets up. He would not, he says, put his hands into the pocket of the conscientious Dissenter. "It was not that he had any fault to find with the estimate of the churchwarden, but it was the principle of the thing which he objected to. He, for one, would never consent to call on Dissenters to wash the parson's dirty linen. (Loud applause followed this piece of wit, for it is a standing joke among the opponents of church-rates to apply this phrase to the parish surplice.)" He moves that the meeting be adjourned.

Mr Owen, a factory owner and a Dissenter, then speaks—but he surprises the meeting by saying that he cannot vote against the rate. "Having bought my property", he says, "subject to a certain deduction for Church rates, I cannot, as an honest man, turn round and vote against a Church rate, and so put the money into my own pocket: it would be robbery to do so." It is also, he says, the law of the land: and he considers that by refusing the rate he would be robbing the poor, who have a right that a place of worship should be provided for them by the owners of real property. This makes an impression, and the rate is accordingly voted without any more trouble.

But matters did not in fact always turn out so satisfactorily; and finally the Act of 30 & 31 Vict., c. 109, abolished the power of enforcing a church rate after 31 July 1868. It was contemplated that the vestries would make, and that the parishioners would accept, voluntary rates: but this was hardly ever done. The rights of the parishioners in their parish church remain, but their obligation to maintain it has been removed. This worried Victorian Churchmen more than it does ourselves: few Churchmen nowadays realize that there was ever such a thing as a church rate. And everyone has accepted the voluntary principle—which seemed to Churchmen in the past a contemptible thing, not worthy of a national Church, and only fit for Dissenters.

All vestry minutes contain regular accounts of the voting of rates, and there are usually detailed accounts of the collecting of them.

At a meeting on 5 June 1704, the vestry of Uffington, Berks., agreed to pay £23 10s for the repair of the steeple. On the 12th they voted that a 10½d tax be made for repairing the steeple, and for buying a new surplice, a new bible and prayer book, and a canopy for the pulpit. On 13 May 1715: "At a Vestry call'd then by ye Churchwardens & overseers of ye Town of Uffington concerning Rebuilding ye Ilse [*sic*] call'd Balking Ilse, it was agreed y^t it should be rebuilt." On the 29th it was agreed to get advice concerning bringing in the inhabitants of Baulking and Woolstone in the matter. On 3 July it was agreed that a 4d tax should be raised towards the rebuilding of the aisle. On 10 December it was agreed that a 2d tax should be collected for it. There follow "The Accounts of Joseph Green & Richard Deane Churchwardens for ye town of Uffing^{ton} for ye Yere 1715. And also ye Receip^{ts} of a 4^d per l in a tax gathered throughout ye parish for ye Repairing of Balking Isle."

On 9 June 1717, the vestry agreed to a 3d tax for the repair of the church.

The Newbury vestry met on 15 September 1719, and resolved:

Whereas by a former order of Vestry it was then Judged necessary to erect & build a new Gallery on the Southside of the said parish Church, and make Seats and pews therein for the better accomodating and Seating the Inhabitants of the said Parish And Whereas Samuel Slocock and William Russell (present Churchwardens) in pursuance of the said Order have proceded and built the said Gallery and made pews in the same and have this day produced the Bills of the Expence thereof amounting to the Sūme of Sixty and Three pounds one Shilling and one penny halfpenny, We the said Minister and Churchwardens and Inhabitants of the said parish now present do hereby allow and approve of the said Bills & Summe of Sixty Three pounds one shilling and one penny halfpenny and agree that the same be paid and discharged by a Rate on the parish aforesaid And we also order that the said Churchwardens do at the Expence and Charge of the parishioners of the said parish erect & build one other Gallery on the North side of the said parish Church and make pews therein answerable to the said new Gallery on the Southside of the said Church and when the same is finished that a Rate or Rates be made and levyed on the parishioners for defraying the Charge and Expence thereof . . .

The vestry of Gainsborough, Lincs., appointed a committee on 22 July 1734, to report on the parish church. They reported that Francis Bickerton of York, and Francis Smith of Warwick, had declared the church unsafe, and that Smith had made a plan of a new church that could be built for £3000.

They thought that the money should be raised by a pound rate upon the houses and lands of the parish, two parts to be paid by the owner, and a third part by the tenant. They had objections to taxes upon trade, or any branch of it, which would prejudice the trade of the parish. They objected also to a tax on malt, ale, coals, etc., because that would be unequal, and most affect the middle and lower sort. But the houses and lands in the parish were, by the laws of the nation, purchased subject to the duty of repairing and maintaining the parish church. They were of opinion that the duty should be charged for twenty one years.

The Comm^{ee} have therefore proceeded to compute ye Value of the Lands & Houses in the Parish, & to calculate what Annual Fund will be necessary to discharge ye s^d Sum of Three Thousand Pounds & Interest, in ye Compass of Twenty One Years, in order to judge what such Annual Paym^t will amount to in the Pound: And it appears to them, That ye Estates chargeable therewith will raise such yearly Paym^t by a Rate of Twelve pence in the Pound; and that Sum, it is hoped, may be lessen'd by voluntary Subscriptions, & the Remainder made an easier Charge upon the Parish, & less liable to any Misapplication or Mismanagement, by granting Annuitys for Lives; as has been done in the Case of the Parish of Shoreditch & other Places.

They did not think that it would be a burden upon the inhabitants,

but on ye Contrary, they cannot help thinking that ye Parishioners in general, when they are fully apprized of ye sev^l Matters now laid before them, will approve of so good a Design, & heartily concurr therein, & make it easy to their Circumstances if ye Expense is abridged in some unnecessary Ornaments, or even in some Conveniences of Life.

On 16 September 1735 a vestry was held, and the report was agreed to, and a committee was appointed to apply to Parliament for an Act enabling the parish to rebuild the church according to the method proposed in the report.[1]

There was a contested rate in the parish of St John's, Newcastle, in 1800. Thomas Fenton, Henry Sunderland, Matthew Brown, and John Darnell, the churchwardens, painted and ornamented the church at a cost of £452. The parishioners refused a rate to pay off the debt. They said that the expenditure was wanton and profuse; that it had not been sanctioned by a general meeting of the parishioners, and recorded in the parish book; and that the churchwardens had wasted the goods of the church. A case was drawn up and submitted to the recorder, R. H. Williamson. He thought that a rate for the full sum expended might be legally resisted; but advised the parishioners to take another

[1] Fac. 9, 68.

opinion: Mr Swabey was applied to, and said that the conduct of the wardens had been irregular, and that the expenditure had been profuse. Finally, the parishioners agreed to pay £320 by a church-cess, and to raise £140 by a voluntary subscription.[1]

There were, of course, other ways of raising money.

On 17 April 1770, the churchwardens of Chesterfield were authorized to apply to the treasurer of the Navigation Scheme, or to Messrs Wilkinson, for the loan of £120, "to be disbursed in paying off Workmens Bills and other contingent Expences attending the late Rebuilding of the North Isle of the Church".

When Battersea church was rebuilt in 1775–7, thirty pews were leased for ninety-nine years at thirty guineas each—producing £945.[2]

The Wandsworth vestry was told on 26 December 1750 that Matthew Shrubb was willing to lend £150 at 4 per cent. They resolved that £163 should be borrowed, and the workmen paid. Shrubb was paid off on 13 July 1763. When the church was mainly rebuilt in 1780, three maiden ladies each advanced £300.

The vestry of Long Ditton, Surrey, decided in 1775 to demolish the old church and to build a new one. On 8 April 1776, they met and discussed the raising of money. It appeared "from a Survey beforehand, and Calculation made by experienced Surveyors that the sum of Sixteen Hundred Pounds woud be requir'd to finish the said Work". Already £221 had been subscribed, and a further £179 could be reasonably expected from the parish. A brief had been granted by which it was hoped to raise £400. It was moved that the remaining £200 should be borrowed on annuities for the lives of the lenders, and that a yearly sum of £64 should be raised by a church rate.

On the 21st Robert Taylor's plan was adopted, and the tender of Edward Gray, of St George's, Hanover Square, was accepted. The estimate of £1600 did not include the pewing and other matters. In the event, the total amount spent was £2836. The brief brought in more than was expected—£444 18s 8d. New College, Oxford, gave £21, and the font and the altar were given by the rector, the Reverend Mr Pennicott.

Dr Hutchinson of All Saints', Derby, raised money by personal magnetism. He wanted to rebuild the church, against the wishes of

[1] See E. Mackenzie, *A Descriptive and Historical Account of the Town and County of Newcastle upon Tyne*, 1827, p. 343.
[2] J. G. Taylor, *Our Lady of Batersey*, 1925, p. 109.

the Corporation and the majority of the parishioners, and, on the night of 18 February 1723, he admitted a large body of workmen, who dismantled it, and began to demolish it. The opposition then gave way, and the doctor took on himself the responsibility of raising all the money, without any help from the parish. Whenever he could think of any likely subscriber, he paid him a visit, and even went to London to beg. Even the Christmas waits were invited indoors, and persuaded to give a guinea.

He succeeded in raising something over £3000, including a grant of £102 from the Corporation. A brief brought in £598 5s 6d, but there was still a deficit of several hundred pounds. So he sold six burying places in the vault for six guineas, and proposed to sell forty of the principal seats in the church. As the seats had hitherto been unappropriated, there was considerable opposition. Finally a compromise was reached, and he was allowed to sell by auction eight double seats in the best part of the church; they realized £475 13s.

Hutchinson was a tiresome man, and peace was only restored when he resigned in 1728. Obviously he was in the wrong; but we owe him a debt of gratitude for being the begetter of Gibbs's magnificent new church.[1]

[1] Hutton's *History of Derby*, 1791, and J. C. Cox, *Notes on the Churches of Derbyshire*, Vol. IV, 1879, pp. 90–2.

7

THE RAISING OF MONEY: BRIEFS

THE RUBRIC in the Order for the Administration of Holy Communion directs that "Then [after the Creed] the Curate shall declare unto the people what Holy-days, or Fasting-days, are in the week following to be observed. And then also (if occasion be) shall notice be given of the Communion; *and the banns of Matrimony published* [the last clause has, without authority, been omitted in modern editions of the Prayer Book] and Briefs, Citations, and Excommunications read."

Papal briefs[1] were abolished at the Reformation; there were episcopal briefs before the Reformation, and a few afterwards. But normally a brief was a royal warrant authorizing a collection for some charitable purpose in church, or sometimes from house to house (a Walking Brief). There were abuses connected with them, and an Act—4 Anne, *c.* 14(3), 1705—was passed to remedy these. This provided that all copies of a brief should be printed by the Queen's printers, and that it should be numbered, and carefully delivered to the authorities of each church; and that it should be given back by them, duly filled in and signed, within a certain time, together with the money collected, to the distributor, who was to give accounts and return the brief to the Court of Chancery, he himself being allowed expenses and a reward for his trouble. But there were still complaints about the fees charged, the time that was taken, and the small profits that resulted.

On 9 February 1816 Lord Shaftesbury moved that an account be laid before the House of the sums produced by briefs for the repair of churches during the ten years ending 2 May 1815. In 1821 a Bill was introduced to the Commons for abolishing all briefs, with the exception of an annual collection for church building. A committee sat in 1822 and took some evidence, but nothing further seems to have been done. In 1828 the system was finally abolished, though the Incorporated

[1] The *Oxford English Dictionary* defines a brief as a "Pope's letter on matter of discipline to person or community (less formal than bull)".

Church Building Society, which had been granted briefs of its own, was allowed the benefit of royal letters for its own funds—but these too were abolished in 1853.

The firm of Byrd, Hall, and Stevenson began to act as undertakers for briefs in 1754. On the death or retirement of Hall, Byrd and Stevenson continued until the death of Stevenson in 1777. Thomas Stevenson and Co. then continued the business, and afterwards William Stevenson and Thomas Dudley. John Stevenson Salt began to act as agent in 1799: after the death of his uncle W. Stevenson in 1807 he acted as partner with Dudley. Dudley resigned in 1813, and Salt then acted alone.

The Salt collection of briefs has been handed over to the British Museum, and only a list, and a few odd copies, are in the Salt Library at Stafford.

The standard work on the subject is *Church Briefs*, by W. A. Bewes,[1] which gives a useful list of all briefs issued from the time of the Commonwealth until 1828. But most of the book is taken up with the earlier period: there are only fourteen pages about the reign of Anne, none about the reigns of the first two Georges, and only twelve about the reign of George III. Nor does Bewes seem to have been very interested in briefs for church repair: he gives very few examples, and none for the eighteenth century.

There is usually very little about briefs in the parish records, except for notes on the sums collected; but interesting details, and sometimes plans, can be found in the records of Quarter Sessions. Application for a brief was made to the justices, who heard the evidence of workmen and received their estimates and, if they approved—as they usually did—forwarded the application to the Lord Chancellor.

Three things must be remembered about briefs:

1. The wording is stylized. Because a brief, or a petition, begins "Whereas the Church of Anytown is a very ancient building", it cannot be assumed that the church is (or was) very ancient. Even if—as happened once or twice—it was a church that had been built a few years before, and, having been carelessly built, was already in need of repair, it might still be called a very ancient building. The architects are invariably referred to as "able and experienced", but it would be unwise to assume that they necessarily were. Petitioners for briefs were told what words they were to use.

2. It must not be assumed that the workmen who surveyed the

[1] 1896.

church, and who presented the estimates, were necessarily responsible for carrying out the work when it was done. Sometimes one or other of them did make the design, but often they were simply tradesmen who had inspected the building. Some reputable architects did survey for briefs, and if one of them was concerned, it is more likely that he planned the repair or rebuilding. But it is not safe to suppose that he did, without a definite statement to that effect; or a signed plan such as is still sometimes to be found attached to the petition; or other evidence.

3. Nor must it be assumed that the work was necessarily done. There were parishes whose churches were described as ruinous and decayed, and in urgent need of rebuilding, which obtained a brief, and then found that they were little better off as the result of it. All that they did was to patch up the church, which, in spite of the surveyors' prophecy of impending ruin, survived to be restored in the nineteenth century, and is still standing to-day. Sittingbourne church, Kent, was burned in 1762, and a brief was asked for in 1763. The estimates are among the Quarter Sessions papers in the County Record Office at Maidstone. The total came to £2089 0s 3d, but nothing like this was actually spent. George Dance surveyed the church, and found the walls, pillars, and arches good and strong. The church was not rebuilt, but was given new roofs: the work was done by John Boykett of Milton for £488 2s 3½d.

There were also, of course, many churches that were substantially altered in the eighteenth century, but were so heavily restored in the nineteenth that they now show no traces of it at all. In such cases a brief may be the means of calling attention to work that would otherwise have been forgotten.

Sometimes, though this is not common, an account of the whole procedure has been kept among the parish records.

At Cheam, Surrey, the rector, churchwardens, and other inhabitants, appealed to Quarter Sessions in 1741. The church was out of repair, and they had been told by the surveyors that the body must be rebuilt from the foundation.

Your petitioners therefore humbly pray that your Worships will be pleased to examine John Sanderson, Surveyor, John Devall, Mason and Robert Broughton, Carpenter, men of good Judgment Honesty and great Experience, and who have viewed the ruinous condition of the said Church & made an Estimate of the Charges of rebuilding the same and repairing the Tower, who attend to declare upon Oath the Truth of the Premisses, what they think the Charge may reasonably amount to; and to certify the same unto the Right Honble the Lord High Chancellor, To the End his Lordship may be pleased to grant unto the Petitioners, his Majesties Letters Patents to enable them to ask, receive and gather the charitable contributions of his Majesties subjects in such places as his Lordship shall think fit.

And your Petitioners etc.

The workmen's estimate was £1082 7s 5d. After the meeting of Quarter Sessions, the following petition was drawn up:

To the Rt Honble Phillip Lord Hardwick Baron of Hardwick in the County of Gloucester Lord High Chancellor of Great Brittain.

May it please your Lords. to be notified that at the General Quarter Sessions of the Peace held at Southwarke in and for the County of Surrey on Monday the 12th day of January inst. It appeared unto us and others his Maties Justices of the peace assembled in open court upon the Humble petition of the Rector, Churchwarden . . . [continues as in their petition] and wee haveing now examined the truth of the premises in open court do humbly certifie to your Lords. that it appeared to us upon the oaths of John Sanderson, Surveyor, John Devall mason & Robt. Broughton carpenter men of good judgment honesty and of great experience now taken and examined in open court that the charge of pulling down rebuilding the Church and repairing the Steeple, besides the old materialls will amount to the sum of 1082.7.5 according to the best of their skill and judgment. Wee therefore humbly presume to recommend the sad misfortune & calamitous condition of the petitioners unto your Lords. consideration humbly praying your Lords. to grant unto them his Maties gracious Letters Pattent for a collection of the pious and charitable benevolence of contributions of such of his Maties well disposed subjects as shall be willing to contribute to so good, laudable & religious a purpose in and through such citties, counties & places as your Lords. shall think fit & convenient all which nevertheless wee humble submit to your Lords. great wisdom & are

Yr. Lords. most obt. servts . . . [names].[1]

There was much industrial development in Staffordshire in the eighteenth century, and Quarter Sessions were constantly being kept busy with appeals for briefs. The following is a selection from those in the later part of the century, which will serve as examples.[2]

1772, April: Gratwich Church was decayed and dangerous, the north wall was fallen down, and the church was supported only with

[1] Parish records in the Record Office, Guildford.
[2] These are in the County Record Office at Stafford. The Diocesan Registry at Lichfield, which contains much material about eighteenth-century church building, is inaccessible to searchers.

props. Charles Trubshaw's estimate for rebuilding was £1150 10s. The brief was issued at Michaelmas 1773, and the church was rebuilt in 1775.

1773, January: the parish of Madeley had raised very large sums which they had laid out in endeavouring to support their church: but it was ruinous and must be taken down and rebuilt. Several able and experienced workmen had surveyed it, and made an estimate of £1490.

October: the church of Longnor was dangerous, and also too small to contain the population. The truth of this was confirmed by the oath of William Billing, whose estimate for rebuilding was £1224 2s. The brief was issued at Michaelmas 1774. The rebuilding was begun in 1780, but another brief was asked for in 1783. The church had been taken down and in part rebuilt, but the parish was unable to finish it. In October 1799 an appeal was made for a third brief. Part of the walls must be rebuilt, and raised six feet higher in order that galleries might be erected. The roof was at present propped with sundry deal poles. Joseph Billinge had made an estimate of £1250. A plan and elevation are attached to the petition. The brief was issued at Easter 1800.

A further brief was petitioned for in January 1813. There is a note,

> To Prove the Estimate call—
> Isaac Billinge)
> the Architect)

His estimate was £1001 10s 2d.

Bagnall made a petition in 1782: the estimate for rebuilding was £1155 13s 11½d exclusive of old materials, "as will appear by the plan and estimate of Thos. Hubbard an experienced Builder". The brief was issued at Michaelmas, and there was a further brief in 1813.

1783: the chapel at Longton (or Lane End) was a modern structure built by subscription in 1761, at which time the population did not exceed 500. It had been found by a late survey to be very much out of repair; and, owing to the increase of population, a new chapel was necessary. There was another brief in 1795, and another in 1827, when the rebuilt church had become ruinous because of coal mines underneath it, and Benjamin Brough of Lane End had made plans for repair and enlargement.

1787: the church of Ipstones was ruinous and decayed, and the greatest part of the church and steeple must be rebuilt on a much larger plan. There is a note, "To prove the plan and Estimate please to call John Clowes". Clowes was called, and said that he had viewed the old church and found it dangerous. His estimate was £1431 14s, exclusive of old materials. Two more briefs were granted—in 1792 and 1800.

In 1789 an appeal was made for rebuilding the chapel of Warslow in the parish of Alstonfield: attached to it is an estimate by Matthew Billing for £1018 12s 6d. A further brief was asked for in April 1807. It was stated on the testimony of Joseph Billinge that the chapel was decayed, though the inhabitants had done all in their power to keep it in repair. It must now be taken down and rebuilt and enlarged. The inhabitants had been increased by the lead, copper, and brass mines in the chapelry. He gave an estimate of £1119 15s 5d.

A further petition was presented in October 1812. Only £253 10s had been collected on the former brief, and £856 5s was still needed. A brief for that sum was issued at Michaelmas 1813. The chapel was rebuilt in 1820.

In 1790 there were four cases. A brief for Mucklestone in 1786 had only produced £310 1s 9¼d, which had already been expended in taking down and rebuilding the church. It could not be completed: the rebuilding had cost about £1300, and the tower was in a ruinous state and could not be taken down and rebuilt without further help.

Hanley chapel had lately been taken down in order to erect a new one. But it was not finished, and could not be completed without assistance.

At the April Sessions, Bloxwich presented its case. The chapel was an ancient structure, greatly decayed and in danger of falling down. It must be enlarged and rebuilt: the tower must be altered and repaired, and a wall must be built round the chapel yard. It had been carefully viewed by Samuel Whitehouse, whose estimate was £1207 15s, exclusive of old materials. A further brief was given in 1804.

Milwich church was stated in October to be ancient and decayed. It had been viewed by skilful architects, whose estimate for rebuilding was £1235 5s. The brief was issued at Easter 1792.

1791: Adbaston church must be rebuilt, and the tower rebuilt as far as the bell windows—besides many other material and necessary repairs to the tower. A brief—for £1488 18s 10d—was issued at Easter 1792, and others in 1796 and 1800. But the rebuilding was not done.

1792: Castlechurch needed to be rebuilt: "The Architects William Mottershaw and William Dudley will produce the plan of the Church & prove the Estimate thereon." The brief was for £1591 9s 8d.

1794, May: Calton chapel must be taken down and rebuilt. "Calton Chapel. To Execute the annexed plan with the whole of the outside of new Stone, the inside stocoed, the Isles laid with stone, the Pews, Desk and Pulpit of the best Oak and neat Workmanship, the roof also of oak covered with Lead sheeting of proper thickness and strength will cost exclusive of the old materials the sum of £1181:12:0." William White, architect, signs the petition. The brief was issued at Easter 1795.

July: Marston was to be rebuilt according to the plan and estimate herewith produced. These are by William Dudley: the estimate was £1490 17s 10d. A further brief was needed in 1815.

In October Joseph Billinge presented his estimate for rebuilding the chapel at Quarnford: it amounts to £1605 19s. The plan and elevation —the latter carefully but clumsily drawn—have survived. There was a further brief in 1812.

1797, January: the tower of Bilston church was a very ancient and ruinous structure, and so low that it was necessary to be taken down and rebuilt. There was no vestry room, and the staircase to the galleries was so narrow and in such bad plight that it must be taken down and widened. Randle Walker's estimate was £1395.

In April William Dudley gave an estimate for repairing Butterton church, for which a brief had previously been granted in 1777. The walls must be raised 6 ft. higher, and there must be a new roof; the church and chancel must have new floors, pews, pulpit, reading desk, etc. This would cost £1009 3s 8d.

1798, January: by virtue of an Act of Parliament passed in the thirty-fourth year of His Majesty's reign, £1350 had been raised to enable the parishioners of Tipton to take down and rebuild their church. This had been spent; and there remained due for the purchase of the land, and burial ground—for the church had been removed to a new site—and for other expenses, the sum of £737 17s 10d. It was also necessary that galleries should be erected. And on 16 December last many windows had been destroyed, and the rest very much injured, by a hurricane. A further sum of £320 10s was wanted. John Keyte had made an estimate of the expenses as stated.

These are typical, and it would be wearisome to the reader to give many more: a few examples from other counties are given in the Appendix.

It only remains to be said that by the end of the century there was a good deal of dissatisfaction about briefs. The antiquaries, who were beginning to teach people to appreciate old churches, felt, with some reason, that the petitions greatly exaggerated the dilapidations, and that the schemes for remedying them were too drastic. Gresley, Derbyshire, had a brief for £2000 in 1786: there was to be an entirely new church by Joseph Wyatt of Burton. A writer in the *Topographer*[1] agreed that the church was out of repair but did it really need rebuilding? "Would not less than half the money, that a new church would cost, make the present all that could be wished?" In fact, the brief produced very small results, and only repairs were done.

The ordinary vestrymen were beginning to think that briefs were a waste of time and effort. The wooden steeple of Beenham, Berks., was struck by lightning on 6 July 1794, and was destroyed, together with the gallery and much of the church. An estimate of £600 was made for rebuilding. An appeal was circulated in Berkshire, Buckinghamshire, and Oxfordshire, stating that the parishioners were anxious to raise the money "without the assistance of a Brief, which must be some time in collecting, and to which too many have lately refused their contributions". Nearly every parish in Berkshire contributed, and £579 14s 11½d was collected.

[1] No. VII, p. 433.

8

ACTS OF PARLIAMENT

FOR THE formation of a new parish, or for the authority to raise special funds for the repair of rebuilding of a church, an Act of Parliament had to be obtained. The vestry would draw up a petition, and find someone who would bring it forward. The church-wardens' accounts of St Catherine Coleman for 1736–7 contain a mention of £2 2s paid to Mr Tayler Bates "for Drawing Plans of the Church and Glebe to lay before the Committee of the House of Comm.ˢ".

As things were, the procedure had to be piecemeal. The only large provision for new parishes was the Fifty New Churches Act of 1711. But there were many petitions from particular parishes, as the need arose, which were dealt with as reported in the Commons Journals: a list of Acts is given in the Appendix to this book.

An important case was that of Greenwich. On 6 April 1711, a report was presented to the Commons: the steeple had fallen on the night of 28 November last, and in the judgement of skilful workmen it was incapable of repair, and must be rebuilt. The petitioners produced plans of the intended new church, with an estimate of £6260 4s 2d. The parish was not able to raise the sum, and the parishioners prayed that, as they had for "40 years past contributed to the building of St Paul's, and other Churches, by a Duty of Coals; and, as St Paul's is near finished, and the Duties granted probably may produce more than enough for that service", the sum of £6000, "or other such sum, as the House shall think fit, may be assigned for rebuilding the said church at Greenwich".

A committee was appointed to consider this, and also to examine the whole question of church building in London, Westminster, and the suburbs. The result was the Act of 1711 for imposing a duty on coals to build Fifty New Churches. Greenwich was the first of the Fifty to be finished.

The passing of the New Churches Act was followed by a number of petitions from parishes which hoped to benefit from it: Rotherhithe,

1714; St Botolph's, Aldersgate, St Giles in the Fields, St Botolph's, Bishopsgate, and St Catherine Coleman, 1718; and St George's, Southwark, 1732.

Petitions are always more interesting when they give the names of the workmen who had surveyed the church, or who had designed a new one. These appear, for instance, in the cases of St Botolph's, Aldersgate, 1711 (Mr Blissart and Mr Smith); St Botolph's, Bishopsgate, 1723 (Richard Groswell and William Groswell, carpenters, and Edward Ireson, bricklayer); St Mary Magdalene, Woolwich, 1731 (Matthew Spray, bricklayer, and William Reynolds and John Henslow, carpenters); St Catherine Coleman, 1732 (Henry Flitcroft, William Cooper, and John James); St George's, Southwark, 1732 (William Lessaw, mason, and John Townsend); St Leonard's, Shoreditch, 1735 (Flitcroft and Cordwell, who had surveyed the church after the fall of the tower in 1716); St Olave's, Southwark, 1736 (George Dance); All Saints', Worcester, 1737 (John Bird and Richard Squires, carpenters); St Botolph's, Aldgate, 1740 (Benjamin Glanville, surveyor); Islington, 1750 (Benjamin Timbrell, James Steere, and George Ufford); All Saints', Hertford, 1765 (John Taylor, architect, Thomas Hill, carpenter, and Samuel Kynaston, bricklayer); Battersea, 1774 (Richard Dixon and Joseph Dixon, surveyors); St James's, Toxteth Park, Liverpool—a new church—1774 (Cuthbert Bisbrowne, surveyor); St John's, Portsmouth—a new church—1787 (John Monday and John Shean of Portsmouth Common, builders: the church was to be built under the inspection of Nicholas Vass of Portsmouth Common); St James's, Clerkenwell, 1787 (James Carr and Joseph Carter); Saffron Walden, 1791 (Robert Brettingham); and All Saints', Southampton, 1790 (John Groves and George Byfield), and 1793 (Willey Reveley).

They are most interesting when the hearing of the evidence is reported in some detail.

On 9 March 1735 the Commons heard the report on Gainsborough, Lincs., given by Francis Smith of Warwick. (Smith, "one of the most successful master builders of the eighteenth century", was by now 63 years old, and decidedly stout.) He said that in November 1734 he came to examine the church, and had made a detailed report of its bad condition. It was in danger of falling, and could not be repaired. He had made an estimate for rebuilding the church, but not the steeple. This was £2834 7s; but if the ornaments were left out, and it were built plain of stone, it would abate £100 or something more. If brick were used, the saving would be much greater.

Abraham Hayward, mason, and Francis Bickerton, surveyor of building, confirmed Smith's evidence. Bickerton's evidence was confirmed by William Morton and Benjamin Silverwood, who had assisted him.

Edward Goddard, mason and bricklayer, said that he had viewed the church in February 1735, with another mason, two carpenters, and some of the parishioners. "He said that he had been concerned in the Repair of *St Mary's* Church at *Nottingham*, which he apprehended was in as ruinous a Condition as the Church of *Gainsborough* now is; but he owned that it did not lean quite so much, and that it was built of *Ashler* Stone, and not propped." He thought that it could be repaired for about £500.

Joseph Madder, Francis Williamson, and Samuel Barnes, who had assisted his survey, gave evidence to the same purport. Madder said that he had been concerned in the repair of Burton Church, Notts., which was in a far worse state.

It was finally decided to bring in a Bill for rebuilding, which was passed on 8 April 1736. £5230 was raised by parochial assessment, and by a duty on coals brought to the town pursuant to the Act. On 27 January 1740 it was stated that £2210 10s 4d would be needed to finish the work, and a further Bill was passed to enable it to be raised.

The design of the new church used to be ascribed to Gibbs. T. Mozley in his *Reminiscences chiefly of Towns, Villages and Schools*,[1] says "The body of the church, by Gibbs, is a noble piece of building, however incongruous, and notwithstanding Mr Britton's fierce denunciations." There must have been a tradition to this effect, and indeed Smith was associated with Gibbs at All Saints', Derby, and Ditchley, and his style is strongly influenced by him; but the evidence in Parliament, and the report of the building committee at Gainsborough, in the Lincoln Diocesan Record Office[2] make it as certain as anything can be that Smith made the design himself.

The petition for Wapping, presented on 26 January 1756, produced some disagreement. Evidence was given on 9 March. George Dance said that the walls were only two bricks and a half thick, there was no steeple, and the church was not built in a substantial manner. It was in a generally poor condition, and the floor in most places was five feet below the surface of the ground. £500 would repair the church so that it would stand for forty or fifty years, but it could not be repaired effectually. A new church would cost £4000 or £5000.

[1] 1885, Vol. I, p. 160.   [2] See p. 92.

James Steer, surveyor to the Hand in Hand Fire Office, St Thomas's Hospital, and Guy's Hospital, supported Dance. He said that it was practicable to raise the floor; but the galleries must be taken down and raised, and then there would be no room for the people in the galleries to stand upright. But he did not think it possible to raise the floor above the level of the churchyard, and the foundation was too weak to raise a superstructure upon. He said that the church might be supported, but he did not advise its repair. Bolton Manwaring, surveyor to London Hospital, said that he had surveyed the church, and would advise building a new one. Henry Keene, surveyor, said that he also had surveyed the church. "That it was built as substantial as was necessary for a Church of that Height; but if he was to build a Church now, should build it thicker, because he should build it higher." He had found no part of the building unsound, and thought that it would last many years more. If care had been taken to carry off the water, it would be safe. Matthew Fairless, builder and surveyor, said that he never saw so old a building so upright. He gave an account of the buttresses and the galleries, and said that, if a little money were laid out, it could be made safe and wholesome. He said "That, to repair the Church, and remove the Things complained of, and make it drier and to beautify it, would cost between £4 and 500. and make it more convenient than ever: That the Dampness may be removed, if the Gutters are taken care of . . . That it would be dangerous to build a heavier Church, and thinks a new Church is not necessary: and that he would go to the old Church as soon as any other; and that, with moderate Repairs, it will last Three or Fourscore Years."

But he did not carry conviction, and a Bill for rebuilding was passed.

The Clapham vestry agreed on 16 October 1773, that a new church should be built, and a petition was drawn up and presented to Parliament. Kenton Couse, who made the plans, gave evidence before the Commons on 26 January 1774, and the Bill passed the Commons on 14 February.

In 1777 a petition was made for a new Bill to enable the trustees to raise a further sum of money. A report was heard on 14 February: they had raised £7719 11s 6d, and spent £7686 2s 2d. £1368 18s 1d now remained for bills unpaid and work contracted for, in order to complete the whole.

Couse said that a contract had been entered into with John Hanscomb for building the church at £5000. Several other offers had been made, but Hanscomb's, though not the lowest, was thought the most eligible. There were some exceptions in the contract, in case deeper foundations were required, and also if piling or planking were necessary. When the contractor began to dig, he found all sorts of soil, and it was all very full of springs. The trustees directed him to order that the foundation should be piled and planked; and it was raised higher than had been proposed in order to get above the springs. That was one of the chief reasons for exceeding the estimated expense. There was also an exception in the contract of the pulpit, altar, and reading desk. And drains had to be made in the churchyard, and locks on the pews were not mentioned in the contract. The committee had given the orders for the extra works, and Hanscomb was preferred to lower contractors because some of the trustees had asked for him. He did not consider his estimate extravagant.

Couse was asked whether he thought that Carrick and Burton, who offered to contract for £4750, could afford to do the work in a proper manner. He said that he thought not. The estimate in his own mind had been £5300.

Was the £5000 to make the church complete for Divine Service? No. The pulpit, desk, and altar were postponed.

Had the painting, glazing, and every other necessary work been done? Yes. The Bill was passed.

The Church Building Act of 1818,[1] like the previous Act of 1711, provided not only for the building of the churches, but for the formation of parishes. Since then, Parliament has had less and less to do with these matters. The establishment of the Ecclesiastical Commissioners in 1835 gave the Church a certain amount of independence. The formation of new districts, the alterations of boundaries, the acceptance of conveyances of land for new churches, the substitution of new parish churches for old, etc., became the business of the Commissioners.

In 1843 Sir Robert Peel's Act made it possible to form a parish without an Act of Parliament. It could be established by means of an Order in Council on the recommendation of the Ecclesiastical Commissioners.

It seems strange to modern Churchmen that Parliament should ever have come into it at all. But it did not worry Churchmen in the eighteenth century. The Church of England was part of the constitution, and obviously Church and State were connected—on the lower

[1] 58 Geo. III, c. 45.

level of the parish, and higher up as well. What authority other than Parliament could there have been for attending to these matters? And anyhow, Parliament was an assembly of Churchmen: the Churchmanship of many of them may not have been of a very high order, but they were all members of the Church of England.

We have to look back through the nineteenth century, and it is difficult to forget the Oxford Movement, and such things as the Public Worship Regulation Act—to say nothing of the Life and Liberty movement, and all the twentieth-century developments, which have separated Church and State so thoroughly that the Establishment now means very little.

We are sure that we do things better—and obviously the simple eighteenth-century methods would not suit the present time. But what would an eighteenth-century Churchman have thought of our present system—a bureaucracy, costing ever more and more, and constantly issuing reports on one thing and another? One thing is certain: he would feel that the Church as he knew it—the Church of England by law established—had disappeared, and that something like a sect had taken its place. He would, as we said, be fairly well at home on the P.C.C., though it would be a shock to him to learn that he would have to put his name on the electoral roll, and to stand for election. He would be quite at home in the business of obtaining a faculty. But it would seem strange to him that Parliament had so small a concern with what was still supposed to be the national Church, and that the successors of Francis Smith, George Dance, and Kenton Couse would never more stand up to give evidence in the House . . . "If the ornaments were left out, and it were built plain of stone, it would abate £100, or something more." That kind of thing had interested them once. And (he would say) it was their business to be interested.

As late as 1842, J. H. Markland, in his *Remarks on English Churches* —an ecclesiological book, based on a letter addressed to the Oxford Architectural Society in 1840—wrote, "the duty of the state—a Christian state—to provide for the spiritual instruction of its subjects, remains—one that will remain as a national obligation, and so long as it is neglected a heavy responsibility rests upon it". He does not think that parliamentary help would put an end to private generosity. He contrasts the lack of interest in Parliament in 1840 with the enthusiasm in Queen Anne's reign.[1]

[1] Pp. 129–30.

The building of the new churches under the Act of 1711 is somewhat outside the scope of this book, but a few things ought to be said about it.

The commissioners appointed under the Act sent a questionnaire to the vestries of the parishes in which new churches were likely to be needed.

The vestry of St Anne's, Soho, appointed a committee on 17 October 1711 which announced on 2 November that it had agreed on the return to be made. The total population of the parish was 8133. There were three places fit for new churches: "in Warder Street in Old Sohoe, A piece of Ground in King Square, another piece of Ground at the end of Litchfield Street, None of which are freehold." The French Minister was possessed of four chapels, none of which were capable of being made parochial churches. There were many Roman Catholics and Dissenters, who did not go to church.[1]

The churchwardens' accounts of St Clement Danes mention some small payments in connection with the questions:

Oct. 13th To Expences on Mr Shreve and others ab^{t} Craven house for a
New Church   3/-
15th To Expences at Capt Jenkins wth some of the Vestry to Consult ab^{t}
the Churches   6
28th To Expences in enquiring after the vallue of the Grange Inn & Craven
house & in measuring the Grange Inn wth the workmen two days   8[2]

St James's, Piccadilly, considered their reply on 7 November: they did not think that there was immediate necessity for building a church, or for the parish chapels to be converted into parish churches.[3]

On the same day, St Martin in the Fields drafted their reply. They said that two new churches would be sufficient. Sites proper for building new churches were (1) On the north side of Long Acre: a piece of ground called the Wood Yard was a proper place for a church, minister's house, and churchyard. (2) Towards Hyde Park.[4]

The parishioners of St Mary le Strand had a very good case, for they had no church at all. There had been a parish church, "then standing where Somerset House is now built". Since its demolition they had been allowed to use the Savoy chapel; but it was too small, and they were liable to be excluded for a year together.[5]

---

[1] Vestry minutes in Westminster Library, A.2202a.   [2] Ibid., B.1062.
[3] Ibid., D.1758.   [4] Ibid., F.2005.   [5] Ibid., G.1001.

When these reports, and the rest, had come in, the commissioners[1] drew up a list of parishes, with the number of new churches suggested for each, which was appended to their report to Parliament dated 23 March 1715-16. From an architectural point of view, it is a pity that many of the churches were never built; but it is certain that, if they had been, many of them would have been an embarrassment to Churchmen in the future, and that by now a large number of them would have been pulled down. What would the twentieth century be able to do with three large additional churches in the parish of St Giles, Cripplegate, or four in the parish of St Giles in the Fields?

The surveyors appointed for the scheme were Nicholas Hawksmoor and William Dickinson. Sir Christopher Wren and Sir John Vanbrugh both made suggestions. Dickinson resigned in August 1713, and was succeeded by James Gibbs—who was superseded by John James in December 1715. Gibbs, a Tory and a Roman Catholic, was not acceptable to the new Whig government.

Nor was the Churchmanship of the new reign favourable to the continuation of the scheme on its original scale. The churches so far built had been extremely expensive, and it became clear that the complete scheme would not be carried out. In the end, the number of churches fell far short of the proposed fifty.

A few old churches were rebuilt: St Alphege's, Greenwich, St Mary Magdalene, Woolwich, St Giles in the Fields, St George's, Southwark, and St George's, Gravesend. The tower of St Michael's, Cornhill, was completed.

Two chapels were bought and consecrated as parish churches: St George the Martyr, Queen Square, Holborn, and St John's, Clerkenwell.

The completely new churches that were built were as follows: Christchurch, Spitalfields (1723-9: Nicholas Hawksmoor, architect); St George's, Hanover Square (1712-24: John James, architect); St George's, Bloomsbury (1720-30: Nicholas Hawksmoor, architect); St George's in the East (1715-23: Nicholas Hawksmoor, architect); St John's, Westminster (1714-28: Thomas Archer, architect); St Anne's, Limehouse (1712-24: Nicholas Hawksmoor, architect); St Mary le Strand (1714-17: James Gibbs, architect); St Paul's, Deptford (1712-30: Thomas Archer, architect); St John's Horsleydown, South-

---

[1] The Commissioner's minutes have at last been discovered, and are in Lambeth Palace. It is much to be desired that a complete account of the Commission's work should be published.

wark (1728–33: the design made jointly by the two surveyors, Hawksmoor and James); and St Luke's, Old Street (1727–33, designed in the same way.)

The later eighteenth century did not approve of most of these churches: they did not appreciate the baroque style of Archer, or the brooding solemnity of Hawksmoor. The nineteenth century naturally did not approve either. Ecclesiologists did not know what to do with them. They were too solid to be altered drastically, so they were left more or less alone, and all that was attempted was a certain amount of redecoration and rearrangement. Now they are appreciated as never before.

But we are not concerned here with anything more than the fact that they were built, and that, having been built, they were given parishes. Churchwardens were appointed, and vestries began to meet, and thereafter they were responsible for the maintenance and repair of the fabrics.

They began at once. St George's, Hanover Square, was consecrated in March 1724–5: already by 4 July the vestry was giving orders for work to be done in the church: Mr Timbrell was to make a pew for the churchwardens, and a christening pew.

St John's, Smith Square, Westminster, was consecrated on 20 June 1728, and in 1730 the vestry made a list of ornaments that were wanting, which they afterwards obtained. In 1742 the church was burned out, and the vestry had to restore it. But that might have happened to any church. On the whole, the lot of the vestrymen of the new parishes must have been a happy one. They were not responsible for maintaining irregular, decaying, ancient fabrics; they had proud, handsome, and solidly built churches provided for them by the Christian generosity of Parliament. The parishes which had failed to obtain help from the Commissioners had reason for disappointment and jealousy. They must have felt sure that, if the thing was to be done properly, it was Parliament that must do it.

9

THE PETITION FOR A FACULTY

AFTER a scheme for alteration or addition to a church has been agreed on—nowadays by the church council, formerly by the vestry—a petition for a faculty must be presented, together with a plan and specification. The citation is then issued, giving anyone who wants to object the opportunity to do so. If there is opposition, the case will be heard in court: if not, the chancellor issues a faculty for the work to be done. The procedure is the same now as it was in the eighteenth century.

Faculties are always a mine of information about work done in churches, and it is curious that they have been so often neglected by those who write about them. But how much more valuable they would be if the plans accompanying the petitions had always survived. Normally the faculty was copied into a book, and this has generally meant the loss of the drawings: there are references to the plans annexed, but they are no longer to be found. Occasionally they survive, either in a separate bundle, or stuck into the book; but at the best, the number is very small compared with the total number of faculties.

The faculties for the diocese of York, from 1747 onwards, are kept in the Borthwick Institute of Historical Research, St Anthony's Hall, York. Plans are plentiful in the nineteenth century, but those of the eighteenth are negligible.

Workington, Cumberland: the church needed enlargement in 1770, and there are plans showing the proposed seating on the floor and in the gallery, with the dimensions of the church as it then was.

Aston, 1777: a plan of proposed new seating.

Wheldrake, 1778: a plan for enlargement.

Thornhill, 1778: a plan of the church, and elevation of the galleries.

Attercliffe, 1779: drawings of a part of the old gallery, a plan, section, and elevation of the intended new one, and a drawing of the outside of the east window, with a new top. Also of "The East End within" and "The East end with the intended alterations".

Barlby, 1780: a plan of the "Ichonography of Barlby Chapel" (i.e., the arrangement of the pews).

York, All Saints', Pavement, 1781: a petition to take down the chancel. There is an elevation of the east end after the operation, signed by William Belwood, architect.

Holmfirth, 1788: a plan of the seating.

Guisborough, 1789: a plan of the seating.

Kinoulton, Notts., 1792: there are two elevations of the south side of the proposed new church, unfortunately not signed. The first is the more elaborate, and has a porch in the middle with Tuscan pilasters and pediment, and an arched doorway with keystone. The second, rather less ambitious, has a window instead of a doorway.

Marfleet, 1793: south elevation of the proposed new chapel, and a plan, signed by George Pycock, Hull.

Bubwith, 1794: a plan of the pews drawn by Thomas Moody.

Just in the next century, there is a plan and elevation of the new church at *High Hoyland*, 1803, signed by Geo. Strafford and Son, Wakefield.

The diocese of Lincoln has also kept its faculty papers very well; but these are the only plans that seem to survive:[1]

Skirbeck, a petition for a gallery, 5 April 1751; a sketch of the gallery.

Wyberton, 1760: a plan and elevation of the proposed new chancel.

Owersby, 1762: the parishioners had caused an estimate of a new church to be made, and a plan drawn, by experienced workmen. There are a plan and south elevation, unsigned.

Hemingby, 1764: a plan and an elevation of the new church. The estimate is signed by "Jnọ Clark Briklar", "Jnọ Clark joyner", "Robrṭ Haddock". There is a note: "Sṛ Whe are thorly sardifide with our Workmen and our Bondsman so we need not make no Skrupel So we shall be glad that you would Send the facklty as Soon as you Can as Witness our hands . . .".

Horsenden, Bucks.: drawings show the church as it was, and as it was proposed to make it—by pulling down the nave, and building the tower at the west of the chancel. The faculty was given on 16 December 1765.

Panton: it was desired to build a new and smaller church in 1768; there is a plan of the seats.

Ketton, Rutland: the bishop in 1774 requested a commission to examine and report on the church. He sent two plans, showing the church

[1] In the Diocesan Record Office, Exchequer Gate.

before and after the suggested reduction by pulling down the transepts.

Stainton in the Vale, 1780: the parish had "contracted & Agreed with a proper Workman to build them a new Church of the dimensions above specified and according to the plan hereunto annexed, in consideration of the Lead & Materials of the old Church and the Sum of Ten pounds". A rough plan is annexed.

Mareham on the Hill, 1780: the parishioners were unable to afford the rebuilding of the steeple, and so proposed to take it down, wall up the vacancy, and build a cupola with one bell; and to repair, new pew and floor the church. A plan is given, and an elevation of the new west end, with its doorway, window, and cupola.

Huttoft, 1781: a plan of the present and intended new chancels, by John Hudson.

Yarwell: the petition stated that after heavy snow and rain in 1782 the coping on the north side had fallen and destroyed the roof of the north aisle; the roof of the body of the church was much damaged and decayed, and the south aisle was out of repair. There is a letter from the vicar, H. K. Bonney, saying that "The Bearer thereof Mr Sanderson is the Person who has undertaken to do the Repairs". There are plans of the church as it is, and of the new seats; a drawing of the roof, and elevation of the south side, and a section of the roof. A faculty was given on 20 June to repair the church and remove the north and south aisles.

Kirkby cum Osgodby: petition 22 April 1790, to take away the aisles, repair the middle aisle, put on a new roof, repew, and fit up with a gallery. There is a very crude drawing of the new south side, and also "1789 September 8 A Heastimate of Joseph Kendall Goiner of Markitraison Contty of Lincoln for polin Doun the 2 Isles and the North Wale and Rebeulding the North Wale and the South Wale betwixt the Pilers of Kirkby Church by the Auder of" [the Church-warden].

Stubton: Robert Heron proposed to build a new church at his own expense in 1790. There are two sheets: one showing the plan and south elevation, the other a section (with crude elevations of the east and west ends on the back, presumably drawn by someone else).

Just over the border of the next century, there are William Hayward's two plans for his masterly reconstruction of *Kirton in Holland* church, dated 1803: one shows a rectangular chancel, and the other an apsidal one.

This is very little in comparison with the hundreds of faculties, and it is very tantalizing to read references to non-existent plans. If only the drawings of Gayhurst, Bucks., had survived—assuming that the architect had not forgotten to sign them—how much speculation would have been made unnecessary. As it is, there seems to be no indication as to who designed this remarkable church. I had myself made several fruitless attempts to discover the authorship of Kingston Bagpuize church, Berks. (1799–1800), and had given up hope, when the petition turned up in the bishop's palace at Salisbury, accompanied by John Fidel's plan, section, and elevations of the south front and west end of the church, and his "Particular for Building a New Church at Kingston Bagpuize Berks according to design". Fidel is mentioned in the *History of the Berkshire, South Bucks and South Oxon Congregational Churches*, by W. H. Summers.[1] He came from Lincolnshire about 1760 to work at Becket House, the seat of Lord Barrington, who persuaded him to set up as a builder in Faringdon. He was an ardent Nonconformist, and built a Congregational chapel at Faringdon in the same years in which he was building Kingston Bagpuize church. No church work of his was known until this petition turned up, and nothing else is at present known, except that in 1787 the churchwardens of Buckland paid him £1 5s for "Ladder and Deal", and £3 7s 2d for unspecified work in 1804. It is of course possible that the actual design for Kingston Bagpuize was made by someone else, who is not mentioned; but there is no reason why Fidel should not have made it himself.

It may always be hoped that such plans will turn up; it cannot be said that the whole field has been thoroughly explored yet. Diocesan registries vary very much. Some have kept their registers of faculties, and other diocesan papers, very carefully, and are accessible to those who want to consult them. Some are less accessible, and a searcher may have to pay more than he wants to for the privilege of searching. One or two are not accessible at all. Some dioceses have a properly arranged muniment room, and some have deposited their documents in the county record office. This seems a sensible thing to do: there is no reason why church records should not be readily available to ecclesiologists and historians.[2]

The petition describes the work to be done, and the faculty incorporates the petition. It is seldom necessary to copy out the whole

[1] 1905, pp. 229–30.
[2] The Pilgrim Trust has made a survey of diocesan records, with notes on their availability, but this is in typescript, and not particularly accessible.

document, as the second part merely duplicates the first. The type of wording does not vary much. The petition for Hardenhuish, Wilts., is typical. It states that the church

> is very ancient and run to great Decay and cannot be well and substantially repaired but at a very considerable Expence to the parishioners to render the same decent and fitting for the performance of Divine Service therein And that the said Joseph Coleborne is thereby induced and willing and Desirous at his own cost and charges to pull the said old Church down and to erect and build a substantial handsome and durable new Church on at least an equal or better plan than the present at a more convenient place the better to accommodate the Inhabitants of the said Parish And to finish the Inside thereof in a decent and becoming manner . . .

The new church—by John Wood of Bath, jun. (1728–79)—was consecrated in 1779.[1]

THE CURTAILMENT OF THE CHANCEL

If the chancel was out of repair, a petition was often made for leave to shorten it. This seemed very reprehensible to the Victorian ecclesiologists who thought of chancels as worth having for their own sakes. But the eighteenth-century Churchmen thought of a chancel as a place for the communicants to assemble in, and they could see no point in having a chancel that was longer than the number of communicants in the parish warranted.

The evidence for the use of the chancel by the communicants can be found in *The Architectural Setting of Anglican Worship*, by G. W. O. Addleshaw and F. Etchells.[2] They sum it up by saying that the process by which the medieval churches were adapted for Prayer Book worship was one of "taking the communicants into the chancel for the Eucharist, so that they can be within sight and hearing of the priest at the altar; and of bringing down the priest from the chancel into the nave so that he could be amongst his people for Morning and Evening Prayer."[3]

At the offertory, or before the exhortation—when, according to the rubric, the communicants should be "conveniently placed for the receiving of the holy Sacrament"—those who intended to receive Communion would migrate to the chancel. The habit of remaining in the nave until the moment of Communion, and returning to it immediately afterwards, superseded the older custom in the nineteenth century. It has become almost universal, and many Churchmen have

[1] See p. 184.   [2] 1948.   [3] Op. cit., p. 45.

never thought of anything else. But it is obvious that the older custom is the genuine Anglican one.

Its restoration is much to be desired—at any rate in churches with long chancels. I have celebrated in a large East Anglian church, with a very long chancel and a screen, without even a server: the small congregation in the nave was completely invisible and inaudible. In due course they appeared at the altar rails for a moment or two, and then disappeared again. That is certainly not what the Prayer Book intends.

In the eighteenth century, I myself might well have been in the reading-pew for the Ante-Communion; and then have gone up to the altar with the communicants following me. If I had been at the altar from the beginning, they would have appeared when the time came to make their offering, and would have stayed there.

But, even so, they would have seemed rather few in that large chancel. And if the chancel had been out of repair, and cold and bleak, to reduce it in size would certainly have seemed to me, and to the people, the obvious thing to do. We should have had no idea of a symbolical meaning for the chancel: it was a holy place, because the altar was there, but it had no other significance. And we should have seen no merit in size for its own sake.

Twentieth-century Churchmen who try to promote a family feeling in the Eucharist would probably agree. It can flourish better in a small room than in a large and empty one.

So, in the eighteenth century, there were many petitions like that from Crowhurst, in Sussex, in 1726, which stated:

> That the Chancell of the said Church (being very large & really too big to bear any due proportion to the Church or to be of any use to the parish) by length of time is become so ruinous & decay'd (notwithstanding the Great Expence the p̃sent Incumbent hath already been at in keeping the same up) That the same cannot any longer be well supported with [sic] a vast expense, but by taking part of the same down & shortening it about Ten feet which will make the said Chancell more uniform & proportionable to the Church, Commodious & convenient for the parishioners & will be more compact decent & durable than the same can be made by any other method of repairing.

Similar petitions came from Dodford, Northants., in 1748; from Brixton Deverill, Wilts., in 1760; from Houghton on the Hill, Norfolk, in 1760; from Carlton, Leics., in 1764, from Swepston, in the same county, in 1779; and from many other parishes up and down the country.

Sometimes the needs of the communicants were specially mentioned. The parishioners of Tydd St Giles, Cambs., represented in 1742 that their chancel was "much larger than is required by the inhabitants for receiving the sacrament".

John Marquess of Granby, the impropriator of Bisbrook, Rutland, represented in 1766 that the chancel of the church was large and dilapidated,

And Further that in Case the same be taken down and a new Chancell Erected and built in the stead thereof to be when Built Eighteen Feet in length and Sixteen Feet in breadth a much better foundation will be Obtained to set the same on and when built of such dimensions will be much Larger than what is or in all probability ever will be wanted for the Use of the present and future Parishioners of Bisbrook aforesaid to Communicate in.

The Reverend Thomas Shellard, impropriator of Tytherington, Glos., made a petition in 1778: he desired to reduce the chancel to 24 feet in length, "which will be quite large and amply commodious for all the Inhabitants of the said parish of Tytherington to approach the Communion Table to receive the Holy Sacrament of the Lord's Supper".[1]

A good many Lincolnshire chancels were curtailed.

The chancel of Ruskington was ruinous and too large, and it was proposed to make it about four or five yards shorter, and to sink the roof a foot or two lower. Commissioners reported that this would "make it very substantial and durable as well as more beautiful and uniform", and the faculty was given on 1 August 1708.[2]

At Gate Burton, the rector, Michael Fawell, in 1741, "having consulted experienced Workmen & Artificers proposes to erect and build the said Chancell in a uniform manner proportionable to the body of the Church"[3]. At Withcall in the same year the steeple was in a ruinous and decayed condition, and the north and south walls were out of repair. It had been agreed to lower the steeple and to use the materials for erecting buttresses and repairing the walls. "And Whereas the Chancell of the said Church is decayed therefore to repair the same in a substantial manner it is proposed entirely to take down the East Wall and build a new strong Wall about two or three Yards into the

[1] Gloucester diocesan records, 292a, pp. 217-8.
[2] Episcopal act book 1705-12 (Bp Wake), p. 84.   [3] Fac. bk I, p. 25.

Chancell which by contracting the South & North Walls will greatly strengthen them as well as the Walls of the Body of the Church."[1]

The chancel of Wyberton was ruinous and decayed in 1760, and John Shaw the rector had employed workmen to survey it, who had found that it could not be repaired. He proposed to build an entirely new chancel with brick, new roof it, and cover it with lead, and to finish the inside with stucco in a handsome and decent manner. The new chancel would be 11 ft. long and 22 ft. broad, " & that there may be a space or Area about Ten feet before the Chancell your Petitioner proposes to remove some Common Seats now Standing in the Body of the said Church & to replace them or so many as are wanting in another part of the Church at his own Expence."[2]

Fillingham chancel was out of repair in 1768, and too large. The petitioner said that he was advised to take it down and rebuild it, and to reduce it to 14 ft. "in a circular form outward", so as to make the chancel and church proportionable to each other, "whereby the whole building will be handsome and uniform". The Reverend John Barr, Rector of Ownby, paid a visit, and said that the alteration would be an improvement.[3]

A faculty was given for Saxby on 2 September 1773. The chancel was ruinous and decayed, and must be rebuilt. It was 38 ft. by 17, and out of proportion to the church, which was only 50 ft. long, and much larger than necessary. It was proposed to build an entirely new chancel, to contain in length 26 ft. and in breadth 17 ft., to cover it with flat tiles, "and to finish the inside in a decent and handsome manner, which will be sufficiently large for all purposes".[4]

Petitioners from South Willingham stated on 27 February 1779, that their chancel was 25 ft. by 19 ft. 3 in. The church, exclusive of the chancel, was 49 ft. long, and of the same width as the chancel. The lead had been blown off, and the whole building was greatly damaged in the walls and roof; part of the walls must be taken down. The chancel was too large, and it was proposed to contract it to the length of 14 ft. 3 in., by taking down the east end, and part of the north and south walls, and to rebuild the same with a new wall in a strong and substantial manner, and to cover the roof with lead.[5]

A petition was presented in 1781 by John Loveday of Caversham and Edmund Gibson, rector of St Benet's, Paul's Wharf, who were possessed of the parsonage and rectory of Huttoft by virtue of a lease

[1] Fac. 23 Oct. 1741; ibid., pp. 35–8.   [2] Fac. 6/4.
[3] Fac. 3/18.   [4] Fac. 3/37.   [5] Fac. 3/60.

of twenty-one years granted on 23 June 1779. The chancel was so decayed and ruinous as to be an annual tax upon them, and they prayed for leave to shorten it.[1]

The chancel of Maltby in the Marsh needed rebuilding in 1788—and it was to be on a smaller scale, 20 ft. by 16.[2]

The Rector of Caenby was given a faculty on 28 May 1796, to rebuild the chancel, reducing it to 14 ft. in width and 8 ft. in length within.[3]

North Reston chancel was 14 ft. wide, and 12 in length, and it was proposed in 1792 to erect a new chancel 12 ft. in width and 11 in length.[4]

Petitions to increase the size of the chancel are extremely rare. But at King's Norton, Leics., William Fortrey, who in 1757 proposed to rebuild the church at his own cost, represented "that the Present Chancel is very small, and that if the same was built as broad and as High as the Church now is and will be when rebuilt, and that if Ten Feet and Eight inches or thereabouts were added to the said Chancel at the East End thereof it would make the said Chancel more regular and uniform."[5]

This was not to be a narrow chancel on the medieval plan. "The younger Mr Wing who now resides at Leicester"[6] had planned a splendid Gothic church without anything that the ecclesiologists would have called a chancel, but with an east end the same width and height as the rest of the church, as Fortrey said, lit with three fine windows in the east wall, one of five lights, and two of two. This is one of the few eighteenth-century churches that keep their original liturgical arrangement intact.

THE REDUCTION OF THE CHURCH

The reduction of the size of the church—which means the church apart from the chancel: the nave and aisles—was often planned when the church was dilapidated and too large for the congregation. We must not, of course, look at this operation from the nineteenth-century point of view. The ecclesiologists, who knew what a complete Gothic church ought to look like, were naturally vexed when they found that pieces had been taken down, simply (they said) in order to save money.

[1] Fac. 9/75.   [2] Fac.10/55.   [3] Fac. 10/135.
[4] Fac. 4 Sept.; Fac. 4/42.
[5] Leicester archdeaconry records, in the Leicester Public Library.
[6] J. Throsby, *Select Views in Leiicestershre*, 1790, Vol. II, p. 139.

The parishioners of Great Sheepy, Leics., asked for a brief in 1767: an estimate of £1108 8s 8d had been made for the repair of the church, which included taking down the south aisle. They asked for a faculty in 1779, and the repair was duly carried out. In fact, both the aisles were taken down, and the north and south walls were given round-headed windows; part of the chancel was added to the church, and a Venetian window was erected at the east end. The church was fitted with new pews. And no doubt they felt that they had done well.

But how different the operation seems when described by the *Ecclesiologist*:[1]

Very great and long-continued must have been the neglect of the sheepy churchwardens, to allow of their church needing repair in 1778. They pleaded, however, that it did; and they pleaded their poverty and inability to do it of themselves, and solicited a brief for the purpose, which was granted: but instead of repairing, the churchwardens made use of the money in demolishing, and actually tore down both the north and south Aisle, and then cut the Chancel in two, and added the greater part of it to the Nave.

They then quarrelled with the Font, and removed that entirely out of the way; and, as covetousness is not a vice that grows less when occasions increase for the exercise of it, they then removed the whole of the stained glass and disposed of it; next all the brasses were ripped off the monuments, and sold for old metal; and at the same time a part of an old monument was converted into a Communion-table.

Had not their grandfathers any shame about mutilating their churches? As a matter of fact, they had not. They seldom had much appreciation of old churches; and if they could make theirs neat and compact, and more comfortable to worship in, while at the same time saving the rates for repair—why should they not do so? The churchwardens of Sheepy knew what they wanted to do. They wanted their church to be convenient and uniform, and they saw no point in preserving old things that would not fit in. They were doing, in fact, exactly what we do when restoring Victorian churches after war damage. The modern P.C.C. certainly does not want its church to be larger than necessary; and as for the glass . . . Well, clear it out, and let's have some light.

These operations naturally happened most often in counties where there were large old churches and small populations.

The faculty books of the diocese of Norwich have many examples. West Harling stated in 1733 that they were rebuilding the roof of

[1] Nos. XXIII and XXIV, June 1843, p. 157.

the nave. There was a south aisle which was not wanted for seating the parishioners and was "farr from being any ornam.ᵗ to the ffabrick of the said Church". After the roof of the church had been taken down, the roof of the aisle, which was joined to it, fell down; and as it would cost £40 at least to repair it, and "as the said Isle is of no Service or Convenience and as we shall lay out so much Money in yᵉ Necessary repairs of the ffabrick of yᵉ sᵈ Church this & the next Year", a faculty was desired to take it down, and to apply the materials to the repair of the rest of the church.

It sounds reasonable enough.

Similar faculties, to take down one part or another of the church, were given for Colby (1747), Weybourne (1749), Hargham (1753), Thuxton (1757), Holme next the Sea (1771), East Ruston (1771), Stanford (1772), South Repps (1791), etc.

Thurning is a delightful example of a reduced church. Here the rector was exonerated by faculty (13 January 1719) from rebuilding the chancel, which had disappeared except for the north wall. A petition for a further faculty was made in 1772. Above £100 had been lately spent on repairs, but further reparations and ornaments were needed: a new pulpit, seats, flooring, north door, Creed, Lord's Prayer, and Ten Commandments, a new Communion table, a new hearse cloth, and a new frame for the bell.

All the eighteenth-century fittings remain: three-sided rails, panelling with the usual writings, three-decker, and seats—some benches and some box pews.[1]

An interior like this is dignified, intimate, and furnished-looking, and it is easy to see why eighteenth-century Churchmen liked to worship in such surroundings rather than in larger, untidier, and colder churches.

Lincolnshire naturally had a good many reductions. On 28 June 1742 the petition of the minister and churchwardens, and the rest of the inhabitants of Kirmington, showed that the north aisle was decayed and ruinous, and damaging the walls and the middle aisle. They prayed for license to take it down, "and with the materials thereof to erect & Build a Strong Wall to support the North side of the Middle Isle . . .".[2] A similar petition was made in 1774 for the removal of the south aisle.

---

[1] Some of the woodwork came from the chapel of Corpus Christi College, Cambridge, in 1825.

[2] Fac. 2/15.

Faldingworth asked for a faculty in 1744 to remove the north aisle: the scribe who was writing out the faculty got bored, and wrote that the north aisle "is by length of time &c", and left it at that.[1]

Lusby needed rebuilding in 1751, but the parish only consisted of ten families, and the church would be large enough if twelve feet were cut off the west end.[2]

The south aisle of Waithe was in a ruinous condition in 1756, and the parishioners prayed for leave to take it down, and to apply the materials to building a porch on the south side, and the repair of the church.[3]

In the same year, South Ormsby represented that their south aisle must be taken down: the church without it would be large enough for the parishioners, if a gallery was erected at the west.[4]

In the next year, Middle Rasen Tupholme prayed for licence to take down the north aisle, and sell the materials to wall up the church, erect a loft or gallery, and repair and beautify the church in a decent manner.[5]

In 1759 Welton wanted to take down the south aisle, and apply the lead and other materials to making up the wall between the arches, and supporting one pillar with a pier, making two large windows, and erecting a new pulpit and sounding board.[6]

Conisholme prayed in 1762 for a faculty to demolish the north aisle and take down the upper part of the steeple.[7]

The vestry of South Willingham in 1766 decided to take down the north aisle and porch, and to wall up the arcades.[8]

Hatton made their petition in 1769—for leave to take down the north aisle, and repair the rest, new roof and ceil it, new floor and pew: also to rebuild the south wall, and put two new windows into it, take down the steeple, and rebuild the end adjoining it with a cupola.[9]

Edlington complained in 1770 that their north aisle "from time immemorial hath served no other purpose than as a place to lay Lumber". It was now ruinous, and they desired to take it down, and to sell such of the materials as could not be worked up again, and erect a new desk and pulpit, "and also to put into the said North wall two large Gothick Windows; And further to repair and ornament their said Church as becomes a place of religious Worship."[10]

There are many other similar examples.

[1] Fac. 10/111.   [2] Fac. 2/26.   [3] Fac. bk I, pp. 160–1.   [4] Fac. 2/37.
[5] Fac. 2/42.   [6] Fac. 2/45.   [7] Fac. bk I, pp. 262–3.   [8] Fac. 3/14.
[9] Fac. 9/66.   [10] Fac. 3/26.

THE COMPOSING OF THE PETITION

The petition is usually written in a stilted, would-be legal style, which is not very interesting. But sometimes the writers have evidently taken some trouble over their composition, and some individuality appears.

At Moorby, Lincs., where the belfry needed to be taken down, the archdeacon was thus addressed in a rather servile petition (25 December 1781):

> Rev^d S^r We, whose Names are underwritten, the Rector, Churchwarden, and principal Parishioners of Moorby in the County of Lincoln, and Deanery of Horncastle, having from a just Sense of Devotion to God as well as a due Regard to the Injunctions given by you upon your parochial Visitation at our Parish Church of Moorby aforesaid a sincere Desire to promote the Service due to God and by providing every Decency which can be deemed requisite in a Place legally appointed for that sacred Duty, industriously provided for making the Alterations and Repairs enjoined by you at your Visitation afores^d . . .[1]

etc.

The parish clergy still sometimes address dignitaries in that kind of way.

Sometimes a few words will make all the difference between a petition that remains in the memory, and one that does not.

The petition from Gayton, Northants., in 1725 shows

> That the steeple of the parish Church of Gayton aforesaid is so very Low being only thirteen yards and a halfe high and the Bells hanging about eight or nine yards from the ground the Inhabitants of the West part of the Town of Gayton aforesaid have several times Complained that they could not hear the sound of the bells over the trees and houses when they were rung or tolled to Call them to Divine Service that if the said Steeple be raised about four Yards Higher it will then be high enough to Carry the sound of the bells over the trees and houses . . .

The mention of the bells and the trees suggests a picture of a pleasant village on a sunny Sunday morning.

But the petition from Grimoldby, Lincs., in 1767, gives an impression of gloom:

> The said Church by its situation is very much exposed to high Winds & Storms, and the Lead upon the Roof had been frequently blown off or

[1] Fac. 4/4.

damaged, and the Repairs neglected, for reasons which will always subsist; the difficulty of getting such repairs done by proper Workmen, & the great Expence of every small Job, and the too frequent & notorious Impositions of Workmen in Bills for Lead Work, whereby small defects are too much neglected to be repaired . . .[1]

The voice of the incumbent can be heard here: we have often heard the like.

Nor is Hackthorn, Lincs., very cheerful in its petition for a faculty to repair the roof and erect a ceiling: "the said Church being quite open to the Roof is very cold, and in the Winter dangerous to the Inhabitants many of whom are very old".

The petitioners from Eskdaleside in the North Riding of Yorkshire, who wanted to rebuild the chapel on a more convenient site in 1762, gave an unusual historical note: the chapel was situated in a low, damp place by the river, "and was put there out of superstitious veneration for the memory of an ancient Hermit who is said to have resided thereabouts".[2]

Expressions of opinion on aesthetic matters naturally occur seldom in petitions. The petitioners say that they want to beautify their church more often than they say that it is beautiful already. The parishioners of Seaton Ross, in the East Riding of Yorkshire, in 1788, said that Mr Constable, the proprietor of the tithes, proposed to rebuild the church, "finish it off well, make it warm, light, and commodious. The whole Church will then be one new, uniform, complete fabric, perfectly decent, and in all respects becoming the House of God."[3]

But they sometimes express appreciation of their church. The vicar and churchwardens of Pinchbeck, Lincs., on 10 February 1732, say that their church "is a very large, beautiful & handsome one": they want to adorn it still more by erecting a singing gallery.[4]

The petitioners from Dunstable in 1770 write in a style which is not unfamiliar to members of modern advisory committees: they want to take down the porch at the west end, "which to us is quite useless, and so Justly excites Reproach from all Strangers, as Eclipsing and Spoiling the Beauty of the Arcade".[5]

The petition of Sarah Wingfield and the rector and churchwardens of Tickencote, Rutland (1791), shows a most unusual antiquarian interest. It

---

[1] Fac. 3/17.   [2] York diocesan records, R. IV. F.1762/1.
   [3] Ibid., R. IV, F.1788/4.   [4] Fac. 2/9.   [5] Fac. 3/20.

Sheweth

That the Parish Church of Tickencote within your Lordship's Diocese of
Peterborough is perhaps the most Ancient Saxon Building in Britain which
by length of time is in so dangerous a State that in the opinion of a very able
Surveyor and other experienced Workmen it is become necessary to take
down all the Nave of the said Church West of the Chancel Arch to add
outside Buttresses to the said Arch for its support and to repair or case with
stone the whole of the East end Walls . . . Your petitioners therefore humbly
hope that your Lordship will be pleased to permit them and the said Parishioners at their own expence to repair or rebuild the s$^{\underline{d}}$ Church upon the
Old foundations which they intend to do so as to preserve the uniformity of
the Ancient Architecture with the east end thereof.

The architect was S. P. Cockerell.
Lord Torrington

crawl'd forth . . . to view Tickencote church, when Behold it was almost
pull'd down. And what is more strange, is now rebuilding with stone, from
the old model exactly, at the expense of Mrs Whitfield of Stamford (a
woman of much taste she must be, and a staunch churchwoman I warrant
ye) . . . When finished, which this summer will complete, it will exist (ages
after all others of this stile are gone) a model of Saxon architecture and to the
honour of this lady.[1]

"Saxon", of course, at this date, meant Norman, and this church
must be the first real attempt at Norman revival. The interesting
church of Allerton Mauleverer, Yorks., rebuilt about 1745, is mostly
Gothic, but has a front that may be intended for Romanesque. But at
Tickencote there is suitable ancient ornament, and the quite certain
intention of being "Saxon".

As a matter of fact the line between plain eighteenth century and
Norman was quite thin, provided the windows were not too large,
and the Classical detail was kept to a minimum. In the nineteenth
century it was not unknown for this kind of work to be converted into
Norman by adding shafts and zig-zag moulding. Charles Anderson's
Ancient Models or Hints on Church-Building gives a pair of small illustrations of "an old barnlike chapel, rendered decent, if not ornamental,
by the introduction of details in the Norman style".[2]

Chalford, Glos., was built in 1724 and reconstructed in Norman in
1841. The south wall of Ham church, Wilts., was rebuilt in 1733, and
restored in 1849: the windows are eighteenth-century within, and
Norman outside.

[1] *Torrington Diaries*, Vol. II, p. 17, under 30 May 1792.   [2] 1841, p. 104.

A transition from Classical to Romanesque could be made easily, and more satisfactorily than from Gothick to Gothic. Such development was not uncommon in the early nineteenth century. But it was not very popular: the classicists thought that Norman was rude and debased, and the Gothic revivalists thought that it was undeveloped. And it did not lead anywhere in particular. But Tickencote deserves mention as a really good first attempt, by a classical architect trying to work in what he must have considered to be a rather barbarous style.

THE COUNTER PETITION

If parishioners objected to a petition, they could make a counter-petition. In 1746 some of the parishioners of Haxey, Lincs., sent a petition to the Archbishop of York. The chancel was being taken down, and it was to be contracted. The parish contained seven hamlets besides the town of Haxey, and was very populous, and if the chancel were contracted, there would not be room for the parishioners. They had had the vestry room at the east of the north aisle viewed by the workmen employed by Mr Sandys to rebuild the chancel, and they had found it in good repair, except for one pillar at the east end, which could be sufficiently repaired at a small expense, and which the petitioners would cause to be repaired. If the chancel were contracted the vestry room must be demolished, and another would have to be built in another place, which would cost £100; or else the vestry and chancel, which was before a regular and convenient building, would, by such contraction, become very irregular and inconvenient.

They prayed that the chancel should be built in the same manner and of the same size as it was before.

Martin Sandys, the impropriator, wrote a reply on 23 July. The scheme for shortening the chancel did not come from him, but from Mr Bradley the rector, who had said that it would be for the benefit of the parish, and that the parish would agree. So he had ordered his undertaker to draw a plan, and obtain permission. Then the parish had, after all, objected, and he must answer their petition, which "has neither Law Reason or Good Manners in it". He had called in a scribe so that his Grace might be the better able to read his thoughts. The parish was very large and rich, and if they would take on themselves to rebuild the chancel, he would freely give his consent.

The memorandum, carefully written by the scribe, says:

1. That the consent of the ordinary, patron, and impropriator only is by law necessary to make the contract.

2. To the second—

The Objection made here can I apprehend have no weight, for let the parish be never so numerous they can have no right in the Chancell otherwise than to attend the Sacrament, and the single Question is whether the Chancell when contracted will be large enough to contain the Parishioners at A Communion; Two or three Neighbouring Clergy may be appointed to view the Premises and examine into this point, and if upon Enquiry they report to your Grace that the Chancell when contracted will be sufficient for the purpose aforesaid I hope your Grace will be well Justifyed in giving your consent to it.

3. It does not concern the impropriator whether the vestry is repaired or not.

4. Since the chancel is the property of the impropriator, "and he has the whole Burden of repairing it, his conveniency in contracting it is to be Considered and not the Parishioners on Account of their vestry room".[1]

There is no record of a faculty being given.

Parishioners of Bow Brickhill, Bucks., the church of which stands on a hill above the village, addressed to the Bishop of Lincoln a Petition and Remonstrance of the Inhabitants against an attempt to pull down the parish church and convert the materials into money. They showed:

1. That the church was situated on a hill less than a furlong from the upper part of the town, and not more than three from the lower part; it commanded an extensive view and was a noted landmark.

2. Divine worship had always been exercised there, until about 130 years ago, when it was first omitted because of the decay of the church: the parishioners then assembled in a school house erected by Mr Perrot.

3. As the parish church was further than the school house, some of the principal inhabitants refused to go there after the roof had been rebuilt—and so divine service was occasionally held in the school house "under Various pretences as badness of Weather, Shortness of the Days and other Pretences, by which Means the said Church by Degrees became less and less frequented and was at length intirely Deserted" (except for weddings and funerals). The school house had come to be known as the chapel.

4. The school house was the property of the trustees of Perrot's Charities, and divine service was held there by their consent.

[1] Fac. 9/72.

5. The school house was not big enough for burying the dead, and all the land round it belonged to the trustees.

6. The parish church had always been the burying place.

7. The present attempt to pull down and sell consecrated things was unbecoming and a bad example.

8. The pretence of convenience would not be answered if the inhabitants had to continue to go to the parish church to bury the dead.

9. Perrot's trustees might refuse to accommodate the parishioners after the church was down.

10. If they should continue its use, there might be commissioners of charitable uses who might decide otherwise.

The petitioners hoped that the bishop might think it more prudent, safe, and expedient to repair and support the church, which might be done for the expense of about £60.

There are two letters from Browne Willis to the Archdeacon of Buckingham.

The first, which is dated 3 March 1755, says that he had gone over to Bow Brickhill and viewed the church, "which is a pretty good building". He had an estate in the parish, and therefore asked the archdeacon to interpose and to oblige the parishioners to restore the church. He says that the rector is unwilling to repair the chancel, "tho it is scarce 20 years agoe since it was repaired by Mr Hore or Hoar the then rector, who new built the east end, & put in the East Window". Neither the rector nor the curate had been resident for over thirty years. This, says Browne Willis, was not his business: "However I cannot be Passive in regard to the church, as I have had a Zeal in all places to which I bore any Relation to promote the ornamenting the churches; and so as I reserve & appropriate somewhat out of my small income to bestow on publick work, shall be ready to assist & contribute to this . . .".

A further letter is dated 5 April. There had been no answer to the previous letter. Browne Willis had worked up in the parishioners a disposition to raise £60, and hoped that the archdeacon would encourage them. "I have on this prospect got the chancel surveyed by Two very experienced workmen; & can with the little interest I have be Answerable for the Remainder of the Estimate above the 60l which you have here enclosed . . .".

The estimate is for £79 0s 2d, made by Thomas Taylor and John Bent, and dated 13 March 1756.[1]

[1] Fac. 9/58.

At Brockenhurst, Hants., the vestry agreed in 1760 that the church should be repaired, and the tower taken down, and in the room thereof a tower with a steeple or spire be built. There was some opposition, and fifteen parishioners signed a statement: "we whose names are hereunto subscribed dissent to any Spire being built or erected on the present Steeple or Spire of Brockenhurst Church, or any other that may be rebuilt." However, the faculty was granted on 20 February 1761.[1]

The proposal of the Reverend and Honourable W. B. Cadogan to extend St Giles's, Reading, has already been mentioned. The Berkshire archdeaconry records[2] show that his application for a faculty was opposed by many of the parishioners, who said that they had been "greatly incommoded in their Seats" by "great Numbers of the lower order of the people from other parishes", who came to hear Cadogan preach Enthusiasm. Mr Emlyn of Windsor had examined the church, and was of opinion that the north wall could be repaired for £143, whereas the supporters of Enthusiasm wanted to spend £335 "merely to indulge the said Wm. Bromley Cadogan in his design of extending the North Isle . . . for the Crowd of Strangers that resort thither to hear the inspired Brethren of the Gospel". The application for a faculty was refused.

[1] Winchester diocesan records.   [2] C. 160, ff. 421–37.

10

THE BISHOP'S COMMISSION

EVERY diocese has now a permanent advisory committee, the members of which have to be ready to visit any church, and report on schemes for alterations or additions. In the eighteenth century, if a petition was made for a major project, a special committee was appointed to go and investigate, to examine witnesses if necessary, and to make a report. We are more concerned with aesthetic and historical questions: they were more interested in the rights of the parishioners and with accommodation. But the procedure is much the same, and it would not be too misleading to head this chapter The Advisory Committee, rather than The Commission.

The records of the Peterborough diocese are more than usually complete in their accounts of such commissions. Here are notes on seven cases, selected from the register of faculties in the registry at Peterborough. They are kept together to show the working of a diocese in the eighteenth century, and the care that was taken in these matters.

The parishioners of Green's Norton applied for a faculty in 1718: the tower and spire were cracked and dangerous, and they prayed the bishop

> to appoint Comm^{rs} as well Experienced Workmen as others by all Lawfull ways and means to enquire into the State and Condition of the said Steeple and the Decays thereof, and if upon a Return to Your Lordship from the said Comm^{rs} it be so found that the said Spire and Tower must be taken down and new built, that Your Lordship upon the new building of the Tower of the said Steeple would be pleased to Grant to your Petitioners Your Lordships Leave and License to take away the said Spire and not to new build it.

On 25 June the Reverend Charles Palmer, Vicar of Towcester, and John Lumley, Gentleman, Surveyor, of the Town of Northampton, were appointed to view the church. Their report was made on 8 July.

Wee whose names are underwritten having this day taken a View and Account of the Decays Cracks & other failures and Defaults in the Tower of the Steeple of the Town of Greens Norton in the County of Northton do hereby declare our Judgment and opinion concerning the Great Danger there is of the said Steeple falling and thereby of doing damage to the Church of Greens Norton if not also of the Loss of many lives should the said Steeple fall whilst the Inhabitants are in the said Church, and though at psent the Tower and Spire of the said Steeple do yet stand, yet do we verily believe that the said Steeple will not stand long but will fall in Case that there should be any great or tempestuous Wind, not only the Walls of the said Tower bulging out in Several places and the middle parts of the said Tower being built of Small Stones which are decayed in several parts, but many cracks in Several places go through the Walls on each side in Several parts of the said Tower as appear by the pticulars which wee have taken of them and are ready to produce upon occasion

> Charles Palmer Vicar of Towcester
> John Lumley a Freemason and Surveyor of Northton.[1]

On 22 March 1721–2 a commission was appointed to report on Stoke Doyle church. They held an inquiry in the church on 9 April, and William Sutton, carpenter, Thomas Lawford, plumber, Thomas Bellamy, joiner, and Richard Perkins, mason, gave evidence.

William Sutton of Kettering in the County of Northampton Carpenter disposeth that he has taken a view of the old Church of Stoke Doyle aforesaid, and that it contains in length with the Chancell Ninety two ffeet within the Walls, and in breadth with the North Isle Thirty Six ffeet, and that the whole ffabrick is at psent very Ruinous and out of Repair, that the New Church intended to be built according to the Modell now Shewn unto him at the time of this his Examination with the Chancell it contains in length Sixty one feet within the Walls and Twenty four feet in Breadth, and that the same when built will be very convenient and much more Comodious than the psent Church and a very Great advantage to the Rector and the Inhabitants there as he verily believes That the Seats of the said New Church according to the said Model or Draught will hold One hundred and Twenty People, there being ffive double Seats which will hold Eight people in Each Seat and Sixteen Single Seates will hold ffive in Each Seat; That a little Portico near the Steeple and a little Door into the Chancell will be very convenient That according to Information given him and as he believes the whole Number of the Inhabitants of the said parish at psent consist of about Seventy Souls men Women and Children and therefore believes that the said New Church according to the said Modell will be large enough to

[1] For an account of Lumley see H. M. Colvin, *A Biographical Dictionary of English Architects, 1160–1840*, 1954, p. 372.

hold all the Inhabitants, That the Spire of the said Steeple is very much out of Repair, and if the same be taken down and converted into a Tower Sufficiently to be repaired it will be very Convenient and no ways pjudiciall or Detrimentall to the Rector or any of the Inhabitants, and if the Alteration is made as proposed it will be very convenient and Ornamentall and no ways Inconvenient or pjudicial to any person concerned as he verily believes & further says not Will: Sutton.

Thomas Lawford, plumber, Charles Drew, mason, Thomas Bellamy, joiner, and Richard Perkins, mason, said that they were present when Sutton viewed the church; that they had examined the model or draught with him, and that they agreed with what he said. It is not stated who had made the draught.

In 1723 Thomas Cartwright, lord of the manor and patron of the church of Aynho, asked for a faculty to take down the old and ruinous church, and to build a new church at his own cost.

Edward Wing, carpenter, Francis Blencow, mason, Joshua Wigson, mason, and William Bennett, carpenter, met the commissioners in the church on 19 August, and gave evidence. "Edward Wing A Witness produced and Sworn deposeth as followeth. That the Church of Aynhoe aforesaid is Soe much decayed and ruinous that it cannot in his Oppinion be repaired but must be new built he having Viewed it." He then described the dimensions of the old church and of the proposed new one. He went on to say

> That the Church intended to be built is to be made Two feet more Westward towards the Steeple and at the West end of the Church is to be built one intire Gallery about five feet and a half Wide with a Stair Case at each end and That the South Wall of the Church is to be agreable to the Modell or Draught as to the Door and Windows with a proper pediment over the door to rise about four feet nine inches above the parapet Wall and the North side or north Wall of the said Church to be answerable to the south side as to doors Windows & pediment That round the whole Church & Chancell is to be a parapett Wall about 3 feet 3 Inches high to hide the roof That the inside of the whole Church and Chancell is to be ceiled and a Cove Cornish round it.

The plans that were produced were all of Wing's own drawing. The others declared that they had viewed the church, and believed that it must be pulled down. They had also examined the plans and approved of them. The commissioners sent in their certificate to the bishop on 10 August, and the faculty was issued on 30 September.[1]

---

[1] There is an account of Wing in Colvin, op. cit., p. 686-7.

When Thomas Howit presented a petition for a faculty to rebuild the chancel of Dodford church in 1748, commissioners were appointed, and asked five questions: Was the chancel quite out of repair? Was it longer than was necessary to contain the inhabitants? Would the chancel if rebuilt be large enough for the inhabitants? Had the principal owners any objection? Was the intention of pulling down the old chancel made known to the parishioners, and had they any objection?

Three witnesses gave evidence, and their answers were satisfactory.

When it was proposed to rebuild the church at Daventry, the commissioners met at the Swan Inn on 5 February 1752 and examined William Hiorn.

William Hiorn of Warwick Builder aged 35 years or thereabouts—to all the Interrogatories he Deposes & says that he well knows the Church of Daventry afores^d as it now stands, that he can't tell how long it is since the same was erected but that it consequently must be very antient thro' its present decayed Condition that it is in dayly danger of ffalling down that he this Deponent the better knows the same having surveyed the Walls Building & Roof thereof That it is not possible to repair the same being so much Decayed and that whatever Sum or Sums of Money shall or may be laid out in repairing the same would be throughing [sic] the same away That the same Church is useless as it now stands it being absolutely unsafe for People to assemble therein for the Performance of divine Service That he this Deponent is well acquainted with the nature and quallity of the Plan of a new Church intended to be built in the Room & Place of the present old Church which Plan is annexed to a certain Petition of the Minist^r Churchw^s Parishioners and Inhabitants of Daventry afores^d in this business exhibited & now shewn to this Deponent at the time of his Examination that he well knows that such intended new Church when built will be much bigger more regular & uniform & will hold a much greater Number of People to meet & assemble in for the Performance of Divine Service than the pres^t old Decayed Church That he this Deponent doth not know what Sum of Money is raised or subscribed for to Defray the Expence of such intended new Church & finishing the same but has heard & believes that the Sum of eighteen hundred Pounds or thereabouts is Raised or Subscribed for for the Purposes afores^d That the Shell & the Tower so high as the Roof of the said intended new Church is agreed (with able Workmen) to be erected for the Sum of Thirteen Hundred & eighty Pounds or thereabouts & that to finish the same will take about the Sum of one thousand Pounds more And further this Depon^t saith not^2m

Wm Hiorn.

Samuel Cattell of Daventry, carpenter, and John Banks of Daventry, inn-holder, gave evidence to the same effect.

The faculty was given on 9 February, and the church was rebuilt by David Hiorn, William's brother.[1]

On 2 May 1753 the vestry of Wicken agreed that it was necessary to pull down and rebuild a considerable part of their parish church. Thomas Prowse, Esq., had proposed to repair and rebuild at his own cost what was ruinous, and rebuild the chancel. They stated this in their petition for a faculty, and said that it was thought necessary to shorten the chancel, "in order to Distribute a more proper Light from the East Window". When shortened, according to the plan proposed by Thomas Prowse (who was his own architect), the chancel would still be long enough.

Commissioners were appointed, who met on 5 September. They first examined Nathaniel Arnold, carpenter, of Wicken, who was born there, aged 35 or thereabouts. He deposed

> That the Walls of the Parish Church of Wicken afores.ᵈ as also of the Chancell were very much decayed and out of their place and so ruinous that it was Hazardous For any Person to be near them & that there was an absolute necessity to take down the same that the Chancell was longer than the new one building by about Six or eight Feet that the s.ᵈ Chancell now building will Contain about twenty Feet in length and the Width of the old one to wit ab.ᵗ Fifteen Feet That the Chancell now building will be big enough to contain the pres.ᵗ and so far as can be seen to the Contrary the future Inhabitants of Wicken for the Celebration of the Lord's Supper And all other necessary Purposes of the said Inhabitants that by the said Chancell being shortened the Body of the Church will receive a much better light than it did by the old one that the same is building up with very Substantial Materials of all Sorts and when built will bear a much Proportion [sic] with or to the Body of the Church than the old One did Also that the Church when Compleated will contain more in the Clear than the old one contained and as it is about to be fitted up when Compleat will contain decently a much larger Congregation And that M.ʳ Prowse pays the People & Workmen as they go on And that he this Deponent has heard & believes that M.ʳ Prowse Will Compleat the Body of the said Church as well as the Chancell at his own Expence And further this Dep.ᵗ saith not——
>
> Nathaniel Arnold

John Bason of Wicken, mason, who was born there, aged 63 years, gave evidence to the same effect. He said that he had several times built

[1] See Colvin, op. cit., pp. 286–8.

buttresses to support the walls: the side walls of the chancel hung outwards a foot and a half or more out of the perpendicular. He ended by saying that

> M.ʳ Prowse has paid for a great deal of Work & Materials already done & has actually agreed with this Depon.ᵗ & the other Workmen concerned in the Premisses for the doing what is further necessary And that this Depon.ᵗ is well assured that M.ʳ Prowse being a Gentleman of Hon.ʳ will punctually perform such part of his Agreem.ᵗ and finish (if he lives) both the Church & Chancell in a Substantial & Compleat manner.

This of course satisfied the commissioners, who reported favourably. The faculty was given on 4 September. The nave was rebuilt after the chancel: an inscription gives 1758 as the date, but the work was finished after Prowse's death in 1767.[1]

A petition for a faculty in 1779 stated that the chancel of Maidwell church was in ruins. James Scawen had repaired, new pewed, very commodiously fitted up, and ornamented the church; the passage into the chancel was walled up, and the altar,[2] Communion table and rails were at the east of the church. Permission was sought to remove the remains of the chancel, and to place the monuments in the church.

William Smith, notary public, of Peterborough, visited the church by himself. A member of a modern advisory committee is often disposed to pay a solitary visit, especially when the proposal is controversial, and it is expedient to see the church unhindered by the incumbent and the dissident members of the P.C.C. But Smith's report was in entire agreement with the vestry. He said that

> such Old dilapidated Chancel is altogether useless, that the said Church is more compact and usefull without it, being very handsomely new pewed and fitted up and large enough for the parishioners of the aforesaid commodiously to attend Divine Service; and that it would be better to take away the said Old Chancel and clear the ground thereof than to let it remain, provided the said Monument and Monumental Inscriptions above mentioned are removed and put up and placed as above proposed.

The nineteenth century, of course, did not agree, and the chancel was rebuilt again by St Aubyn, Son, and Wadling, in 1891.

These reports vary in interest: some give a vivid impression of the

---

[1] Ibid., p. 479.

[2] "Altar", in eighteenth-century usage, often means the place of the altar; what the ecclesiologists called the *sacrarium*, and we call the sanctuary.

proceedings, others are more formal. Obviously William Hiorn has been faithfully reported. John Bason's voice can just be distinguished, but either he was prompted, or else what he said has been somewhat touched up. But almost every report transports us satisfactorily back to the eighteenth century.

Commissioners were usually appointed in the Lincoln diocese, and their reports are generally given in the faculty papers, though they are less full and interesting than those in the Peterborough diocese.

Congerstone, Leics., presented a gloomy petition in 1716. The church was in danger of falling, and some seats were wanting, but the estate of the whole parish chargeable to the repairs of the church did not exceed the yearly value of £160; and all the estate, except for £20 per annum or thereabouts, was in the hands and occupation of tenants. The parish had been at a considerable expense, in taking down and new erecting a pillar and arch for the support of the church; and their estate and circumstances were so small that they were incapable of repairing it with lead, and therefore wished to sell the lead and other materials towards defraying the charges of tiling or slating, the addition of new seats, and other alterations. Commissioners were appointed on 1 September. They reported that the representation was just, and that, since the issuing of the commission, the whole roof had been taken down and rebuilt in the same manner as before, with new wood and lead, by the assistance of Sir Clobery Noel and Charles Bennett. They also represented that a partition wall between the church and steeple. and a passage with a door through the wall of the steeple, might be made without damage or danger to the church or steeple,

> & w.^d be for the greatr: Decency & Security of the s^d Church, & further that there is a Gallery & severall new Seats wanting & old ones to be repaired, wch if repaired, or as they rather recommend, rcmovcd & taken away & new ones built & erected in their places w.^d be for the greater Decency of the s.^d Church & conveniency of the Parishioners & Inhabitants.[1]

The commissioners for Coningsby made their report on 21 April 1741.

> We whose names are subscribed the neighbouring Clergy & others the Inhabitants of the Parish of Coningsby having viewed the Chancell of the Parish Church of Coningsby do certify whom it may concern that the said Chancell is fifty feet in Length, twenty feet in Breadth, & near sixteen feet

---

[1] Episcopal act book, 1715–23 (Bp Gibson), p. 63.

in Height & that if it is taken down & rebuilt One of twenty eight feet in Length twenty feet in Breadth & about sixteen in Height will be in no Sort detrimental but more rather decorous & advantagious to all Persons at present concerned or thereafter to be concerned therein.[1]

West Rasen was reported on by commissioners on 3 March 1746–7. They had inspected a certain ruinous building contiguous and opening into the church: they certified that it would be necessary to take it down, and that to do so "will be no detriment or prejudice to the forsaid Church but rather (as there is now no further Occasion for the use it was built) advantageous."[2]

John Grubb proposed to take down the nave of Horsenden church, Bucks., and rebuild the tower at the west end of the chancel. A commission was appointed on 20 May 1765, consisting of the Rector of Great Hampden, the Rector of Monks Risborough, and John Carruthers of Princes Risborough. They made their report on 30 May. They had viewed the church, and found that the facts mentioned in the petition were strictly and literally true.

And further it is our Real Opinion, That the Alterations proposed by John Grubb Esquire The Patron will Contribute greatly to the Advantage of the Parishioners, the Decency of the Place set apart for Divine Worship, And in our Judgments is a Thing in all Respects proper to be done.[3]

On 21 April 1772 Edward Jackson, mason, of Doncaster reported on Tetford church, Lincs. He said that the ruinous north aisle might be taken down with safety to the body of the church. The old materials would make a substantial wall. Half the south aisle could be repaired, but he preferred that it should be demolished; and the chancel should be contracted. The vestry agreed, and sent in their petition on 5 May. A commission was appointed on 4 June, and made their report five days later. They had viewed the church, and thought that when contracted it would be large enough for the parishioners. The proposed alterations could be made without endangering the body of the church or the chancel. The commission consisted of three local clergymen, with John Reynolds, bricklayer, of Louth, and Matthew Robson, stonecutter, of Louth.[4]

On 17 March 1774, the Bishop of Lincoln wrote to Philip Day of Ketton, Rutland, builder, John Hubbard and William Wright, of the

[1] Fac. 2/14.   [2] Fac. 2/22.   [3] Fac. 9/74.   [4] Fac. 9/89.

same place, carpenters, and Robert Hibbings, of the same place, mason. Sir John Rushout, Bt., had said that the north and south aisles (i.e., transepts) were out of repair, and that he was desirous, with the bishop's leave and licence, to reduce and repair the church according to the plan annexed (two unsigned plans of Before and After)— "which Alteration he apprehends will add strength to the Steeple and the body of the Church without defacing the ffabrick". They were empowered and requested to view and report. Their report is written on the back of the sheet: it is favourable. They are not sure of the exact value of the lead, but think that it will be nearly sufficient to pay for the repairs.[1]

The commissioners appointed to view the chancel of Moulsoe, Bucks.—the Rector of Great Linford, the Minister of Lathbury, and the Vicar of Newport Pagnell—reported on 30 September 1773, that it must be rebuilt, and that a new chancel of 18 ft. long by 15½ wide and 12 ft. high, would, when ceiled, be equally useful and convenient for the parish. They therefore prayed that the rector might have leave to take down the old chancel, and rebuild it with stone as described. Permission to do this was, for some reason, given by letter, without a faculty.[2]

A petition was made in 1781 for leave to shorten the chancel of Huttoft, Lincs.: it was accompanied by a plan of the present and of the intended new chancels, by John Hudson.

Commissioners were appointed, and met in the church on 1 June. They reported that the chancel was covered with thatch, of little or no value. There were no monuments, and contracting it would be attended with no inconveniences to the parishioners. It was so much out of repair that it must be taken down.

And we do Certify that a new Chancel of the Width of fourteen Feet six Inches, and of the length of Seventeen Feet, in the Clear, will be sufficient for the purposes of the parishioners assembling for Divine Worship. And we do further certify that there will be Occasion for a Window at the East End, which should be Six Feet in Height and five Feet in Breadth, in the Square, and an Arch in part thereof, to Spring three Feet six Inches in Height.

The Communion rails were to be placed 7 ft. from the east wall, and the screen was to be taken down. The new work was to be built in a firm and substantial manner (details given). The faculty was granted on June 20.[3]

[1] Fac. 9/76.   [2] Fac. 9/78.   [3] Fac. 9/75.

Here are a few more examples, taken at random from the records of different dioceses.

On 2 November 1747 commissioners were appointed to view the old church of Fonthill Gifford, Wilts. William Beckford had undertaken to build a new church "on the south part of his park nearer the center of the said parish in a good and sufficient manner". They gave their approval on 17 December.

The vestry of Brimpton, Berks., presented in 1748 a petition for a faculty. The timber belfry must be taken down, and they had agreed to build a brick tower on a new foundation at the west end of the church, according to the plan annexed (which is unfortunately unsigned: it would be interesting to know the authorship of this very striking design). The Vicars of Bucklebury, Beenham, and Thatcham, and the Rector of Wasing, were appointed a committee to inspect the belfry and the place where the new tower was to be, and to certify whether it would be beneficial or prejudicial. Three of them turned up to do so, and reported that it would be "highly beneficial & Ornamental, and in no way Detrimental, to the Church or Parish". A faculty was therefore given, on 21 July, and the tower was built. It is still there, but it can only be seen from inside: in 1869 it was faced with flint, gothicized, and given a spire by J. Johnson.

Commissioners were always appointed in the diocese of York. In 1770 the chapel at Chapelthorpe in the West Riding was in decay, and the parishioners feared that it would fall. It could not be repaired, and would have to be rebuilt. A petition was sent to the Archbishop of York praying for licence to pull it down, and to build a new chapel, 7 ft. longer than the old, with a breadth of 40 ft. On 22 June 1771, the archbishop issued a Commission of View and Inquiry to the Reverend Michael Bacon, D.D., Vicar of Wakefield, and others of the clergy. They inspected the chapel and on 28 June reported that it would be advisable to take it down and rebuild it.

At the very end of the century—in January 1800—the Rector of Dogmersfield, Hants., and Sir H. P. St John Mildmay represented to the Bishop of Winchester that the parish church "was a very antient Structure & in so dangerous a State of Ruin as to be unsafe for the Congregation to assemble in for ye purpose of Div Worship, and was situated at a very inconvenient Distance from the greater part of the parish as well as from the Parsonage". Mildmay wished to take it down, and build a new church on part of the glebe lands. On the 24th commissioners were appointed, who came and viewed the church, and gave their consent.

Mildmay's church, finished in 1804, was abandoned when a new church, by Benjamin Ferrey, was built in 1843. It is of brick, Gothic, with a low embattled tower. Though pathetic, it has a certain determined dignity.

II

THE FACULTY

THE USUAL subjects of faculties[1] are, the repairing, enlargement (or sometimes contraction), or rebuilding of the church; the erection of pews and galleries, and the allocation of the seating in them; the building of burying places or "dormitories", or the construction of vaults inside the church; occasionally the erection of a monument (though most of them were put up without a faculty); the adornment of the church or chancel with paving, altarpiece, rails, or wainscoting; and occasionally the demolition of a church. Such things as the removal of a corpse, or the extension of a churchyard, or—in towns—the cutting off of part of it to widen the road, do not concern us here.

THE DATE OF WORK INDICATED BY FACULTIES

Faculties are, of course, invaluable for fixing the date of a particular piece of work. All the books seem to say that the aisles of Richmond, Surrey, date from 1750; but the faculties make it clear that only one of them is of this date.

The first faculty in the papers of the archdeaconry of Surrey is dated 15 June 1699. The parish was increasing, and His Majesty had given £200 towards the enlargement of the church. A new aisle was to be added on the north. The second was given on 14 March 1749. The plates and arches over the south arcade were rotten, and a new plate must be put in, and the decayed parts of the rafters must be removed. And it was necessary "to take down the Stone Arches and Peers and put a Substantial Breastsummer of Timber under the plates

---

[1] Faculties, by the beginning of the eighteenth century, are usually in English, though faculties for pews may be in Latin for some time afterwards. There are, however, a few general faculties in the early eighteenth century written in an elementary kind of lawyers' Latin: e.g., the title of the faculty for Burton Overy, Leics., in 1706—"*Consensus D.ni ad Reparand Basilicam anglice 'The Steeple' Eccliae parochialis de Burton Overy*". The faculty-Latin word for a gallery is *pergula*. The dictionary meaning of the word is a lean-to used as a shop, a studio, school, lecture room, brothel, or vine-arbour. So it is as good a word as any.

thereof And to support the same with Columns of Timber as that of the North Isle". Also, "the Windows of the said Isle are very much decayed and too small and low at the head and the porch very much dargens [sic] the same so that it is necessary to take down the said Isle and porch and rebuild the said Isle which will make the Church mor [sic] light and convenient and to raise the pews higher and Arch the said Isle as the North Isles by taking away the Bearers of the said South and Middle Isles . . .".

Ockham, in the same county, has a brick chapel, containing Rysbrack's monument to Peter first Lord King, who died in 1735. Local histories say that the date of the chapel is not known; but the faculty for building it was given in June 1734.

Wonersh was rebuilt at the end of the century, and one would assume that the top of the tower is of the same date.But a faculty was given on 3 October 1751 to take down the timber spire, and rebuild 12 or 13 ft. of the tower—and then carry it 5 or 6 ft. higher "like a battlement wall", in order to cover the bells.

It is, of course, possible that the work mentioned in a faculty, or part of it, was, for some reason, not done; but this is not very common. It can usually be assumed that it was; and sometimes there is a certificate that the work had been finished. When a church was rebuilt, a commission was often appointed to allot the seats, and there is a certificate signed by them when this had been done.

THE WORK DESCRIBED

The faculty usually gives a detailed account of what is to be done. This may sound rather complicated, if it is a question of fitting in pews or galleries, making entrances to them, removing pillars or arches, and making adjustments to what was there already. It will sometimes be necessary for the researcher to stop, and ask, "Now where exactly were they putting this, and what could it have looked like?" One advantage of approaching these matters through the documents in the vestry safe is that it is possible to get up and walk into the church, and look around. Obviously far more information can be got, in a far shorter time, by working on an accumulation of documents in a diocesan registry, or record office; but, away from the church concerned, it is not always possible to visualize exactly what was proposed; and all that can be done is to copy out the proposals exactly, though the meaning may be somewhat obscure.

If there is to be a new church, it is usually described carefully. A faculty for Carlton, Leics., was issued on 3 May 1764. The chancel was to be contracted: "The East End thereof to be built on the old Foundation with a handsome Bow or Venetian Window therein." The church, when rebuilt, was to be of the same dimensions as before, and built on the same foundations,

except Ten ffeet and a half which will be taken from the West part or End of the Chancel and six Inches on each side of the same which will be taken from the Chappel Yard to make that part of the Chappel which is to be built thereon uniform and equal to the other part thereof, and the walls of the s^d Chappel to be fifteen Feet and a half High with three Windows on each side, The Roof of the s^d Chappel & Chancel to be covered with Swithland Slate and underdrawn, with a handsome plain Cornish round both; The Walls on the Inside to be drawn with good Morter; The Floors to be laid with Brick Quarries, and the Chappell to be new pew'd with oak or Deal, and a handsome reading Desk and Pulpit of the same, The Steeple to be rebuilt at the West End of the said Chappell with Stone or Brick sufficient to hold two Bells with oak Frames and Wheels.

But it would hardly be possible to picture Twickenham church from the description in the faculty, without reference to "the plan proposed by the afore mentioned Mr John James annexed to the said Certificate". The faculty simply says that the new church "is to be rebuilt part on the old foundation and part on the new", and mentions that "the two Additionall Breaks on the South and North sides of the said Church doe each of them containe in length Thirty and Three ffeet and ffour inches and in Breadth ten ffeet and ffour inches . . . which said Breaks on the North and South sides of the Church are designed to be rebuilt by a charge, distinct from that of the Church, as likewise that in the Chancell".

And the faculty for Nuneham Courtenay, Oxon (1762), is very uninformative. The Rt Hon. Earl Harcourt is given leave to take down the old church, which is ruinous, too small, and damp, and to build a new church of freestone, cover the roof with copper, and fit up the inside in a neat and decent manner at his own expense.

SUBJECTS OF FACULTIES

I. CHURCH DEMOLITION

The eighteenth century was not sentimental about old churches, and saw no point in spending money on the repair of a church that was inconveniently placed and seriously dilapidated. The purpose of a church was to accommodate the parishioners; and why should money be spent on repairing a church to which they did not want to go? If there were sufficient room in a more convenient church, the obvious thing to do was to pull down the unwanted building, and to use the materials for repairing the church that was more accessible and less ruinous.

The benefices of Raithby and Hallington, in Lincolnshire, were united in or about the year 1707. By the middle of the century, Hallington church was in ruins, and the inhabitants attended divine service at Raithby. A petition showed that "Whereas the Church of Raithby is an old Large Building and very much decayed and out of Repair and the Parishioners, who are only the Inhabitants of one Farm and two Cottages, are at a great Expence and Charge in upholding and supporting the same", a faculty was desired to sell and dispose of the remains of Hallington, and apply the materials and money to the repair of the church and chancel of Raithby, and the erection of convenient seats for the parishioners. The bishop replied,

> Let a Faculty be granted to the Purposes of the Petition above written, the State of the Churches being first viewed by two Neighbouring beneficed Clergymen, & a Certificate of the Truth of the premises being returned under their Hands and Seals
>
> John Lincoln
>
> June ye 5th 1753

This is endorsed with the commissioners' approval on 13 June, and the faculty was granted.[1]

Elsewhere there is the account of the rector for pulling down Hallington Church. £32 19s was received for the lead and the bell. The total of his disbursements was £62 2s 7d, including £18 18s 7d paid to "John Chatterton the Undertaker for Work & Materials about the Repair of Raithby Chancel".[2]

A faculty was issued on 8 October 1750 to demolish the church of Scrafield. Hameringham church was only a mile away, and large enough to contain the inhabitants. The materials of Scrafield would be used for repairs.[3]

Calceby was ruinous and dilapidated in 1752, and the inhabitants were attending church at South Ormsby. A faculty was given on 3 November to sell the materials of Calceby, and to apply the money

[1] Fac. II/29.   [2] Fac. 10/74.   [3] Fac. 9/71.

to the repairing and beautifying of South Ormsby, and making pews for the inhabitants of Calceby.[1]

In 1772 a faculty was given to take down South Heighton church, Sussex. On 7 February 1769, a violent storm of thunder and lightning had fallen on the church, "whereby the Walls of the said Church were pierced through, the Roof thrown down, and the whole Church received so much damage as to render it quite unserviceable for divine Worship and unfit to be repaired". It was badly situated and inconvenient: there were very few parishioners, and they could not bear the expense of rebuilding the church in a tolerably decent manner. Tarring Neville church was situated in a valley about half a mile away, and was large enough for the inhabitants of both parishes.

Leave was therefore given to take down South Heighton, and repair Tarring Neville with the materials.

A petition was made by the parishioners of Huttons Ambo, in the North Riding, in 1800. There were two towns, High and Low Hutton, and there were a church and a chapel of ease, the former at High, and in the centre of the parish, and the latter at Low, half a mile away. Divine service was held at the chapel only every third Sunday. The church had lately undergone a thorough repair; the chapel was of no use, and the parishioners were unable to afford the expense of repairing it. A faculty was given to take down the chapel, and repair the church with the materials.[2]

II. THE ALLOCATION OF SEATING

Enough has been said already about pews and galleries. The allocation of seats may be rather a dull business; but occasionally there is a pleasant sentence. A faculty assigned to a certain worthy in Somerset a pew that had belonged to his uncle—"In which said seat room or place of sitting his said Uncle decsd. sate quietly and undisturbed even to the Time of his death."

The usual form of faculty is something like this (which assigned a pew to John Maw in Epworth church in 1739):

Whereas it hath been made known to Us on the part and behalf of John Maw the Younger of Epworth in the County of Lincoln Gent, that the said John Maw was and is a Parishioner and Inhabitant of the said Parish of Epworth and with his ffamily constantly resorts to the Parish Church of

[1] Fac. bk I, 1738–71, pp. 110–11.
[2] York diocesan records, R. IV. F.1800/3.

Epworth aforesaid to hear Divine Service and Sermons when performed therein, and that he the said John Maw not having any convenient Seat or Pew in the said Parish Church to sit stand and kneel in to hear Divine Service & Sermons when performed in the said Parish Church, did by and with the Consent of the Minister and Churchwardens of the said Parish erect and build on a vacant Space of Ground a certain Seat or Pew in the said Church situate in the South East Corner of the South Isle containing in length nine feet ten Inches and in breadth three feet ten Inches and a half, which Pew or Seat is no ways prejudicial to any of the Parishioners or Inhabitants of the said Parish, wherefore he the said John Maw hath humbly prayed our Licence or Faculty for appropriating and confirming the Said Seat or Pew to him and his Family so long as he or they continue Parishioners and Inhabitants of the said Parish exclusive of all other And Whereas We the said Chancellor rightly and duly proceeding did at the Petition of the Proctor of the said John Maw decree the Rector & Churchwardens of the said Parish in special and all others in general having or pretending to have any Right Title or Interest in the Premises to be cited to appear at a certain competent time and place then and there to shew Cause if they or any of them had any why our Licence or Faculty should not be granted to the said John Maw for the purposes aforesaid, with Intimation that if they did not appear at the time and Place and to the Effect aforesaid We did intend and would proceed to grant our Licence or ffaculty to the said John Maw to the Effect aforesaid And whereas on the due Execution and Return of the said Citation with Intimation & calling all Persons as well in particular as in general, & none of them appearing, they were pronounced to be in Contempt and in Pain of such their Contumacy a Licence or Faculty was decreed to be granted to the said John Maw for the purposes afores^d (Justice so requiring) . . .

The date was 1 August 1739. It is sad to reflect that so imposing a document is considered to have conveyed no real right at all.[1]

III. FIREPLACES

Fireplaces in private pews are generally regarded as indefensible corruptions by those who write about the Church of England before the Oxford Movement. But it would be hard to resist the plea set forth in the preamble to the faculty given on 28 November 1740 to Sir Jeremy Sambrooke:

Whereas It hath been set forth and represented upon us by Sr Jeremy Sambrooke of Gubbins in the said Parish of North Mimms In our Diocese of Lincoln Baronet, and John Alkins Clerk Vicar of the same, that their Parish

[1] Fac. bk I, 1739–71, p. 7.

Church in the south Isle of which He the said S.ʳ Jeremy Sambrooke and his
Family have Their Pews for their Attendance on Divine Service repairable
at his Sole Costs & Charges, Is, by being Situated below the Ground or Level
of the Church Yard, so Cold and Damp, that it is truely Incommodious &
Unsafe for Him and His Family, in the Winter Season to be there so frequently & so long as they are Required & Disposed to be . . .,

Sir Jeremy had requested leave to erect a fireplace 3 ft. in breadth
at the east end of the said south aisle, "Undertaking and Ingageing at
the same Time to have this Fireplace so Skilfully and Decently made
that It shall be no disfigurement, but rather a decoration to the Fabrick".[1]

IV. DORMITORIES

Places of burial that were also used as family pews have been mentioned already; but faculties were sometimes given for places of burial
only—either the enclosure of a certain space in the church, or the building of a "dormitory" on part of the churchyard, adjacent to the
church and opening into it. Edward Curtis made a petition on 27
May 1727. He had lately rebuilt the church of Wilsthorpe, Lincs., at
his own expense. There was in the chancel a place on the north side
about 13 ft. in length and 10 in breadth, in which Sarah his wife lay
buried: he wished to fence it with an iron rail as a burying place for
himself and his family.[2]

In 1704 the Rt Hon. Henry Earl of Kent desired to take in land
from the churchyard of Flitton, Beds., and build a dormitory 33 ft.
2 in. by 13 ft. 9 in. Commissioners were appointed to view the ground,
and report whether they could find "That by the Taking to the Dormitory from the said Churchyard the Piece of Ground aforesaid it can
be any ways injurious to the Church or Chancell of Flitton aforesaid,
or the Foundations thereof; or obstruct or hinder any Light, or Lessen
the Proffitts belonging to the Vicar; or Damage the Parish aforesaid."
They decided that it could not, and the faculty was accordingly
issued.[3]

At a vestry held on 11 June 1715 at Great Gaddesden, Herts., the
Hon. Henshaw Halsey requested "that he might have leave to en-
close a peice of the Church: Yard 26 feet long and 19 wide or thereabouts adjoyning to the North side of the Chancel and East end of the

---

[1] Episcopal act book, 1723–61 (Bp Thomas), p. 394.
[2] Fac. 9/20. [3] Fac. 9/22.

North Isle of the said Church and to erect a building thereupon for the Enlargem.ᵗ of the Chancell and for a buriall place for himselfe and ffamily to be buried in". The vestry agreed, the petition was presented, and the faculty was given on 2 July 1715.[1]

On 12 November 1728 the vestry of Amersham, Bucks., agreed to the proposal of William Drake of Shardeloes. The family had used the chancel as a burying place, but now it was becoming too full. Adjoining the chancel on the north side was a building 18 ft. 6 in. by 12 ft., used as a vestry, which would make a commodious burying place. If he could have it, he was ready to erect another building on the north side of the present vestry room, equally commodious, to take the place of it. The faculty was given on 3 February 1728–9.[2]

On 26 May 1733, Viscount Torrington said in his petition that he was desirous to build a dormitory on the north side of the church of Southill, Beds., 30 ft. in length and 20 in breadth, abutting south and west on the church and chancel, and east and north on the churchyard, containing one vault, and one room over, with a door or passage. The vicar had approved. The petition has a note appended, "*ffiat* R. Lincoln".[3]

V. MONUMENTS

Most of the monuments erected in churches during the eighteenth century were, as we have said, certainly put up without a faculty. But occasionally there is mention of one.

A faculty was granted on 6 October 1726, to John Baker Dowell, executor of Robert Bridges of Woodchester, Glos., who was desirous to erect a monument to Bridges and his relations in the chancel.[4]

On 18 November 1742 a confirmatory faculty was given to Elizabeth Trafford, relict of Sigismund·Trafford, who had caused a vault to be built at the east end of the north aisle of Tydd St Mary church, Lincs., and had erected a monument against the north wall, over the vault—"which said Monument is not, nor can be any ways prejudicial to the Fabrick nor incommodious to any of the Parishioners".[5]

A faculty for the monument of the Earl of Shelburne at High Wycombe, was given on 9 June 1752—though the monument was not erected until some years later.

---

[1] Episcopal act book, 1705–12 (Bp Wake), pp. 256–73.
[2] Fac. 9/23.   [3] Fac. 9/19.
[4] Gloucester diocesan records, 279a, pp. 150–1.
[5] Fac. bk I, pp. 45–8.

THE CONFIRMATORY FACULTY

If work has been done without a faculty, it can be regularized by a confirmatory faculty afterwards.

It was stated in 1713 that the old timber tower and belfry of Somerford Keynes church, Wilts., were very much dilapidated and ruinous and dangerous, and that they had been taken down, and a new tower of stone had been built. The seats had also been altered and transposed, and Edward Foyle had at his own cost built a decent and commodious gallery. A faculty on 20 March ratified the alterations, and the disposition of the seats.

A faculty was issued for Wilton on 6 October 1751. The Hon^bles Robert Sawyer Herbert, Esq., and George Sawyer, Esq., trustees of the last will and testament of the late Rt Honble Henry Earl of Pembroke and Montgomery, had lately enlarged the chancel of the parish church by erecting, building, and adding to the east end thereof an additional new building containing in length 15 ft. and 19 ft. broad—a vault or burying place for the late earl. The faculty confirmed the building.

In 1754 it was stated that the seats and pews at Steeple Ashton were old, ruinous, and much decayed. They had been removed, and decent and convenient pews had been erected by the parish. A faculty was given on 17 June to confirm the work.[1]

Tooting church was enlarged in 1773–4 by Messrs Arnold, bricklayer, and Garrood and Overton, carpenters. On 14 July 1774, it was agreed to send the plan of the new work to (Doctors') Commons to obtain a faculty confirming the work.

Wandsworth obtained a faculty on 17 November 1779. The church was old and ruinous, and the committee had caused the walls on the south side, and great part of the wall at the east end, to be rebuilt; had caused the north end, and all other walls, to be considerably raised and refaced; and had new roofed the church in a strong substantial and workmanlike manner. The faculty confirmed the alterations.[2]

In 1756 Edward Turnor, the impropriator of Wragby, Lincs., stated in a petition that the chancel was ruinous, and that he had lately caused it to be taken down and rebuilt "with brick in a strong substantial & workmanlike Manner and covered the same with Lead at a great Expence". There was a small private aisle or chapel on the north,

---

[1] Salisbury diocesan records, in the Diocesan Registry.
[2] Surrey archdeaconry records.

which had fallen into decay, and "which was of no use, but a recep-
tacle of idle people & Boys to loyter in during the time of divine Service", which had been taken down. He asked for a faculty confirming
the work.[1]

William Holgate, churchwarden of Thorganby, was given a confirmatory faculty on 14 October 1776. He had at his own cost repaired
and reseated the church, as directed at the archdeacon's last visitation,
and had taken down the north aisle.[2]

The parishioners of Flixborough composed a rather verbose petition
on 15 June 1789. The church was ruinous and dangerous, and half a
mile from the village. The parishioners had agreed to pull it down,
and build a new church in the centre of the village. The new church
had been erected and fitted up, and would be fit for use in the course of
next month. A faculty was asked for the removal of the old church,
and it was hoped that the bishop would be pleased to come and consecrate the new one as soon as possible.

> We the Rector and Inhabitants of the Parish of Flixborough are apprehen-
> sive of deservedly incurring your Lordship's Displeasure for taking any Steps
> in this Business without first consulting your Lordship, which Omission we
> trust your Lordship will have the Goodness to forgive for the following
> Reasons.
>
> If the Work had not been set about in the Month of June last, when your
> Lordship was engaged in your Visitation and probably could not have
> attended to this Business it must have been defered till another Year, because
> the Parishioners who are all Farmers and Tenants at rack Rents could not at
> any other Time spare their Horses and Waggons; and if the Work had been
> defer'd, it was probable that several voluntary Donations, which have en-
> abled the Parishioners to undertake this Work, might not at any other Time
> be procured; and the Sum required being considerably less than a thousand
> Pounds, we were informed that a Brief could not be obtained, so that the
> Parish must have remained without a Church for a long Time, perhaps for
> ever.[3]

Willoughton had been rebuilt at a cost of upwards of £200. The
parishioners desired a faculty to ratify, confirm, and approve their
doings and transactions therein—which was given on 27 May 1795.[4]

Lissington church was rebuilt, after it had fallen down, exactly the
same size and dimensions as the old church. A faculty was desired to
confirm the building, and the disposal of useless bells and materials—
besides which the parishioners had expended upwards of £100, and

[1] Fac. 10/73.   [2] Fac. 3/49.   [3] Fac. 4/29.   [4] Fac. 6/28.

were proceeding to new pew and fit up the church decently. The faculty was given on 16 June 1796.[1]

THE SELLING OF MATERIALS

Small parishes with dilapidated churches often found the raising of money impossible without selling something to help with the cost of repairs. Many faculties were given to parishes in poor and rural counties, such as Lincolnshire, Norfolk, and Suffolk, to sell lead or unwanted bells. Here is a selection from the many faculties for Norfolk.

Dilham, 29 November 1700: the petition showed that the church "is much dilapidated and out of repair both in the Lead and Timber of the Roofe, and the Buttresses of the said Church are much decayed, and the porch of the said Church was fallen down, And that the charge of repairing the said Church and porch will amount to sixty pounds at least". Leave was given to the parishioners to take down a bell and convert the same, "and the moneys that shall be raised by sale thereof to lay out towards the repairing and amending and beautifying" the church.

Antingham, 11 March 1702-3: a faculty to sell three bells to repair the church. An endorsement dated 25 May 1703, authorized the churchwardens to take down the walls of the ruined church of St Margaret to repair the steeple and church of St Mary's.

A further faculty—4 May 1764—authorized the sale of two bells to repair the church; and another—1 June 1764—authorized the sale of the lead.

Tunstall, 11 January 1704: by reason of the falling down of the roof and other dilapidations no divine service had been held in the church for forty years. But Mrs Elizabeth Jenkinson of Boxtead, widow, impropriatrix of the great tithes, had at her own expense put a new and substantial roof upon the chancel, and was willing that the inhabitants should have the use of it. But to make the chancel a decent and fit place to serve God would be a charge too great for the parishioners. And therefore they desired leave to sell a large bell, hanging in the old decayed steeple, to repair, beautify, and adorn the chancel.

Irstead, 6 August 1709: the church was in decay. Able and sufficient workmen had estimated the cost of repairs at £42 10s. Two small

[1] Fac. 4/46.

bells were to be sold, and the money used to amend, repair, beautify, and adorn the church.

Roudham, 1 October 1714: the steeple and church were in great decay, and the parish wished to sell a useless bell, and lay out the money towards reedifying and beautifying the church and steeple.

Attlebridge, 20 December 1720: To sell two bells for the repair and ornamenting of the church.

Upton, 27 March 1727: above £200 had been spent in the last few years, but all the seats were decayed, and the leads of the roof needed repair. The estimate was £200. Three split bells were to be sold, and the money was to be applied to repairs.

Little Ellingham, 1729: the church was decayed in the walls, roof, and steeple. The roof of the church and steeple must be taken down and the walls repaired. The lead was to be sold towards the doing of the same, which would amount to £40, and the roof was to be covered with tiles instead, which would take the further sum of £114 for finishing the work.

And so it continued throughout the century. For instance, faculties were given in 1733 for Brunstead, West Harling, Guestwick, Felthorpe, West Raynham, and Burgh next Aylsham; in 1734 for East Raynham and Edgefield; in 1738 for Oulton and Great Ellingham; in 1739 for Baconsthorpe; in 1741 for Matlask; in 1742 for Melton Constable and Little Fransham; in 1743 for Sisland, Morston, and Hempstead; in 1746 for Little Barningham and Cockley Cley; in 1747 for Colby, Southery, Gillingham, and Didlington; in 1748 for Kirby Bedon; in 1749 for Tuttington, Mundham, and Billingford; in 1750 for Roydon; in 1751 for Hardingham; in 1752 for Swanton Novers; in 1753 for Crostwick and Arminghall; in 1754 for Fundenhall and Mattishall Burgh; in 1755 for Hassingham and Wickmere; in 1756 for East Harling and Carlton Rode; in 1757 for Thuxton and Longham; in 1760 for Rougham and Bradeston; in 1761 for Great Dunham; in 1762 for Moulton; in 1763 for Bawdeswell, Drayton, Booton, Freethorpe, West Barsham, Honingham, and Coston; in 1765 for Hoveton St John and Little Brandon; in 1765 for Stoke Ferry, South Lynn, and Beeston Regis; in 1767 for Cromer, Alby, Gresham, Little Dunham, and Letheringsett . . . and so on.

Similar faculties were often given for Suffolk parishes—among many others, Lidgate, 1794; Little Wratting, 1710; Bawdsey, 1711; Little Finborough, 1725; Ashfield, 1745; Claydon, 1759; Stoke by

Nayland, 1763; Aldringham, 1766; Benacre, 1768; Wangford, 1769; Somerleyton, 1772.

This is the story of some of the picturesque patchings and debasements which still survive in many East Anglian churches. The Victorians found them repulsive, and removed them if possible, and said unkind things about the eighteenth-century churchwardens. To us they do not seem so objectionable, and we have some sympathy with the parish authorities, who had to maintain large churches—sometimes more than one to a village—with limited funds, in a district which is not remarkable for Church fervour. We are experiencing the same difficulties in the twentieth century; and it is not uncommon for parishes to apply for a faculty to remove lead, and to sell it to help in the raising of money for church repairs.

In counties that were not blessed with so many large old churches, and where the population was larger and more prosperous, such ways of raising a few more pounds were seldom resorted to.

12

THE WORK IN PROGRESS

IT IS always interesting to be able to see the church in the process
of being built.

The laying of the foundation stone might be a mixture of ecclesiastical and civic pomp. Mrs Philip Lybbe Powys gives a description
of the proceedings at All Saints', Southampton:

> On the 3rd August 1792 the first stone of the new church, called All Saints,
> was laid. We saw it from a stand erected in the High Street just opposite,
> and the windows of every house were filled with company to see the pro-
> cession of mayor and aldermen, attended to and from the other church by
> a vast concourse of people. A very fine sermon was there preach'd by Mr
> Scott, and an anthem sung. When divine service was over, about half-past
> one, they all proceded to the spot where the inscription, on a glass plate, was
> read with an audible voice by the town-clerk, signifying "that the first stone
> of All Saints' Church was laid on the 3rd of August 1792 by Mr Donellen
> Grand Freemason". They call'd for silence when he read it, and it was then
> placed by him between two stones, and let down by pullies; then a prayer
> was read by Mr Scott.[1]

In the course of the building, difficulties sometimes occurred, and
alterations were made in the design. Eighteenth-century churches,
particularly in towns, have a way of looking as though they had been
there for ever; and some of them are so familiar that it is hard to
imagine that they might have looked different. But the parish records
take us back to the time when they were coming into existence.

The vestry minutes of St Nicholas', Deptford, give a few glimpses
of the building of St Paul's, one of the Fifty New Churches. There
is an account of the choice of a site; and the progress of the work,
which began in 1712, is mentioned from time to time. On 6 October
1717, a resolution was carried that,

> Whereas the New Church is now so far advanced, that the Plaistering,
> Glazeing, and other Works and materials there may Suffer very much for

[1] *Passages from the Diaries of Mrs Philip Lybbe Powys*, 1899, pp. 273–4.

want of a Person employed to look carefully after them, It is therefore agreed That Samuell Priestman who by an Act of Vestry Dated the 1ˢᵗ Septᵣ 1712 was chosen the first Sexton of the New Church, be ordered and appointed to watch and take Care, that the Works of yᵉ said Church and Parsonage House there to be built be preserved from Spoil and Damage.

Gibbs was chosen as surveyor for rebuilding St Martin in the Fields at the end of November 1720. On 23 May 1721, the commissioners "Resolved that the Ground Plann produced at this Board by Mr Gibbs Surveyor be the Ground Plann for the Church and the same was signed accordingly". (The same with the superstructure.) "Ordered that Mr Gibbs the Surveyor do prepare a Modell of the New Church according to the Plann and uprights signed this day at the Board . . ." On 12 June Gibbs was ordered "to prepare each side of the Modell with severall sorts of Windows according to the two coverall uprights delivered by him to this Board, which is to be Approved of by this Board". On 4 August Christopher Cass was chosen as mason. On 15 August the bricklayers were ordered to appear before the Board on Tuesday next. On 12 September Thomas Hinton was elected clerk of the works.

31 October:

The Modell of the Church prepared by Mr Gibbs being Veiw'd it was put to the Vote whether the Windows Expressed on the South Side of the Modell being the Rusticated Windows on a plain Ground should be the Form of Window to be Used for the Church or not it was Carried in the Affirmative. Ordered that the Basis of the Steeple be raised higher than is Expressed in the Modell but left to the Judgment of Mr Gibbs how much higher it shall be raised.

The work was begun, but on 26 April 1722 a letter was received from Gibbs:

Sᵣ I was this afternoon inspecting the Brickworke of the Church of Sᵗ Martin's and upon finding the materialls and worke insufficient have Putt a Stop to the work so that I desire Sumons may be sent to morrow morning to Call a Committee exactly at Four a Clock tomorrow in the afternoon from Sᵣ Yᵣ Most Humble and Obedient Servᵗ Jaˢ Gibbs
The reason why I mention 4 a Clock is because its inconvenient for some of the Committee to meet sooner.

It was decided that the brickwork was to be taken up and relaid, but the bricklayer—John Witt, of the parish of St James, Westminster

—was to continue, provided he discharged his foreman. Hinton was dismissed, and James Browne was appointed in his place.

In October alterations in the portico were proposed, and it was decided to make it wider. In April 1724 an alteration was made in the design of the steeple.

The interior decorations were begun by the end of the year. On 4 February 1725 it was resolved that a subscription be raised to complete the decorations. On 27 September

> M.ʳ Churchwarden Turner Reported to this board from the Commee of Vestry (appointed to Consider of the Decorations and Ornaments proper for the new Church) that they were of Opinion that the outward plain moulding of the Pannelling (in which the King's Arms are) and the Outward plain moulding of the Pannells on each side of the King's Arms and the ends of the Flowers in the said three pannells Should be Guilded and that having since Consulted with M.ʳ Gibbs Surveyor about Guilding the above said Mouldings, he was of Opinion that it would be unnecessary Save only the two mouldings under the Arch over the Church. It is therefore Ordered that the two last mentioned Mouldings are only to be don accordingly.

On 4 October the vestry was told that the commissioners had declared that they had completed the church, and delivered the keys to them. It was consecrated on 20 October.[1]

The church of Rotherhithe was in a poor condition at the end of the seventeenth century, and in 1685 the vestry agreed to have it surveyed. The surveyors made their report on 22 September 1686:

> Wee whose Names are hereunder Written have been Called by the Justice and Church-wardens of the pish of Rotherhith to view yᵉ want of repaire of the parish Church, do find the said Church to be much out of repaire and that if it be well repaired yᵉ Said Walls and Roofe are Sufficient and Serviceable to remayne and Stand as they now are Witness our hands yᵉ day and year above said

Witness Tho: Perriman	Tho: Denning	
Geo: Dining	Henry Bullock	} Carpenters
	Henry Colebeck	
	Henry Sumers	} Bricklayer

On 20 April 1687, the vestry ordered that repairs be done: the cost was £1200. But on 17 November 1700, it was again decided that a survey

---

[1] St Martin's parish records in Westminster Library. Vestry minutes, F.2006; commissioners' warrants for payments on account, 1722-5, F.6033; bills and receipts for rebuilding and furnishing the church, 1724-8, F.6036.

must be made, and an estimate for a general repair. Some alterations were made, but by the end of 1705 it had been agreed that the church must be rebuilt. An Act of Parliament was to be obtained, and a brief was granted in 1707. The faculty was given on 12 April 1714, and by 7 June 1715 the new church was "near Finish'd and Pew'd". The vestry agreed that the gentlemen managers appointed for the rebuilding had power to seat the inhabitants. In 1716 a further Bill was introduced to the Commons.

On 13 July 1718, the vestry agreed that the top of the tower, which had not been rebuilt, was to be repaired, with boards or otherwise, at the least expense possible.

In 1737 there was another Act of Parliament to enable the parish to finish the church and rebuild the steeple. The tower was presumably begun after this, and the sanctuary is said to be of the same date. But the tower was completed later. On 19 June 1746 the vestry passed a resolution that the trustees should see to the rebuilding: in case they did not comply,

We do Order, that the present Churchwardens Mr. Isaac Wright and Mr. Robert Sanders do immediately after Employ able Workmen to Raise the Tower about Eight feet; Advance the Bells higher, and Stoco over, and Finish the Tower in, or near such a Manner, as is particularly mention'd in a Letter sign'd by Mr Benjamin Glanvill Surveyor, so that the whole Charge and Expence do not Amount to more than the Sum of Three Hundred Pounds, which Money shall be Collected by the sd Churchwardens in their Church Rate.

The tower has a stone dated 1747.

On 5 March 1754, the vestry passed the following resolution:

We the Rector, Churchwardens, & other Inhabitants of the Parish of St. Mary Rotherhith assembled in Vestry pursuance to notice given on Sunday last in our Parish Church to consider of the most effectual methods that may conduce to the settling of the Acct between Mr Dowbiggin (for rebuilding the Steeple and making other alterations relating to our said Parish Church) and the Trustees thereof. It appearing unto us that the said Mr Dowbiggin being desird at several repeated Instances by the said Trustees to determine & adjust the same, which hitherto he has neglected to do, We do therefore unanimously resolve, & desire that the two Church Wardens for the time being, with the Vestry Clerk do call upon the said Mr Dowbiggin and declare these our final resolutions that if the said Mr Dowbiggin does not within the space of one month (to be computed from the date hereof) exhibit his Acc^{ts} and settle the same with the abovesaid Trustees, that he shall be proceeded against by a due course of Law to Oblige him thereto.

The body of the new St Peter's, Wallingford, Berks., and the base of the tower, were built between 1760 and 1767. The vestry books contain no mention of building operations during these years, and it is impossible to say whether Sir Robert Taylor, who completed the church, made the design. The contractors were Joseph Tuckwell and William Toovey, who were paid £834 17s 0½d "in building and covering in the shell of the church, and carrying up the tower to the height of 38 feet".

In 1767 the vestry agreed that the church should be paved, pewed, and stuccoed, and Sir William Blackstone was to procure a plan and estimate from Mr Taylor. In November it was ordered that the church be fitted up according to Mr Taylor's plan. Harry Fowler was to glaze the windows, and Solomon Gunston of Watlington to finish the ceiling and cornice. The pewing was done in the next year by John Cox and Richard Absolon. The church was consecrated in 1769.

After more money had been raised by a brief in 1773, it was decided to complete the church with a spire. Taylor at this time was rebuilding Long Ditton church, Surrey, and had made a design for a Gothic spire, which was rejected: he produced a similar design for Wallingford, and made two estimates for building it: in freestone £480, in Barrington stone £560. The vestry agreed to the former. The spire rises from an octagonal base, with open cinquefoiled arches: it is of a peculiar and unforgettable outline—very slender, divided by flat projecting bands with sunk quatrefoils, and pierced with elongated openings. There is a drawing among the parish papers which shows pinnacles at the angles of the tower; these were not built.

It must have been interesting to the people of Wallingford to see the spire in process of being built. Blackstone made a contract with Emmanuel Williams on 22 February 1776, and he completed the work by the next year.

When the work was completed, the workmen were often given a treat. The vestry minutes of St Thomas's, Southwark, have no references to the rebuilding of the church, except for the following, on 1 July 1702:

> The question was put whether five pounds should be allowed for a Raiseing Diner for the workemen that built the Church it was Carryed in the Afermitive—

The question was put whether forty Shillings of the said five pounds Should be allowed to Treat the Master workemen and the Treasurer it was Carryed in the Afermitive

And the question was put wether ye Remaining three pound should be Allowed to Treat ye workemen it was Carryed in the Afermitive.[1]

The trustees for building St Mary's, Birmingham, voted five guineas on 7 September 1773, "as a treat for the rearing of the said chapel".

[1] Vestry minutes in the London County Record Office.

13

THE FITTING UP OF THE CHURCH
AND THE CONSECRATION
OR REOPENING

THE NECESSARY fittings for a church were the altar, rails, pulpit, desk, pews, and font; there would also be the Commandments, etc., and the royal arms. These would be provided by the parish, unless anyone offered to pay for any of them.

The churchwardens' accounts of Lighthorne, War.,[1] contain

The account of Ephraim Hunt And Thomas Mann Churchwardens Tacking Down and Rebuilding the Church and Tower at Lighthorne Which was Began in the year 1773 and Finished in the year 1774 and at the sole Expence of the Right Hon^Bl Lord Willoughby debroke [sic] Thomas Green Thomas Webb and Thomas Mason being the Freeholders of the said parish Likewise all Carriage And the Expences of Carriage and the Furniture of the Church and Tower And Chancell Dun at the Expence Of the Occupiers of the Land of the said parish P^d to Samuel Eglington and John Mantun For Tacking Down and Rebuilding the said Church and Tower and Likewise Pewing and Building the Gallery and Finishing the same.

The total was £791 18s 2d.

The accounts for 1774 contain payments for furnishing:

for the Commun Tabl	5	7	2
p^d for the new Kings arms	8	8	0
p^d for paint in the fant	0	5	0
p^d for paintin the Alter Rails	0	13	0
p^d John mantun for making The alter Rails & Table and a new fant	4	3	2
p^d the Carriage of the Alter Table & Rails & the fant from Kingtun	0	2	6
p^d Mr Winn for to frames & Hangin up in the Church	3	4	0
p^d A trete to Mr Winn for putting up the Commandments	0	11	0

[1] In the Warwickshire County Record Office.

THE ALTARPIECE

It was not part of the parish's obligation to provide an altarpiece, but eighteenth-century Churchmen liked to have one if possible. When St James's, Duke Place, in the City of London, was rebuilt in 1727, and fitted up in 1728, it was agreed that there should be no altarpiece—only the Creed, Lord's Prayer, and Commandments, "and Likwise Moses and Aron in ye Pear next ye Window". But St James's was rather poor and obscure: a well-appointed church would have an altarpiece, and it would be as fine as they could make it.

In 1726 an altarpiece of dark grey marble of the Doric order was set up in Tewkesbury abbey. It was designed by John Ricketts of Gloucester. John Copner of Haresfield, freemason, contracted to work and erect it; but he died before the work was done, and Ricketts completed it.[1]

On 19 May 1739 a faculty was given to the parishioners of St Michael Coslany, Norwich, to raise the pavement of the chancel, and to new pave it with fine Portland stone and black marble dots; and to erect an altarpiece 18 ft. high, divided into five parts or panels, and painted with the Resurrection in the middle panel, and the four Evangelists as witnesses of the Resurrection. On each side of the middle panel there was to be a Corinthian column to support an open pediment, on which was to stand, carved on a pedestal, a pelican; and round the top part seven golden candlesticks with other ornaments. This is typical of the more elaborate altarpieces. The Usual Writings were almost always there. As to paintings, there was no customary subject: almost anything might be chosen.

On 2 March 1720–1 the vestry of St Clement Danes "Resolved that the Glory wch is to be over the Alter in the Church be painted & that it be done by Mr Kent". During the year several bills were paid for work done at the altar, and Kent was paid £63 for the picture. It was removed in 1725 by order of Dr Gibson, Bishop of London, as it was supposed to contain a portrait of the Pretender's wife (St Cecilia), and some of her family (angels).

On 2 November 1748 it was ordered that the committee for making an altarpiece at St George's, Liverpool, "do agree with Mr Coppuck to paint an Altar Piece in such scripture-historical manner as the said Comittee shall fix".

In 1755 £500 was spent for pictures at the east end of St Mary

[1] J. Noake, *Rambler in Worcestershire*, p. iii.

Redcliffe, Bristol, by Hogarth: they represented the High Priest's servants sealing the tomb, the women at the tomb, and the Ascension.

High Wycombe had a painting of the Conversion of the Britons to Christianity by St Paul, the work of John Hamilton Mortimer, "the Salvator Rosa of Sussex": it was given by Benjamin Bates, M.D., in 1778.

The altar painting at All Saints', Bristol—the Annunciation—was painted by John Simmons of Bristol, who died in 1780.

Bledlow, Bucks., has a Dead Christ painted in 1768 by Samuel Wale: the altarpiece to which it belongs has been moved from the chancel, but has fortunately not been taken from the church.

The *Gentleman's Magazine*[1] said that Linton church, Cambs., had been recently repaired, with a new altarpiece, "one of the most striking remnants of Gothic architecture supposed to be known". There was a picture of the Blessed Virgin Mary, "executed with all the elegance of antient performances".

Kingsey, Bucks., rebuilt in 1780-2, had Christ bearing the Cross.

St Paul's, Bristol, completed in 1795, had St Paul at Athens, by Edward Bird, R.A.

The vestry might undertake the erection of an altarpiece. On 18 April 1716 the vestry of St Thomas's, Bristol, agreed that "a fair altarpiece of Flemish oak" should be put up at a cost not exceeding £170. This was replaced when the church was rebuilt in 1791-3.

At Ilfracombe an agreement was made between the churchwardens and Elias Harris, joiner, of Combe Martin, on 17 July 1718. Harris agreed "to sett up in the parish Church of Ilfordcombe The Lord's prayer, and Ten Commandments in four tables made of red deall or heart oak of the same extent and bigness that Those Tables were wch were last sett up and to witt the Character Every way agreeable to the pattern that he hath produced and to adorn the Tables with ffluted Pillesters Cornishes and Cheribims". He also agreed to keep them in repair for twenty years.[2]

At Kenn, Mr Garrett was paid £42 for erecting an altarpiece in 1753.

In 1762 the vestry of Charles church, Plymouth, ordered new altar rails, and new steps round the Communion table, "with some carv'd work to Decorate the Altar Piece, such as shall be approved of by the Minister and Churchwardens".[3]

---

[1] 1797, Pt. I, p. 368.
[2] F. Nesbitt, *Ilfracombe Parish Church*, 3rd ed., 1937, p. 60.
[3] J. P. Baker, *The Church of Plymouth called Charles Church*, 1915, p. 20.

At Chesterfield "In the Summer of 1795 the new Altar piece was Compleated and likewise the new steps, the altar by Daniel Hodkin the Ends and Rails by Jno Glossop the Stone work by Joseph Cowley & William Bainbridge."[1]

But private donors often adorned the east end at their own expense. Poole, Dorset, was given a very handsome altarpiece by Richard Pinnell in 1736. When the church was rebuilt by Kent and Hannaford in 1819–21, it was kept and replaced, and is still there. It is of the Corinthian order, with a dove in glory in the pediment and a pelican on the top.

In 1715 Richard Thursby gave an altarpiece to Hanslope, Bucks.

Martock, Somerset, had an "elegant superb altar-piece in stucco plaster, erected at the sole expense of John Butler Esq.". In the centre were twin-wreathed Corinthian columns supporting an entablature and an arch: the entablature was continued above panelling, with pilasters, at the sides. The ornaments included the implements of the Passion, cherubs' heads, a glory, and medallions of the lamb and pelican.

Other examples of private gifts are given in Chapter 5.

Old topographical writers loved to describe the finer specimens of altarpieces. Here is Malcolm's account of the altarpiece of St Paul's, Covent Garden, which was new when he wrote the *New View of London*.[2] It was

> adorned with eight fluted columns painted in imitation of porphyry, of the Corinthian order, and an entablature painted white, and veined. The inter-columns are the Commandments, done in black characters on white, under a Glory, environed with painted Cherubim within an alcove, and these between two Seraphim carved. Above all which is an arch, with the Queen's arms on the key-piece, between two handsome vases, and all under a painted festoon curtain extending on part of the roof so as supposed to let fall before the whole.

At St Anne's, Limehouse, the east window forms the reredos; but when Malcolm described it,

> the Commandments, Creed, and Paternoster, are on the sides of the window, in panels, inclosed by pillars. The space above represents a sky, glory, and cherubim withdrawing curtains. A real festooned curtain hangs in the window. Seven golden candlesticks are placed on the arch of the window, the cornices, and over the Decalogue, Creed, and Paternoster.

[1] MS. vestry minutes.   [2] 1807.

David Hughson describes the glorious altarpiece (1703) at St Saviour's, Southwark, which was 35 ft. high:

> It consists of an upper and lower part; the latter is adorned with four fluted columns, and their entablature of the Corinthian order; the intercolumns are the Commandments done in black letters, on large slabs of white and veined marble, under a glory (exhibiting the name *Jehovah*, in Hebrew characters) and triangular pediments, between four attic pilasters, with an acroteria of the figures of seven golden candlesticks replenished with tapers; the whole is under a spacious circular pediment belonging to the Corinthian columns, which are placed between the Paternoster and Creed; each under a pediment, between small pilasters. The upper part is adorned with four pedestals, and between them two attic pilasters, with a small compass pediment; on these six, and one on the middle of the pediment, are placed seven lamps, and in the centre of this upper part is a glory in the shape of a dove descending within a circular group of cherubims, all very spacious and finely painted, and presented to the view, as it were, by the withdrawing of a rich curtain painted in festoons, behind all which is a five light window the arch whereof is enriched with the figures of six swans, and an angel.[1]

A great deal has been written about the degradation of St Saviour's in post-Reformation times, and it was indeed a badly treated building. But an altarpiece like this would be compensation for many shortcomings.

Nichols's *Leicestershire* mentions a few altarpieces in the county. That of St Martin's, Leicester, was set up in 1719 by Benjamin Garland and John Brothers. It was ornamented with a painting of the Ascension given by Sir William Skeffington. Loughborough had an altarpiece of the Doric order, of Norway oak, the altar itself of alabaster, on an exquisitely wrought frame of iron, ornamented with vine leaves, grapes, etc. In 1775 the royal arms were newly painted by Bagnall; Moses and Aaron, Time, and the Huntingdon arms were washed out, and the Creed, Lord's Prayer, etc., painted in gold.

The altarpiece at Stapleford remains: when Nichols wrote, it was "just completed by Brown of Derby, and is beautifully formed of marble, with borders, of black, statuary and dove colour. In the centre is a neat tablet, with the emblems of hope and eternity, an anchor suspended on an encircled serpent; and at the top a handsome urn."[2] The whole church was the gift of the Earl of Harborough.

[1] *A History and Description of London, Westminster and Southwark*, Vol. IV, p. 498.
[2] *The History and Antiquities of the County of Leicester*, 1795, Vol. II, p. 340.

William Stretton describes the altarpiece at St Peter's, Nottingham:

The altarpiece was painted at the expence of Alvery Dodsley, M.D., by Edward Dovey, an artist of no mean abilities, who lived on the west side of Bridlesmithgate, and lies buried in St Peter's Church yard, opposite to the chancel door. It was a representation of the Last Supper, Christ and his apostles being under a sort of pavilion with a niche in the centre, in the forground were Corinthian columns, with gilt capitals, supporting a rich entablature, whole length figures of Moses and Aaron in their priestly habiliments being on the two sides, over which were two angels presenting a portrait of Her Majesty Queen Anne, the whole surmounted by a rich crimson canopy bordered with gold. The present figure of Christ's Passion in the Garden of Gethsemene [sic] was painted by Barber, of Nottingham, in 1815, together with some other alterations of Dovey's painting, but the caps and entablature, with the crimson canopy, are as painted by Dovey, except that the portrait of her Majesty was taken out where the dove is now represented.[1]

Newcastle had some good average specimens. The altar of St Nicholas' was "very sumptuously and yet decently adorned" in 1712, when the chancel was wainscoted at the expense of the Corporation. In 1783–7 the arrangements of the church were altered under Messrs Newton and Stephenson: the altar, which had stood away from the east wall, was moved up against it. Part of the old wainscot remained on each side. In 1818 Sir M. W. Ridley presented a picture by Tintoretto of Christ washing the feet of the Disciples.[2]

The altar of St Andrew's was beautified in 1781, when a subscription was made for procuring new silver plate and a new altar cloth. The picture of the Last Supper, by Luca Giordana, was given by Major Anderson in 1804.

The beauties of this superb painting cannot, however, be seen to advantage, in consequence of the bad light in which it is placed. In order to remedy this defect, it has been proposed to build up the east window, and to enlarge and raise the old window on the south side of the communion-place.[3]

At St John's,

The communion-table of this church was given by Mr Robert Crow in 1712; and Lady Musgrave, in 1754, bequeathed an altar-cloth and cushion.

[1] The Stretton Manuscripts, 1910, p. 147.
[2] E. Mackenzie, A Descriptive and Historical Account of the Town and County of Newcastle upon Tyne, 1827, pp. 246–7.
[3] Ibid., p. 327.

On the altar-piece there is a painting by Henry Mort, representing cherubs ascending and descending in the clouds, under a crimson curtain with gold fringe. In 1800, Mr Fenton, the acting church-warden, and his associates, expended £125 in purchasing a new velvet covering, and in painting and gilding about the altar.[1]

THE PULPIT AND DESK

The pulpit, reading pew, and desk were certainly the responsibility of the parish, and private individuals were not expected to give them —though they often gave hangings to adorn them. Where they were to stand, and what they were to be like, were questions quite often discussed by vestries.

St Catherine Coleman, in the City of London, had been rebuilt by James Horne. On 4 March 1740-1

> The Situation of the Reading Desk and pulpit was taken into Consideration and several Debates thereon arose and the Question being put whether the Reading Desk & pulpit should be Both placed one Side of the great Isles, or one of the one Side & the other of the other. Twas ordered that the same should be placed together on one Side of the great Isle.

At St Martin in the Fields on 5 June 1758 a committee considered that "it would be much to the Benefit of the Congregation and Hearers to have the Pulpit, Reading Desk and Clerke's Desk Removed to the South end of the Pew wherein the same stands to the Edge of the Middle Isle of the Church". On 15 August the committee heard the Reverend Mr Taylor preach from the present pulpit, and also from one in the new suggested position. They could not make up their minds, and a decision was postponed.

At a meeting of the trustees for rebuilding All Hallows', London Wall, on 9 May 1765 it was "Moved and seconded that no Sounding Board be put over the Pulpit which was Agreed to".

The normal position for the pulpit and desk was at the east end of the church; but they might be in the middle, against a side wall, or even at the west, as at the Gothic church of Teigh, Rutland, where the seats are arranged college chapel-wise. At St Martin Outwich, rebuilt by S. P. Cockerell, and consecrated in 1798, they were at the west, in a deep recess.

[1] Ibid., p. 345.

9. Stoke Doyle, Northants, 1722–5
"The same when built will be very convenient and much more commodious than the present Church"

10. Owthorpe, Notts. Church rebuilt and reduced in size about 1750

12. Little Livermere, Suffolk. The arrangement of pews and pulpit in a country church, reconstructed in Gothic in the middle of the 18th century

11. Market Drayton, Salop. The interior after reconstruction in 1787, under Thomas Harding, surveyor. Money was raised by briefs in 1782 and 1786

The faculty for rebuilding Chapelthorpe in the West Riding mentions the removal of the pulpit, reading pew, and clerk's desk from the south side, and fixing them as near as may be to the centre of the west end.[1]

Central pulpits were not as common as some writers have suggested, though of course there were some. Holy Trinity, Clapham, had a magnificent erection. The pulpit of St Botolph's, Aldersgate, which was rebuilt in 1789–91, stood before the altar, against a palm tree, the leaves of which supported the sounding board. It does not seem that there was anything particularly Low Church about the central position. In several churches the pulpit was only moved to the middle at a late date, and the motive was simply to make a little more room for pews in order to accommodate an increasing population. In 1807 a committee was appointed to repair St George's, Southwark. It decided, among other things, to reseat the church entirely, and to alter the form of the pews, according to the plans of Mr Hedger. The pulpit and desk were removed to the centre as part of the scheme. The vestry of St Giles's, Camberwell, agreed in 1817 that there must be more accommodation, and that the pulpit and desk must be moved, and the space converted into pews. J. Bray, of Little Chapel Street, Westminster, was to do the work.

The obvious fault to be found with a central pulpit is that it obscures the view of the altar from the nave—though eighteenth-century Churchmen were not worried by that in the way that we should be. But no such fault could have been found with the pulpit of East Budleigh, Devon, which stood on legs so high that the preacher was well above the top of the screen. This was a most extraordinary and impressive piece of furniture: a large sounding board, surmounted by an angel, hung from the roof above it. Of course it disappeared when the church was restored; but its worst enemies could not have said that it hid the altar. When All Saints', Derby, was rebuilt in 1723–5, the pulpit was placed in the middle, but in 1726 the vestry decided to move it "to yᵉ South Pillar next to it". In 1873 it was moved back to the middle. At this date, the position was definitely adopted for a Protestant reason. At the same time, the marble altar of 1725 was taken down, and a wooden table put in its place. The marble slab was displayed in the church with a polemic quotation from Bishop Ridley about "the old superstitious opinions of the popish mass". The pulpit has, of course, been moved to the side again.

[1] R. IV. F.1771/2.

PAINTING

Painting, apart from altarpieces, was not particularly common— but it was more common than has sometimes been imagined. Often it was nothing more than texts with ornamental borders. In 1730 Samuel Ward was paid 14 guineas for painting in Little Missenden church, Bucks.—blue and yellow curtains with cords and tassels, with black outline and shading, beside the Creed, Lord's Prayer, etc. But it was sometimes more ambitious.

The church which the Duke of Chandos built at Whitchurch, Middlesex, is well known. The whole of the interior is painted, probably by Louis Laguerre and Antonio Bellucci; at the east is the Adoration of Jehovah; at the sides, the Holy Family and the Descent from the Cross. The sanctuary has the Giving of the Law and the Sermon on the Mount. On the nave ceiling are scenes from the Gospels, and on the walls the Evangelists and Virtues. The semidome over the Duke's pew at the west has a copy of Raphael's *Transfiguration*.

The paintings in the ceiling of Great Witley, Worcs., by Bellucci, came from the Duke's chapel at Canons.

Browne Willis's account of the work that he paid for at Bletchley, Bucks., in 1704–7, includes payments to William Wace of London for painting—e.g.,

> For painting the Chancel, painting & gilding the Glory & 37 Cherubs' heads, the 12 Apostles as big as the life, 17 Pannels done with ornament, 84 foot of cornish, three Members inriched, 56 foot 4 inch astical inriched, 26 of 5 Inch hollow round the Window inriched, gilding all the mouldings round the 39 Pannels, painting two Columns, five large Curtains & painting all the wall 3 times in Oyl.................£50

Keighley, Yorks., was beautified in 1710

> with 15 copartments, which contain a short history of the lives of the blessed Jesus, the Virgin Mary, the twelve Apostles, and St. Paul, with the figures of each head set crest-wise; also old Time flying and running, a skeleton, and many Scripture sentences (besides the Creed, the Lord's Prayer, and the Ten Commandments) fit for that holy place.[1]

In 1710 the walls above the arches of Prestbury, Cheshire, were painted with the Twelve Apostles. In 1710 the ceiling was painted to

[1] The Revd. Miles Gale's *Topographical Description of the Parish of Keighley*, quoted in *Gentleman's Magazine*, 1815, Pt. I, p. 495.

imitate panelling, and adorned with the Evangelists emerging from clouds, and the sun in the centre with gilded rays.

The painting of Kingswood church, near Wotton under Edge, Glos., rebuilt in 1723, was unfavourably described by a writer in the *Gentleman's Magazine* in 1830: "The east end is all along the wall painted in the most paltry style of modern beautification, like the frontispiece of a barn theatre or ale-house puppet-show, to represent the sky with a glory and Jehovah in the middle, Belief, Commandments, pelican feeding her young ones . . .".

Rowston church, Lincs., was furnished in 1741 by Mrs Millicent Neate, and a painting was erected at the east of the nave: entablature and pilasters of four bays; above them a large panel with royal arms, supported by consoles and drapery swags; the spaces in the lower part, between the pilasters, filled with the Creed, Lord's Prayer, and Commandments. The roof principal immediately above was boarded in, and painted with cherubs' heads in clouds, and the tetragrammaton.

At St Margaret's, Westminster, in 1763, figures of St Peter and St Paul, painted in imitation of statuary marble by Mr Cassali, were placed in niches on either side of the altar.

In 1764 Ambrosden, Oxon, was given a west gallery, with a picture of the Last Judgement above.

The chancel of St Clement's, Hastings, was painted by Roger Mortimer.

The ceiling of Matlock, Derby., was painted with the four Evangelists writing their Gospels, attended by their symbols. On the wall over the singing gallery was David with a harp, attended by angels— one holding a scroll of music, and the other blowing a trumpet; behind them, Time and Death. Over the pulpit were two winged figures— Christianity, holding in the left hand a church, and in the right a Bible, and trampling on the Crescent and the Koran; and Faith, with a cross in the right hand, and a Bible in the left, trampling on a triple crown and missal.[1]

Wymondham, Leics., was painted by Mr Baker, a house painter, at his own expense. He executed a perspective view of the inside of a church and chancel, with a vaulted roof adorned with panels of roses. The east end of the chancel was adorned with a rustic base and fluted Doric pilasters with a cornice and pediment.

[1] Rawlins's notes in 1827, quoted in J. C. Cox, *Notes on the Churches of Derbyshire*, 1877, Vol. II, p. 522.

PAINTED GLASS

Painted glass was usually the gift of a private benefactor. Among
the Coleshill papers in the Berkshire Record Office at Reading is some
correspondence between the Earl of Radnor and Francis Eginton
about the glass which the earl was proposing to erect in Shrivenham
church.[1]

My Lord
    I Receiv'd your favour of the 20th for which I have enclos'd a Receipt
with my most sincere thanks—I have also enclosed a ruff sketch for the
Church Window in which I have incerted three Sheilds for the Arms you
mention, I have made use of such Ornaments to fill up the Window as I
think would produce the best effect at the least expence but if you should
prefer a more enrich'd Ornament I will send another design the whole
expence of the window according to this Plan would be only 25 Guineas
including every expence except wire work cariage and putting up which
may be done by any common careful workman. the price of the three coats
of Arms if they had been all like the first and second would have been only
9 Guineas but from the great quantity of work which I suppose there must
be in that containing 20 Coats and the Coronet I fear they can not be done
for less than 15 Guineas

Handsworth   I am
Nov.ʳ 24ᵗʰ 1791   My Lord
                                        Your Lordship's most
                                            Obliged and most Obᵗ
                                            Hᵇˡᵉ Servᵗ
                                                Fʳ Eginton

P.S. I suppose the window to be 1 : 8 wide and 10 : 4½ high in the Clear
and that the top is of the form I have drawn it.

The earl replies:

Longford Castle Nov. 26 1791
Sir
    The above is the Sketch of the Window in general, into which I want to
introduce the Shields of Arms as mentioned in my last—I wish to introduce
no painting whatever except the three Shields . . . [The rest of the letter
has been torn off]

Eginton to the earl:

My Lord
    You will herewith receive slight coloured sketches of the Arms &c drawn

[1] D/EPb 83.

of the full size, and also a small sketch of the whole together, by which I hope you will see whether I have a right idea of your Lordships instruction, and I shall be much obliged if you will please to favour me with your remarks when you return the drawings which I must beg the favour of you to do before I can begin the Glass—

Handsworth
  near Birmingham
    March 18th 1793

I am
  my Lord
    your Lordships most
      Obliged and Ob.^t Servt
        F.^s Eginton

My Lord
  Your Lordships Idea of glazing the window in Lozeng formed panes is certainly right and may be easily executed according to the sketch on the other side but in that case would it not be best for me to have the Iron Work made here as it must be made with proper rabbets and will require more skill than common blacksmiths generaly have in that way the lead work may be done by any good Glazier

Handsworth
  March 28th
    1793

I am
  your Lordships
    most Ob.^t H^{ble} Ser.^t
    F.^s Eginton

There are also three letters from Barak Longmate, sen. (editor of Collins's *Peerage*), about the heraldry. They are dated 26 October, 12 November, and 8 December 1792.

There is glass by Eginton at St Alkmund's, Shrewsbury (Faith: a copy of Guido Reni's *Assumption*), St Paul's, Birmingham (1791: the *Conversion of St Paul*, etc., after Benjamin West), and Aston (1793). His work has disappeared from several churches, such as Hatton, War.,[1] and Great Barr, Staffs., where there was an east window after the Reverend W. Peters, of the spirit of a child arriving in the presence of the Almighty.

James Pearson's east window at St Botolph's, Aldersgate, from designs by Nathanael Clarkson, is of the Agony in the Garden, with figures of St Peter and St John.

St George's, Windsor, is not a parish church, but it is difficult to resist the temptation to quote the description of the east window, made by Thomas Jervais from designs by Benjamin West, in *The Thames, or Graphic Illustrations of Seats, Villas, Public Buildings, and Picturesque Scenery on the Banks of that Noble River*, by W. B. Cooke.[2]

[1] See p. 84.   [2] 1811; Vol. I, no page number.

In the centre is our Saviour ascending from the sepulchre preceded by an angel, above whom in the clouds is an host of cherubim and seraphim, and among them is a portrait of the Prince Octavius. In the front are Roman soldiers, whose countenances and attitudes are suited to the awful circumstances of the scene. In the compartment to the right are represented Mary Magdalen, and Mary the mother of James, approaching the sepulchre with spices &c; and in that to the left are Peter and John, who are represented as running in great haste to the sepulchre, according to the apostolic narrative of the extraordinary transaction.

Needless to say, windows like this were most distasteful to the Gothic revivalists, and most of them have been taken away.

THE ENSEMBLE

Eighteenth-century Churchmen liked their churches to be handsome, neat, and regular. The writers of travel books used many adjectives when they wrote about scenery or ruined abbeys; but in parish churches they did not expect anything sublime; and, if they praised them, it was in more prosaic terms.

In the summer of 1803, the Reverend Edmund Butcher made an excursion from Sidmouth to Chester and back, through the counties of Devon, Somerset, Gloucester, Monmouth, Hereford, Salop, Derby, Stafford, Warwick, and Worcester; and described the journey in a series of letters to a lady, which were published in two parts in 1805. Butcher was not specially interested in churches, but he mentions them from time to time. And it is interesting to notice the limitations of his adjectives. This is all that he has to say (excluding such words as "large" and "ancient"): "plain, handsome" (Honiton Chapel); "neat" (Monkton); "handsome" (Taunton); "a neat rural structure" (Westbury); "handsome" (Ludlow); "handsome" (St Mary's, Shrewsbury); "finished in a very elegant manner" (St Chad's, Shrewsbury); "peculiarly neat" (Weston); "a large, handsome modern edifice" (Whitchurch); "peculiarly neat" (Cromford); "in a neat modern style" (South Wingfield); "large and handsome" (All Saints', Derby); "very handsome" (St Philip's, Birmingham); "very neat" (St Paul's, Birmingham); "neat" (Ashted); "a very fine structure" (Tewkesbury). Lichfield cathedral, after Wyatt's restoration, strikes him as particularly neat.

The first idea which occurs on entering Litchfield cathedral is the extreme neatness and simplicity of the whole. The walls and roof are entirely covered with a substantial white-wash, and the greater part of the choir is paved with alabaster and kennel-coal, in imitation of black and white marble. The chapel is in unison with the rest, and the workmanship of the prebendaries' stalls excellent. They were erected at the expence of different gentlemen of the county, and each stall bears the name and arms of the donor. The altar-piece is an exquisite painting on glass. . . .[1]

Eighteenth-century churches are, of course, always regular and neat.

Old churches are often regrettably shapeless, with accretions of various dates. We find this interesting, as evidence of the growth of a church; and we like either to imagine it as it was at first, and to picture the additions being made, one by one, in the succeeding centuries; or else to go backwards, and strip off, in imagination, the various additions, until we get back to the church as it was. Needless to say, the eighteenth century knew nothing about this, and would not have been interested. Only a tiny handful of antiquaries, towards the end of the century, had any idea of the dates of the various styles of Gothic. A typical old church simply appeared as a very ancient, irregular, and deformed building.

The Reverend William Waterson, who died in 1759, left a manuscript history of the parish of Winkfield, Berks., which is among the parish papers. He was not satisfied with the appearance of the inside of the church, nor did he think that the efforts to beautify it (in 1723) had been very successful:

The Lords prayer & near ye Communion table, being done or procured to be done by ye same busying hand that did the Joiners work, is not, for that reason, worth notice: 'tis much to be wish'd that ye whole was entirely taken down & defaced, & the same supply'd in such a masterly & judicial way, as might adorn & not disgrace ye House of God, or depreciate His Worship & Service there. Before ye old Window was taken down, there was nothing in that part to be seen but bare Walls, & those in many places especially near ye foundation rough & unplaister'd these it's true are now put out of sight, & the Holy-Place somewhat better ornamented than ever it was before, but still the plane as well as the Pensil are wanted, both to adorn ye Place & amend ye Work in a more masterly stile than as yet appears or ever did appear since it was a Church.

An old church must be made as regular and neat as possible—and, to this end, the walls must be plastered. It would certainly never have

[1] Butcher's Excursion, p. 336.

occurred to anyone that it would be interesting to expose traces of Norman windows, or the jambs of an eastern triplet: such things would naturally be covered up. And the roof would be ceiled: unceiled rafters looked mean. Irregular bits of aisle or chapel could be brought into the general scheme by being fitted up as pews; and the rest of the pews would be made as uniform as possible. Of course this was not always accomplished, and there were many country churches that were not "done" (the expression used of Barwick in Elmet church, Yorks., meaning ceiled, pewed, etc.). But it was the ideal. And when it has been left alone, the eighteenth-century treatment of an old church looks very complete and satisfactory. A restored church too often looks scrappy; there are bits of old masonry exposed—broken niches, and scraps that are extremely interesting to antiquaries, but which would have seemed ugly and uninteresting 200 years ago. So many churches have been stripped to the bone, and have been made interesting from a historical point of view—but they have lost the complete and furnished look that they once had.

Cranbrook church, Kent, had somewhat more than the usual things done to it in the eighteenth century. In 1725 the burial place of the Bakers of Sissinghurst, at the east end of the south aisle, was opened, and a pillar fell, bringing with it 50 ft. of the arcade and aisle. The rebuilding was completed in 1728, and the upper part of the chancel arch was rebuilt at the same time. The branch was bought second-hand in 1736; the royal arms were given in 1756 by Thomas Basden, apothecary, of London. There was a good deal of enriched plaster work, a west gallery, and the usual woodwork; the chancel was enclosed on the north and south by rather high panelling.

In the '60s there was a restoration under William Slater (nave) and Ewan Christian (chancel), which was carefully done. The usual clearance of pews and plasterwork was made, and the church was opened out to its fifteenth-century proportions. The branch and the royal arms were kept, and so was part of the pulpit. But the ensemble was lost.

A sensible person has no prejudices against nineteenth-century restorations as such. They were usually necessary, they were often done with care, and in many cases the church was improved by them. They were done at a time when the old parish machinery of vestry, church rates, and pews for householders, was breaking down, and it seemed to Churchmen that the system had had its day, that the pews must go, and that the whole arrangement would have to be altered to meet the new situation. If we had been living then, we should probably have agreed with J. A. Chatwin, who came to the conclusion in 1872 that St Martin's, Birmingham, was hopeless, and that it would have to be entirely rebuilt in the Decorated style. The interior, if it had survived unaltered until the present, would be regarded as a prize-winner: but the parishioners in the '70s were delighted to see it disappear: "We saw, with no regrets, the destruction of that ugly brick building, which successive generations of meddlers and muddlers had tacked on to a fine spire."

No doubt, from a pastoral point of view, they were right—and yet we must regret the sacrifice that was made of the sombre but impressive lay-out of so many Georgianized interiors, with their colour scheme of brown woodwork, red velvet, gold fringes, black and white marble pavement, gilded organ pipes, and white walls relieved with painted hatchments. It was not only the stupid and old-fashioned who were grieved to read such things as the advertisement in the *Builder* of 28 March 1863:

> To Clergymen, Churchwardens, Builders, and others.—To be disposed of immediately, the massive Carved Oak Altarpiece and Wall-Panellings, as at present fixed in the chancel of S. Nicholas Church, Newbury, Berks, together with about fifty feet lineal of Oak Altar Railing; the whole in a good state of preservation. The work is of the Corinthian order, and includes four well-proportioned detached fluted columns, with carved capitals, entablature, and pediments. The Decalogue is written on four raised and gilded panels; and there are also two paintings on panels of Moses and Aaron . . .

The altarpiece had been given in 1719. Until the restoration, the altar stood in the middle of the chancel, and the rails projected as far as to the chancel arch. But when the chancel was reopened, after Woodyer's restoration, on 7 November 1863, the congregation saw something very different: new arches to the chancel aisles, the organ on the north, a new roof, a reredos of seven panels with crocketed heads, a lining of Derbyshire marble to the walls, stalls for the choir, and a low panelled stone screen at the west. The iron gates, for which William Field was paid £3 16s in 1704, were put back later; but the solemn effect of the chancel has gone for ever.

The interior of St Margaret's, Westminster, must have been very impressive. It was a church on which work was constantly done in the eighteenth century, and there were pews and galleries of the period. In 1758 the east end was "wrought into a circular sweep, ending at the top in the form of a half cupola, wrought into squares of Gothic work: under the window, and round the sides of the altar, also variously ornamented in a similar Gothic stile". The sanctuary was entered by a handsome and spacious pointed arch, with Prince of Wales feather capitals. On the side walls were niches with paintings of Moses and Aaron in chiaroscuro. There was a groined ceiling; in the centre, a large division painted with a descending dove. Behind the altar was a copy of Titian's *Meeting at Emmaus*, modelled by John Nost, and carved in lime by Seffrin Alken, of St Anne's, Soho, under the direction of Kenton Couse the architect. The vestry bought the sixteenth-century glass for the east window from John Conyers of Copt Hall, Essex, for £420, and refused to take out any parts that were offensive to the dean. On 8 May 1761, they passed a vote of thanks to the Reverend Dr Thomas Wilson "for his learned and excellent treatise on Ornaments in Churches, in which he had unanswerably justified the acts of the Vestry in causing the late ornaments to be made to S. Margaret's, and more especially the east window". In 1802 a new pulpit and desk had been erected by S. P. Cockerell, and a new ceiling "in the formation of which the general Gothic Style and Character of the building was necessary to be attended to".

But when F. W. Farrar was appointed rector in 1876, the appearance of the interior filled him with horror, and he raised a very large sum of money for restoring it. Scott made the plans; the apse was removed, the windows were restored, and it was entirely refitted. The east wall was rebuilt in 1905. It is now a handsome Perpendicular church, but its former character has gone.

St Dunstan in the West was entirely rebuilt by John Shaw in 1831-3: this is how the old church looked, after repairs by Mr Robinson in 1752:

> The roof or ceiling of the interior is adorned with a spacious quadrangle of deep mouldings, crocket work, an elipsis, roses, &c. of fret work; and above the pillars which support the roof, there is an entablament of painted wainscot extending round the church; on the north, west, and south sides, are galleries of wainscot; the pulpit is of the same kind of wood; and the church is well pewed with oak. In the west gallery is a fine organ.
>
> The altar-peice consists of two columns of the Ionic order, adorned with painted cherubims, over which is a cornice, and in the middle a globe between two Bibles, denoting the wonderful spreading of the pure Gospel over the world: the whole is fenced in with a rail and banister, and the space

paved with marble. In the east window is a figure of *St Matthias*, in stained glass.[1]

At Tewkesbury abbey,

the pewing of this church was till lately extremely irregular, and very un-worthy of such a noble fabric; but, by the munificence and public spirited exertions of the inhabitants and the representatives of the borough, aided by liberal donations, that defect has been wholly removed; and the part appropriated to divine worship, fitted up in a stile of singular elegance, yet perfectly according with the architecture of the building, and the purpose for which it was designed. The uniformity, convenience and disposition of the seats, the peculiarly light and elegant construction of the pulpit, and the *tout ensemble* of the choir, challenge admiration, and almost defy competition.

The designs for these improvements were the production of our very ingenious townsman, Mr Edward Edgcumbe, now resident at Ellesmere in Shropshire, to whom the Editor owes many acknowledgements for his friendly communications; and they were carried into execution by that able architect Mr J. Keyte of Kidderminster. Their performances here will be a lasting testimony to the talents of both, in their respective professions.[2]

This has, of course, all disappeared: the altarpiece of 1725 was taken down in 1848, and none of Keyte's woodwork survived Scott's restoration, which was begun in 1875.

Hurley church, Berks., was described by "Plantagenet" in three articles in the *Gentleman's Magazine* in 1839[3] These are a few of his notes: the ecclesiological terms seem to be his own invention.

The sanctuary or altar-place is spacious, and divided from the chancel by a wooden railing of well-turned spiral balustres; but we did not see any pulvinar or cushion for the convenience of communicants when on the genuflexorium, or kneeling-step, at communion-time. The holy table is neatly made, and stands at the extreme upper end of the chancel . . . The pallium is a decent blue woollen cloth, and so large as to completely hide the table . . .

The altarpiece is of mahogany-coloured woodwork. It is in the Roman style, and consists of a pedestal base, above which are two semicircularly

[1] D. Hughson, *A History and Description of London, Westminster and Southwark*, Vol. IV, p. 108.
[2] W. Dyde, *The History and Antiquities of Tewkesbury*, 2nd ed., 1798, p. 55.
[3] Pt. I, pp. 257–63; Pt. II, pp. 27–32, and 139–45.

headed panels and two lateral square-headed ones, all flanked by fluted pilasters, supporting a triglyphed and dentilled entablature, but with a truncated pediment. Between the heads of the central panels, surrounded with a glory of gilt radii, is an inverted triangular gilt space, on which are inscribed the four Hebrew letters signifying "Jehovah". In the central vacuity of the pediment is a small carved and gilded dove, symbolic of the Holy Ghost, in imitation of the gold vessel wherein the Eucharist was kept; but which in primitive churches was suspended, as if hovering over the altar. In the two central panels, on a white marbled ground, is a copy of the Decalogue plainly written in small black Roman Letters; and in the lateral panels, on a black ground, are representations of Moses and Aaron standing on marble pedestals . . .

Directly under the rood-loft beam, and dividing the chancel from the nave, is a well-designed open screen of lime or sycamore, or some such close grained wood, too well, however, executed, to have been made at the public cost, unless in times more munificent than ours, and, therefore, probably the gift of some pious public-spirited parishioner. It is in the Italian taste, and was most likely erected in the early part of the last century. This screen . . . consists of a narrow central semicircularly-headed archway between two wide, flat-headed openings, flanked by rectangular ornamented pillars supporting a neatly-carved entablature, the console or key, and spandrels of the central arch being adorned with finely-cut, flowing foliage. Against the north and south walls of the chancel is a continuation of this screen-work as a return arch, like that just described, but with a console embellished with a beautifully-carved cherub, thus giving to the backs of the manorial and vicarage pews somewhat the appearance of stalls in a cathedral . . . The pulpit . . . is neatly made of wainscot, and is of hexagonal form, as well as the sounding-board, a handsomely inlaid piece of joinery projecting from the capital of an oaken fluted pilaster attached to the wall. The pulpit cloth and cushion are of blue velvet, now much faded . . .

None of this survived the restoration by J. H. Hakewill in 1852, except for Moses and Aaron, who were placed on the new Norman reredos.

The chancel of Hagley church, Worcs., was rebuilt in the Gothic style by Sanderson Miller, for Sir George Lyttelton, in 1752–4. This is how Dr Richard Pococke saw it.

The Chancel is entirely new: the windows are adorn'd on the sides and every part with Gothick ornaments in hewn stone, and all the other part of it is in stucco. On the ceiling and at each end are the arms of the paternal ancestors of the Lytteltons . . . These are all done at the expence of the Dean of Exeter, who gave a Persian carpet as a covering for the Communion table.

The east window is of rich painted glass—date 1569 ... the whole bordered with blue, purple and green glass lately made at Stourbridge. There are three windows each side in the Gothick style with a bordering of coloured glass thrown in pretty Gothick forms.[1]

All of this disappeared when the church was rebuilt by Street.

It is the same almost everywhere. A clean sweep was made by the Victorians. From their point of view they were certainly right. It seemed to them to be unreal and untruthful. Who could defend neatness and elegance if they were achieved with the aid of plaster, paint, and whitewash? If stonework was covered with paint, and roof timbers were hidden by plaster, and the honest irregularities of an ancient building were masked by regular pews and galleries—what could be done except clear away all the shams, and reveal the building as it really was?

Perhaps much of the adornment was too frail to last; and certainly it sometimes concealed defects that would eventually have brought the church to ruin: plaster ceilings were fixed to rotting timbers, and cracks in the wall were hidden by panelling. And it is probable that much of it would have had to go, even if there had been no theory to justify its removal.

But it was generally accepted by the restorers that it must all be swept away in any case. And what was to be done after that? Street or Woodyer could, if they wished, refashion a church into something complete and, in a new way, attractive. But many other nineteenth-century architects simply destroyed without creating anything of their own.

Before Thomas Hellyer of Ryde set to work on Thatcham church, Berks., he made two charming sketches of the church as it was: the exterior with its old texture, and a brick south chapel; the inside with pews and galleries, and hatchments on the walls; sunlit, a bit faded, but very lovable. It seems strange that he should not have been moved to restrain himself. But he was not. He embarked on a vicious restoration: the arcades are his, and so is the chancel arch; a new south aisle was built; the brick chapel was faced with flint, and faked up with new windows and pinnacles; the rest of the church was refaced; and the old fittings were removed from the inside, and new furniture of the dullest kind was provided.

[1] *The Travels in England of Dr Richard Pococke*, ed. J. J. Cartwright, 1889, Vol. II, p. 235.

Very many churches underwent this treatment, and the eighteenth-century ensemble is now very rare.[1]

In their treatment of complete Georgian churches, even the best of the Victorian architects went astray. They reseated them, gave them choir stalls and stained glass, took down the galleries, and sometimes added an open timber roof—which ought to have made them look better; but the more sensible of them must have realized that they had not succeeded. A Tractarian atmosphere is delightful, and we can feel at home in it: but it is different from the atmosphere of eighteenth-century Anglicanism, with "its lucidity, its classical view of life, its freedom from cant and humbug, its objectivity".[2] And it is not easy to combine the two in one church. SS. Philip and James's, Oxford, is a perfectly legitimate and satisfactory expression of Anglicanism, and so is Chislehampton; but they cannot be mixed up.

In many ways, we are not wiser than our fathers: we perform operations on nineteenth-century churches that are as cruel, in their ways, as those that the Victorians inflicted on the churches of the eighteenth century. But at any rate we have learned by now to respect the eighteenth century, and the few churches which the Victorians left unaltered are likely to remain so.

THE CONSECRATION AND REOPENING

And finally, when the work was done, the church was reopened—or consecrated, if it was a new church.

There has never been one official Anglican form of consecration. In 1640 Archbishop Laud proposed to the Upper House of Convocation that a uniform rite should be prepared; but nothing came of it: the time was hardly suitable.

A form was approved by both Houses in 1712, and in 1714 it was revised, but it did not receive the royal assent.[3] The revision did not improve it: the procession to the various parts of the church was left out, and all the prayers were to be said at the altar. But no doubt it seemed solemn and affecting to Churchmen of the time, and it was generally used, with slight modifications, during the century. Occasion-

---

[1] *Bonney's Church Notes*, 1845–8, ed. N. S. Harding, 1937, and *Lincolnshire Church Notes*, 1828–40, by William John Monson, F.S.A., ed. John 9th Lord Monson, 1936, give useful descriptions of many Lincolnshire churches that have since been restored.

[2] Addleshaw and Etchells, op. cit., p. 60.

[3] See R. Phillimore's *Ecclesiastical Law*, p. 1763.

ally the whole order of service was copied out in the episcopal register, and sometimes a note was made of the order that was used. The new church of Chislehampton, Oxon, was consecrated on 27 August 1763, and it was noted that the same form had been used as at Hailey on 4 August 1761. The register of the church records that all things were done decently and in order.

It is pleasant to try to picture the consecration of an eighteenth-century church, and the bishop in the midst of his people. We tend to think of Georgian prelates as we see them in their portraits—perpetually sitting in a chair, with their hands, just emerging from enormous lawn sleeves, resting on the arms. But we cannot picture a consecration without seeing them in movement. And it is certainly an occasion when we can detach them from their palaces, their London houses, and the House of Lords, and see them in contact with their flocks.

It is a pity that on these occasions someone else normally preached the sermon, and that the bishops did not take the opportunity of addressing the congregation. But the preachers no doubt took a good deal of trouble. What they said would be on the lines of the opening sermon in Thomas Bisse's admirable series on *The Beauty of Holiness in the Common Prayer*.[1] He begins,

> Since the worship of God is the greatest and most honourable among all the acts and employments of the children of men, from which as the meanest are not excluded, so neither are the greatest exempted; since the highest among men, even they that sit on thrones, must bow down before the altars of the Most High . . . surely this universal work, or duty of man, ought to be set off with the greatest order and magnificence, *with the beauty of holiness*. When King *David* left instructions to *Solomon* for building the Temple, he gave in charge, that it should be *exceeding magnifical*: and the reason afterwards given is itself exceeding awful as well as just; *for*, saith he, *the palace is not for man, but for the Lord God*. As the house of God, so the worship performed in it should in like manner be *exceeding magnifical*. For it is a work of a superiour and incommunicable nature: it is not a respect paid to our Superiours; it is not an offering made to our Governors; it is not an homage done to our Princes: No; worship *is not for man, but for the Lord God*.

So when Kingswood church, Glos., was consecrated by Joseph Wilcocks, Bishop of Gloucester, on 27 August 1723, Robert Bull, Rector of Tortworth, preached a sermon on *The Necessity and Holiness of Churches*.

But the bishop must have been the chief attraction. Wilcocks seems

[1] 1st ed., 1716.

to have been rather an ordinary bishop, but his visit must have been interesting to the people of Kingswood.

The new church of Hardenhuish, Wilts., by Wood of Bath jun., was consecrated on 4 November 1779.

> This day the elegant new-built parish church of Hardenhuish, near Chippen-ham, liberally erected by Joseph Colborne, esq.; lord of the manor, and patron of the rectory, together with the new church-yard walled in about the same, were consecrated by the right rev. the lord bishop of London, for the . . . lord bishop of Sarum; and an excellent sermon, suitable to the solemnity, was preached by the rev. Dr Frampton to a numerous congrega-tion of clergy, gentry, and others of the neighbourhood there assembled.[1]

The bishop was Robert Lowth, one of the best of eighteenth-century bishops, an excellent scholar, and a very good preacher: "his manner, grave and solemn; his style perspicuous, pure, and nervous".[2]

Silverstone, Northants., was consecrated on 31 July 1782. The peti-tion was presented to the Bishop of Peterborough. It said that the old chapel had been inadequate, and in a ruinous condition: it had been agreed to rebuild it "which being now completed at considerable charge and trouble they humbly hope that your Lordship taking into your consideration the necessity of their Request & Piety of their Intention will be graciously pleased to Consecrate the said Building" —which the bishop proceeded to do.

The bishop here was John Hinchcliffe, who, as a bishop, managed to remain Master of Trinity College, Cambridge, until he was ap-pointed Dean of Durham, when he resigned: he remained bishop and dean until his death. He was "a most pleasing preacher, with a clear and melodious elocution"[3] and a weighty speaker, on the Whig side, in Parliament. "We hear little of him on purely Church questions and in his pastoral capacity, and may conclude that in these points he was neither more nor less than the average bishop of his age."[4] But the eighteenth-century Church did not expect too much of its bishops.

All Saints', Newcastle, David Stephenson's beautiful church, was finished in 1789.

> On Monday, November 16, 1789, the Right Rev Thomas Thurlow, Lord Bishop of Durham, arrived in Newcastle, and was entertained at the Mansion

---

[1] *Gentleman's Magazine*, Vol. XLIX, 4 Nov. 1779.
[2] T. Somerville, *My Own Life and Times*, p. 155.
[3] William Jones, *Memoir of Bishop Horne*, p. 144.
[4] C. J. Abbey, *The English Church and its Bishops 1700–1800*, Vol. II, p. 244.

Liverpool Daily Post and Echo

14. Holy Trinity, Liverpool. A town church, consecrated in 1792

13. Old Dilton, Wilts. The three-decker

15. Quebec Chapel, St Marylebone

House by the Right Worshipful Hugh Hornby, Esq. mayor, and one of the trustees for building the new church of All Saints, the consecration of which took place on the following day. At eleven o'clock, his lordship proceeded to the edifice where the usual prayers of consecration were read with great solemnity, and an excellent sermon preached on the occasion, by the Rev. Hugh Moises, A.M. rector of Greystock, and morning lecturer of All Saints', from Leviticus, chapter xix. ver. 30, "Ye shall keep my Sabbaths, and reverence my sanctuary, I am the Lord." After divine service, the Right Worshipful the Mayor gave a grand entertainment to the bishop, the clergy then in town, the trustees for building the church, the church-wardens, and a number of other gentlemen.[1]

Thomas Thurlow was brother of the Lord Chancellor, and, as one might expect, had had rapid promotion. He was only four years at Durham, and died in 1791.

The chapel at Loudwater, Bucks., was erected by William Davis, and licence was granted on 3 January 1790, for the performance of divine service in it, for three years, or until the consecration of the building by the bishop. The consecration, in 1791, is described in the episcopal act book.

Accordingly on the said twenty-fifth Day of June the said George Lord Bishop of Lincoln came to the Hamlet of Loudwater aforesaid between the Hours of Ten and Twelve in the Morning and being there met by the said William Davis and other Inhabitants of the said Hamlet the said Petition and the Deed of Endowment hereafter Recorded at Page 534 were in due form Presented by them to his Lordship at the door of the said Chapel and the Petition being ordered by him to be read was openly and publickly read by me John Hodgson Notary Publick and which being done his Lordship did in pursuance thereof and at the humble desire of the said Petitioners immediately enter upon the said Work and the following Schedule or Sentence of Consecration was in the course of the Service of the day used on the Occasion then and there by his Lordship's direction openly and publicly read and Pronounced by the Worshipful Thomas Bever Doctor of Laws Chancellor of the Diocese of Lincoln in manner and form following . . .[2]

This bishop was George Pretyman Tomline, the tutor and biographer of William Pitt. He had adopted the name of Tomline on receipt of a legacy from a man who, it is said, had only seen him once. Richard Porson, the classical scholar, disliked him, and said that if the man had seen him twice he would never have left the legacy. But he was a person of ability, though "a little inclined to intolerance, and to an

[1] E. Mackenzie, op. cit., p. 304.　　[2] Episcopal act book 1761–99, p. 530.

over-straitlaced and precise orthodoxy".[1] He worked hard, and visited his enormous diocese with regularity and care. Loudwater, which is an outlying part of High Wycombe, is a long way from Lincoln, but no doubt he would come there from London.

When it was not a new church, there was, of course, no bishop and no consecration. But the parish would do its best to provide an impressive service for the reopening.

Trusley church, Derby., was rebuilt in 1713. The register contains the following note: "The aforesaid sixth of August was ye opening of ye new church, when we had both vocall and instrumentall musick the service read as at Cathedrals an Anthem very well performed Mr Coke being one of ye performers. A Sermon preached by the rector, Severall of ye gentry and clergy auditors of ye whole performance."[2]

At Montford, Salop, "March the fifth [1738], the new Church, blessed be God for it, was opened, rebuilt by that ingenios Architect, Mr William Cowper, junr. of Salop, the Foundation thereof on May ye 19th, Ascension Day, in ye Presence of several Trustees hereafter mentioned . . .".[3] The writer then records the ways in which the money was raised, and Cowper's generosity in refusing to take any money for additional work. The service is not described, but it seems to have been a joyful occasion.

When Holy Trinity, Minories, in the City of London, was reopened after repairs in 1760, the congregation were greeted by a pleasant smell: 1s had been spent by the churchwardens on frankincense, to overcome the smell of paint.

[1] Abbey, op. cit., p. 241.   [2] J. C. Cox, op. cit., Vol. III, p. 338.
[3] Note in the register, quoted in *Shropshire Parish Documents*, p. 233.

14

PROPRIETARY CHAPELS AND
PARISH CHAPELS

BESIDES the parish churches, there were in most of the large
towns, and especially in London, proprietary chapels and
parochial chapels.

PROPRIETARY CHAPELS

The proprietary chapels, built as speculations by, or for, some
particular clergyman, and afterwards leased to others who wanted to
make a living by them, had nothing to do with the parish churches,
except that the vestries sometimes had to rate them. The proprietors
were not always very keen about being rated. The reports of Committees of St George's, Hanover Square, contain one or two notes of
appeals against assessments in the early years of the nineteenth century.
On 3 July 1813,

The Revd Mr Cockburn rated at £300 for the new Chapel in Albermarle
[sic] Street declared that in Consequence of the great Expence of building
the Chapel, and the Restrictions imposed in order to his obtaining a License
for it, together with the allotting a part of it for the Accommodation of 50
Poor Persons without paying for their Seats, the clear annual Income to
himself is only about £45 a Year.

The committee recommended the vestry to reduce the rate to £180.
On 24 June 1819,

The Revd Weedon Butler on Behalf of the Proprietors of Charlotte Chapel
Pimlico rated at £200 produced an Account extracted by himself from the
Books of the Chapel for the last 7 Years, by which it appears that the clear
Income from the Chapel to the Proprietors after paying all Expences of the
Clergyman, Clerk, Organ, Repairs &c has scarcely amounted to £100 per
Ann^m on an Average, tho' before the Erection of Ebury Chapel & Belgrave
Chapel he believes it was considerably more.

The rate was reduced to £100 for the time being.

There must often have been some tension between the parish churches and the chapels; but in these cases the church seems to have acted generously.

Most of the chapels have disappeared without leaving a trace behind them.

St Mary's, Spital Square, Spitalfields, was built of timber in 1693 by Sir George Wheler for the use of his tenants. In 1756 it was rebuilt in brick. By the end of the century it was "going into ruin". In 1809 the friends of Josiah Pratt, Secretary of the Church Missionary Society, told the patron that they were ready to repair it if he would appoint the person whom they chose. He agreed, and Pratt was licensed in February 1810: the chapel was repaired at a cost of about £1000, and reopened in October.

In 1828 the Reverend Richard Tilliard bought it for the Reverend Edward Bickersteth. Then it was sold to the Hyndman Trustees, who repaired it again. It was reseated in 1872, and again repaired in 1884. C. Booth speaks of "hard, devoted work, successful in its way".[1] There were a vicar, curate, bible woman, Church Army captain, and other workers. The Holy Communion was sparsely attended, but there were about 50 people in church at 11 a.m., and 100 at 6.30 p.m. But it came to an end about 1911. The pulpit is in St Alphege's, Edmonton, and there are a few odd papers in the record office of the County Hall. Otherwise, everything has vanished.

Westminster has lost almost all its chapels, of which there were a good many. Charlotte chapel (afterwards known as St Peter's, Buckingham Gate) was superseded by St Philip's, Buckingham Palace Road, in 1888. Booth reports: "On Sunday evening a genuine, though not numerous, working-class congregation . . . The ritual is low, with evening communion, and the services plainly conducted, so that plain people can follow them."[2] But this did not last very long. The church was handed over to the Russians, who used it until it became unsafe, and was taken down a year or two ago. The site is now part of Victoria Coach Station.

St Mary's chapel, Park Street—or the Duke of Westminster's chapel—was demolished in 1882. Queen Street chapel was converted into offices about 1888; Curzon, or Mayfair chapel, was demolished in 1899.

---

[1] *Life and Labour of the People in London*, 3rd Ser., *Religious Influences*, Vol. II, 1902, pp. 13–15.
[2] Ibid., Vol. III, p. 118.

Ram's chapel, Homerton,[1] disappeared quite recently.

St Marylebone—the vestry of which, as we have seen, was quite incapable of making up its mind to provide church accommodation—had several proprietary chapels. Portland, or Foley chapel, Great Portland Street—built in 1750–66, and consecrated in 1831 and known as St Paul's—was pulled down in 1908. Titchfield chapel (of which John White, the local surveyor, wrote in 1799, "This Chapel has not been Warmed there being no means of doing it without some inconvenience to the Occupier of the Beer Cellars underneath") has gone.[2] This was the same as Welbeck chapel, Westmorland Street (afterwards known as St James's): these variations in name are common in proprietary chapels, and decidedly confusing. The *Marylebone Mercury* reported: "I understand that the church has been what is termed in commercial circles a 'failure' since the death of Mr Haweis, and that the congregation for some time past has never exceeded fifty in number. It is stated that flats are to be erected on the site of the famous chapel."[3] Some of the fittings went to St Anne's, Brondesbury.

Portman chapel (St Paul's) built by Mr Portman in 1779 is still there. (This has sometimes, not unnaturally, been confused with St Paul's, Great Portland Street.)

Brunswick chapel also remains. There are a few papers about this among the Portland papers in the St Marylebone Public Library. One is a printed paper announcing an auction by Mr Christie at his Great Room, Pall Mall, on Thursday 12 May 1796, at one o'clock. It is described as

A SPACIOUS ELEGANT CHAPEL, built in an uncommon substantial Manner, and finished in a Stile of simple Elegance. The Situation surrounded by most respectable Inhabitants, with easy Access to the South and North Fronts Formed on a large Scale, with Pews sufficient to hold a Congregation of at least One Thousand in Number with great Facility; and completed with elegant Pulpit, Reading Desk, and Vestry mechanically constructed, with sliding Shutters and Sashes, for the Purpose of throwing it occasionally into the Chapel. A neat Belfry and Bell. Under the Chapel are spacious Cellars sufficient for containing Four Hundred Pipes.

The chapel was disused for a time, and then taken over by the Church Army. It has been given a horrid Victorian front, a new roof, new seats, and window tracery; but the back part remains more or less as it was.

[1] See below, pp. 196–7.   [2] Portland papers, in the St Marylebone Public Library.
[3] 19 March 1904.

Some chapels have been superseded by parish churches. Margaret chapel was built in 1776 for "public worship on the Principles of Natural Religion apart from Revelation". It then belonged for a time to the sect of Bereans,[1] and was for two years a proprietary chapel. After a spell of Irvingism, it was taken by Frederick Oakley, and made a centre of Tractarian worship. Then All Saints', Margaret Street, by William Butterfield, the model church of the Ecclesiological Society, took its place.

Quebec chapel (1787) has been superseded by Walter Tapper's beautiful church of the Annunciation.

Most of the proprietary chapels outside London have also been disposed of, demolished, or superseded by parish churches.

There was one at Twickenham. About 1720 Captain Gray built a row of houses called Montpelier Row, and a small chapel in 1727. After his death, the houses were sold to different people, and the chapel was sold also. It was never consecrated, and after the building of St Stephen's church in 1873 it was used as a hall. In this century it became completely derelict: all the glass in the windows was broken, and the interior contained nothing but the tottering gallery.

Proprietary chapels have acquired a bad reputation; and there is certainly not much to be said for the way in which some of them were run, or for the clergymen who ran them. The ecclesiologists, in the nineteenth century, naturally detested them.

In 1846 a writer in the *Ecclesiologist*[2] mentioned a west end chapel which had a "lady's closet" and a "gentleman's closet" behind the altar, "where, at a rent proportionable to such a privilege, gentlemen and ladies have respectively the privilege of imploring, supplicating, and praising their LORD, unknown to all but their equally honoured companions".

Ten years later the Reverend F. G. Lee helped for a short time at

---

[1] Acts 17. 10–11: "And the brethren immediately sent away Paul and Silas by night unto Berea: who coming thither went into the synagogue of the Jews. These were more noble than those in Thessalonica, in that they received the word with all readiness of mind, and searched the scriptures daily, whether those things were so." The sect of the Bereans, or Barclayans, or Barclayites, was founded in Edinburgh in 1773 by John Barclay (1734–98). He taught that the only source of truth is the Scripture, every verse of which speaks of Christ. The act of faith conveys the assurance of salvation, and unbelief is the sin against the Holy Ghost. There were a few congregations in Scotland, and in London and Bristol, but the sect did not survive for long after the death of Barclay.

[2] No. X, April 1846, p. 142.

Berkeley chapel, where the Reverend W. H. Brookfield would deliver sermons prepared with great care, "but always somewhat deficient in Christian doctrine, such was never mentioned. He was cynical, sarcastic and platitudinarian; sometimes dreary in thought; 'very philosophical' as some said, and often epigrammatic in expression."[1] It is hard to imagine Lee, the rigid High Churchman, and afterwards founder of the Order of Corporate Reunion, in such surroundings, and it need not be said that he felt out of place: this was the kind of thing that the Tractarians disliked more than anything else.

But there is something to be said on the other side, and all the chapels were not as bad as they have been painted.

In 1789 the Reverend Richard Cecil went to look at St John's chapel, Bedford Row, Holborn. It needed repair, and he did not want to take any risks.

> A lady of fortune, however, offered to secure him from any ultimate loss, by her bond, should not the undertaking succeed: but, as the chapel prospered, she was never called on. Yet wishing to testify her regard to Mr Cecil, she gave him a very considerable sum of money toward building the present vestry and the rooms adjoining, to which several other friends contributed; and by whom the expense of building, amounting to several hundred pounds, was defrayed. The former vestry, being very small, was made into a pew, and appropriated to the use of the minister. At the same time a gentleman in the Law offered to lend Mr C. all the money that might be required for the repair of the chapel, without any other security than his note.[2]

Cecil began his ministry at St John's in March 1780. Though an Evangelical, "He was SINCERELY ATTACHED TO THE CHURCH OF ENGLAND both by principle and feeling—to her ORDER and DECORUM", and he "would never break through the order and discipline of the Church, to obtain any partial, local and temporary ends".[3] His views on Church matters were of the classic Anglican kind.

> The Papists treat man as all sense; and, therefore, some Protestants would treat him as all spirit. Because one party has exalted the Virgin Mary to a divinity, the other can scarcely think of that *most highly favoured among women* with common respect. The Papist puts the Apocrypha into his canon

[1] H. R. T. Brandreth, *Dr Lee of Lambeth*, 1951, p. 16.
[2] *Remains of the Rev. Richard Cecil, A.M., with a view of his character by the Rev. Josiah Pratt*, 1849, pp. 17–18.
[3] Ibid., p. 165.

—the Protestant will scarcely regard it as an ancient record. The Popish heresy of human merit in Justification, drove Luther on the other side into most unwarrantable and unscriptural statements of that doctrine. The Papists consider grace as inseparable from the participation of the sacraments—the Protestants too often lose sight of them as instituted means of conveying grace.[1]

He took great care over the services.

He was a great admirer of order, and particularly so in the church. There was, in consequence, much more attention paid at St John's, than in most other places, that all the parts of the service should proceed in regular succession, without any intermission, from the time when it commenced till it ended.

The voluntary after the psalms was abolished. The bell began at exactly 10.30, the organist began to play immediately the bell stopped, and the reader was in his desk to begin the prayers when the organ ceased.[2] Cecil had a feeling for atmosphere in a church, and preferred Gothic churches to the "trim, finished, classic, heathen piles of the present fashion". He could never enter an old church without feeling, "Within these walls has been resounded, for centuries, by successive generations, Thou art the King of Glory, O Christ".

Clearly worship at St John's was very different from what went on at most of the proprietary chapels; and the preaching was far more edifying than, for instance, the elegant discourses of Dr Dodd at Charlotte chapel, Buckingham Gate, which Dr Johnson disliked.[3]

PARISH CHAPELS

The line between proprietary chapels and parochial chapels is not always easy to draw, as a chapel might be first one and then the other. But parochial chapels were something different: an effort by the large parishes to deal with the problem of accommodating their people, without undertaking anything too permanent. The formation of a new parish was a lengthy and difficult business, and the obvious thing to do was to acquire buildings which could be used for worship, without being consecrated, and could be got rid of if they did not succeed. In

---

[1] Ibid., p. 356.   [2] Ibid., p. 20.

[3] "A CLERGYMAN (whose name I do not recollect): 'Were not Dodd's sermons addressed to the passions?' JOHNSON: 'They were nothing, Sir, be they addressed to what they may.'" Boswell's *Life of Johnson* (ed. Birkbeck Hill and Powell), Vol. III, p. 246 (*sub* 1778).

the nineteenth century, after the passing of Sir Robert Peel's Act, it became the fashion to form as many new parishes as possible; and it was soon clear that far too many had been formed. A large number of separate parishes containing a few thousand people, and a single priest, not very well paid, was not necessarily the best way of dealing with the problem of London. A. J. B. Beresford Hope wrote of the

> interminable series of circulars, printed and lithographed, by incumbents of destitute Peel districts which are ever passing and repassing through the post-office. The same story with a few variations runs through them all. The church is either unbuilt, and Divine Service performed in some wretched, pestilential, unsuitable hole, or else it has been built with a debt that is breaking the backs of all who have taken part in that good work . . . In the mean while the poverty-stricken district cannot be effectively worked even in proportion to the means which it has scraped together. A morning spent in posting urgent appeals even in behalf of God's house is a bad preparation for preaching God's word in that house. Besides, the single-handed clergyman is physically unable to work his natural resources to the uttermost . . . The evil is increasing day by day; and if the religious world is not timely wise, there may some day be a terrible crash and collapse of character and influence, not to say a general catastrophe of material reverses.[1]

It was generally agreed that Bethnal Green, for instance, and—later— St Pancras, had been provided with a quite unnecessary number of churches.[2]

Many of the Victorian parishes have had, in recent years, to be merged with others. The eighteenth-century way had a good deal to be said for it.

St Martin in the Fields was a large parish which had a good many chapels at different times.

Holy Trinity, Conduit Street, rebuilt in 1716, was acquired in 1724. It was repaired several times in the century, and disposed of in 1777. It was demolished exactly 100 years later.

Tavistock chapel, built in 1763 by the Russell family for the tenants on the Bedford Estate, was only taken over in 1833. In 1855 it was consecrated (St John's, Drury Lane), and given a parish of its own. It was demolished in 1939.

Long Acre chapel was built in 1721. On 23 December 1757, the vestry of St Martin's, "taking into Consideration the present state of Long Acre Chaple in respect of its having been of late made use of as

---

[1] *The English Cathedral of the Nineteenth Century*, 1861, pp. 16–17.
[2] See also the article in the *Christian Remembrancer*, Dec. 1861, p. 472 ff.

a Place of Worship by the People called Methodists and Apprehend[g] that it would tend to the Advantage of the Religion by Law establish'd in this Kingdom to prevent the like Usage for the future by taking a Lease of the said Chaple or otherwise Renting the same", appointed a committee to treat with the owner, Sir George Vanderput. On 13 March 1758, they proposed to offer £400 for his term and interest in the chapel. He refused, but said that he was willing to take £450. The vestry agreed to this, and took over the chapel, which they repaired.[1] By 1782 there was a debt on it, and they decided to part with the lease. Finally, on 16 June 1784, they sold it to the Reverend Mr Foster for £500.

Clifford chapel, built in 1731, was vested in the Vicar of St Martin's in 1820: it was known as St Matthew's, Spring Gardens. It was acquired in 1882 by the Commissioners of Woods and Forests, and was pulled down in 1903.

Oxenden chapel, Panton Street, was another parish chapel. On 17 May 1677 the vestry were told that Mr Baxter had offered the house wherein he formerly preached to be made use of for the public worship of God, on condition that the parish would pay £35 a year rent. The offer was accepted, and work was "done in the said Tabernacle for building of pews there, and making the said house fit for the worship of God". The bills were to be paid by the people who had pews there.

On 2 December 1725, "The Rev[d]. D[r] Pearce and the Churchwardens represented to this Board that they upon a View of Oxendon Chappel Scituate in Oxendon Street and rented by this Parish were of Opinion that upon setting up in the said Chappel of a Communion Table and Rails and appointing Monthly Sacrament there It would be of great use to the Inhabitants thereof and help to advance the profitts of the said Chappel." The table and rails were accordingly set up. The chapel was eventually disposed of, and demolished.

Archbishop Tenison's chapel (now St Thomas's, Regent Street) was a chapel of St James's, Piccadilly.

At a meeting of the St James's vestry on 24 July 1707,

The Rector in Consideration of the Great increase of the Parish towards Sohoe proposed the purchasing and fitting up of the Chappell formerly used by the French in Berwick Streete for the providing that part of the parish with the better opportunitys for the Service of God which was approv'd by the Board—

[1] St Martin's vestry minutes in Westminster Library, F.2007.

Then he did further propose that the Vestry wou'd be pleased to Appoint som of their Members to have the Care of purchasing and fitting up the Chappell aforesaid which they accordingly did.[1]

The chapel was rebuilt as St Luke's, Berwick Street, in 1838–9, by E. Blore; it has now gone.

King Street chapel was built of wood by Dr Tenison and others; it was afterwards rebuilt in brick. In 1711 the vestry considered the reply to be made to the commissioners for building Fifty New Churches. They said that the chapel in King Street seated 890 placed, and 2000 with standing. (This was in the rough draft: in the reply they said "2200 and upwards".) Berwick Street held about 1300, "for the building whereof there is a debt yet standing out of 900 pounds and upwards". They thought that if a church were needed the best place would be on the Pesthouse Ground. But they did not think that there was immediate need for building a church, or for the chapels to be converted into parish churches.[2]

King Street was partly rebuilt in 1713. In 1766 they got rid of their old organ, which was bought for Berwick Street. In 1767 Berwick Street was enlarged and repaired.

St James's, Hampstead Road, St Pancras, was built as a chapel for the new burying ground of St James's. The ground was purchased from Lord Southampton, who was to agree with the rector and churchwardens about the plan of the buildings; he was to be given a handsome and convenient pew at the east end of the gallery of the chapel, and a proper vault under the east end of it. The trustees met on 13 August 1789, and appointed Thomas Hardwick as surveyor.[3] The King Street chapel was making a profit, and the archbishop had agreed that an advance could be made to the trustees from its income.

The burial ground was consecrated on 19 November, and on 13 February 1790 it was resolved that the chapel be built. The total cost was £2,802. The bricklayer's work was executed by George Malpas, and the carpenter's and joiner's work by Philip Peckham. In 1864 the vestry resolved to sell the chapel to the parish of St Pancras.

Grosvenor chapel, in the parish of St George's, Hanover Square, was built by Benjamin Timbrell and others on a piece of ground leased by Sir Richard Grosvenor.[4]

[1] Vestry minutes in Westminster Library, D.1712.   [2] Vestry minutes, D.1758.
[3] Minutes in the Westminster City Library, D.1715.
[4] Westminster Library, c. 766a.

14 April 1730: Ordered that the Churchwardens be desired with ye Rev^d Mr Trebeck to wait on Sr Richard Grosvenor with the request of the Vestry That he will be pleased to grant ye Inheritance of the Chappell intended to be built to the Parish after the Expiration of the Term of ninety nine Years in order that the said Chappell may be Consecrated.

28 April: Mr Benjamin Timbrell in behalf of himself Mr Robert Andrews Mr William Barlow & Mr Robert Scott Undertakers of the Intended New Chappell near Grosvenor Square made the following proposall to this Board (Viz) That they will get the Inheritance of the whole Ground as well Chappell as Chappell Yard & Vest the fee in the Parish as also build Vaults According to the plan laid before this Board under the Chappell at their own Expence for which they shall be Allowed the Sum of £20 p Ann for Ever out of the proffits that shall Arise from Burying in the said Vaults.

7 May: That the ffee of the Ground intended to be Granted by Sr Richard Grosvenor for Building a Chappell near Grosvenor Square Be Vested in ye Rector and Churchwardens of this Parish Subject to a Lease of ninety nine Years to the Undertakers of the said Building.

On 12 May Timbrell said that he had laid the resolution before the other undertakers concerned with him, and that they had accepted them.

The chapel was leased to the parish on 9 May 1732.[1]

The history of St George's chapel, Hyde Park, was similar to that of St James's, Hampstead Road. It was built in 1765, from plans by John Phillips, as the chapel for the new burial ground of St George's, Hanover Square. But it does not seem to have been used for ordinary services, except for a short time towards the end of the nineteenth century. In 1897 the chapel of the Ascension was built on the site.

On 10 March 1764, at a meeting of the Hackney vestry, "The Reverend Mr Cornthwaite acquainted the Parishioners that he had received a Letter from the Reverend Dr Ballard to whom the Inheritance of the late Mr Ramms Chappell in Homerton had descended that he was willing to accomodate the Parish with the use of the said Chappell for the purpose of divine Service if the Parishioners were willing to take the same." On 17 March the vestry clerk said that all persons willing to subscribe for a seat in the chapel had been asked to send in their names: only one had done so. "The consideration of useing the said Chappell for the purpose of divine Service was thereupon dismissed." On 22 December it was stated that Ballard had applied to

[1] C. 766a.

the bishop to have the chapel licensed for divine service. The vicar desired to know the opinion of the parish: whether it would be for the benefit of the parish to have it licensed, as he was willing to consent to anything which would be for the accommodation of his parishioners. No one thought that it would be.

However, Cornthwaite took it on. On 1 April 1771, he was desired to let the seats at 10s 6d each; he was to be indemnified annually out of the church rate for any deficiency. On 21 December he was voted a sum of £50 "for any loss he may have sustain'd in taking the Chapel into his own hands for divine worship".

Clapton chapel (now St Thomas's church) was built by John Devall, of Buckingham Street, Fitzroy Square, for his tenants, and let by him to Cornthwaite in 1776. Three years later, Cornthwaite told the Hackney vestry that the chapel had occasioned a loss to him of nearly £50 a year, and that as the first term for which he had taken it expired at next Michaelmas, he thought of quitting it from that time. He desired to know whether the parish would take the chapel over. The meeting agreed that the parish church was not sufficiently convenient and commodious, but thought it totally improper to build a new church. However, proper accommodation must be provided; and a committee was appointed to consider the matter. They reported on 31 May that there were more than a hundred parishioners who wanted seats, and it was their opinion that to open the chapel at Stamford Hill as a free chapel of ease would be the least expensive way of accommodating them. However, the parishioners decided on 7 June that they were not disposed to take it, and it remained a proprietary chapel.

Finally, in 1827, it was sold by the owner, Dr George Richards, Vicar of St Martin in the Fields, to Joshua Watson and three other gentlemen, and it was consecrated as a chapel of ease.[1]

In some parishes, schismatic chapels were built, which were "placed on the Establishment" at a later date. The Evangelicals wanted to hear their own doctrines preached, and were much displeased if they did not.

On 13 May 1796 a meeting was held at the house of Mr Montague in Camberwell. "It was the unanimous Opinion of those present, That as the Gospel was no longer preached in our parish Church a Chapel should be built for the alone preaching of the Gospel." On 6 June George Gwilt was appointed as surveyor, and on 17 June he produced a plan. On 5 July Charles Castleman's tender was accepted.

[1] MS. vestry minutes of Hackney.

On 30 May 1797, it was agreed that, as the bishop and the vicar had refused to give their consent to the chapel, it should be licensed under the Act of Toleration. It was opened on 10 September, and was known as Camden chapel.[1] In 1816 the suggestion was again made of placing the chapel on the Establishment. The vicar was approached; but as he thought that the appointment of a minister should be subject to his veto, the trustees would not agree. But the Reverend Henry Melville, minister from 1829–43, was licensed by the bishop, and the chapel ceased to be schismatic in 1844.

St Mary's chapel, Castle Street, Reading, had the same kind of history. The Reverend and Honourable W. B. Cadogan, the Evangelical Vicar of St Giles's, died in 1797. His successor, on 30 July, preached a far from evangelical sermon on *The Probable Causes and Consequences of Enthusiasm*, which was much admired by the *Reading Mercury*, but disliked by the congregation, many of whom seceded, and built themselves a temporary chapel in St Mary's Butts. The permanent chapel, on the site of the old Castle gaol, was opened on 16 December 1798. The builder was Richard Billing, whose conduct does not seem to have been always strictly evangelical: as surveyor to the Corporation of Reading, he took Corporation land on advantageous terms to himself: Albion Place and Southampton Place were built on Corporation property, leased to himself for ninety-nine years at his own valuation.[2] The congregation of the chapel were "partial conformists": "their only difference from the national Establishment consisted in a stricter conformity to the tenets of the early reformers than that observed by some of the regular clergy". Baptism was not administered, and no minister was allowed to occupy the pulpit who did not wear a gown and use the Liturgy.

After the departure of the Reverend Henry Gauntlett in 1808, some of the congregation withdrew, apparently because the trustees would not sanction any alteration in the use of the Liturgy. James Sherman, the first settled minister, came here in 1820, and left for Surrey chapel, Blackfriars, in 1836. He built chapels at Woodley, Caversham Hill, Theale, Binfield Heath, and Wargrave.

In 1836 the trustees reunited with the Church of England. About 200 members of the congregation disapproved, and decided to secede. They secured a site on the other side of the road, and built a Congregational chapel (J. C. Cooper, architect and builder). The village

[1] Minute book in the County of London Record Office.
[2] *Reading Mercury*, 14 Oct. 1833.

chapels became Congregational. The original chapel was enlarged in 1840 with a portico designed by Henry and Nathaniel Briant;[1] a chancel was added in 1842. It still remains, and is in use. The Congregational chapel was closed in 1957, and has been converted into a handsome shop.

[1] Contract advertised in the *Reading Mercury*, 7 March 1840.

15

NINETEENTH-CENTURY ALTERATIONS

IN VICTORIAN propaganda-novels, eighteenth-century church arrangements were always associated with the slackest kind of Church life. A good example is *The Vicar of Roost*, 1860, 'by the author of *The Owlet of Owlstone Edge*, *S. Antholin's*, etc.'.[1]

The hero, the Reverend R. Dove, goes to be curate of Roost under the Reverend Septimus Soaper. At their first meeting, he observes that Soaper speaks through his nose, that his head is shaped like a pineapple, that his colouring is sallow, that there are stains on his waistcoat, and that he is unpleasantly fat and heavy-looking. He notices the works of the Fathers in his study, but Soaper says that he has never read any of them: they came to him from his grandfather, who also left him a hundred sermons, which he has been preaching for twenty years. He says:

> The rage for increasing the number of services is, to my fancy, a great nuisance. And really one had need to be made of cast iron to be able to get through the mere Church work which some parsons cut out for themselves. As to wearing out my strength in teaching a pack of grubby children in a frowzy school, it is what I positively decline doing. The smell of heads absolutely puts a stop to the progress of digestion in my case.

He seldom visits anyone—but he often goes to Mrs Cooper of the Grange, who can be relied on to provide a glass of good ale.

The church is as repulsive as the vicar.

> In the interior is a heterogeneous mass of rickety pews of all shapes, sizes, and colours; a glare of whitewashed walls, and the close, fusty smell of rotting hassocks. The chancel is a sorry sight enough. A common deal table, stained red (its top covered with a piece of scanty baize, which having faded from green to an unwholesome yellow, looks like a very dirty ironing-blanket), occupies the space beneath the east window: the pavement is rough and broken; while three squalid frames contain, in white letters on a ground

[1] I.e., the Reverend F. E. Paget.

of black canvas, the Creed and the Ten Commandments, and the Royal arms of that "pious, glorious, and immortal sovereign, King William the Third"; his heraldic achievement predominating (as did the monarch himself), over the Creed and the Decalogue; and all surmounted with a tablet in blue and gold, in which it is announced that the chancel itself was rebuilt in the year 1774, by the Most Honourable John George, third Marquis of Kingsbury, Earl of Epsom, Baron Newmarket, K.G., Custos Rotulorum, and lay Rector of the Parish of Roost.

The surplice is dirty, the prayer book is dog-eared, and the cushions are full of moth.

Dove tries to work conscientiously, and falls foul of the vicar and Mrs Soaper. The story then becomes farcical, and not—to twentieth-century readers—very amusing. It ends, of course, with Dove leaving Roost; he has been appointed Vicar of Sunnymede. The church at Sunnymede is not described, but obviously it is a complete contrast with that of Roost. We imagine it as correctly restored, with open seats, a raised chancel, a properly vested altar, and a new east window with Middle-Pointed tracery, and glass by Hardman.

What Paget, and others, did in their stories, and the *Ecclesiologist* did in its articles, some did in drawings. As long ago as 1825—fourteen years before the foundation of the Cambridge Camden Society—there had been an anonymous pamphlet called *Hints to Some Churchwardens*, with twelve very amusing coloured plates. Pugin's *Contrasts* came out in 1836—but the purpose was not quite the same, and anyhow Pugin was then a Romanist.

The drawings that best illustrate the ecclesiologists' attitude to the eighteenth century are A. R. Mowbray's in *The Deformation and the Reformation*. There we can see a "miserably debased" church in an untidy churchyard, in which animals are feeding. There is also a choir in a west gallery, with the royal arms on the front, and an inscription, "This CHURCH was Beautified and this singing loft erected A.D. . . . at the sole expense of Dame Margery Meanwell of this Parish. Peter Porty Rector, David Drawl Curate, Sam! Sawyer and David Daub Churchwardens". This is, of course, contrasted with a surpliced choir singing decorously in a properly arranged chancel. Our old friend the rickety altar table has a top hat, coat, and walking stick on it. The drawing of the correct altar (delightfully incorrect by Dearmerite or neo-Caroline standards) is a masterpiece. There is also a picture of a service in an unrestored church, with an immense three-decker: the congregation is languid, and some are sitting facing the west. The contrast here is a service in progress at SS. Philip and James's, Oxford. And there are other illustrations, of contrasted fonts, clerical vestures, and so on.

The drawings were done, says Mowbray, "for the benefit of our younger Churchmen, who will find it hard in some cases to believe my words". We do not disbelieve him. There is no doubt that there were dilapidated churches, in which the worship was slovenly; and, by the middle of the nineteenth century, those that had survived seemed grotesquely out of date. On 14 September 1869 the Reverend Benjamin Armstrong, of East Dereham, went to a service at Gressenhall church, taken by the rector, Parson Hill, who was between 80 and 90 years old, but who still enjoyed his gun and his game of bowls, and drank his daily bottle of port. He found the whole affair "very irreverent and ludicrous".[1]

Armstrong's diary is extremely interesting as an account of how things appeared to a sensible High Churchman. He had restored his own church. On 9 October 1870, he recalled its condition when he came to the parish in 1850.

> Then, the altar was a miserable mahogany table with a covering fifty years old; there was a vile yellow carpet; a Grecian reredos with daubs of Moses and Aaron; no painted glass, and the rail for the communicants intersecting the sedilia. Look at it now—an altar and super-altar of full dimensions with flower-vases always replenished with flowers; candlesticks and candles (now introduced); three altar-cloths changed at the seasons; the windows painted; a stone reredos highly painted and with a central cross; a rich carpet; credence table; Bishop's chair, etc., etc.[2]

And it was not only a question of taste: the services were better attended, and brighter, and people joined in. There can be no doubt about this: even moderate and broad Churchmen, who would not go all the way with the ecclesiologists, agreed that there had been a great improvement, and adopted the new ways themselves. The old order was inadequate to meet the needs of the nineteenth century.

But that does not mean that it had always been inadequate. There is no reason to suppose that eighteenth-century Churchmen were dissatisfied with what was customary in their time. They were impressed and uplifted by the furnishings that seemed so lamentable to the Victorians, and they loved the services of the Prayer Book as they

[1] *A Norfolk Diary*, ed. H. B. J. Armstrong, 1949, pp. 144–5.
[2] Ibid., p. 156.

were performed, in that setting, in the way to which they were accustomed. "Give me good old George the Third and the Protestant religion", said Mrs Bolton in Newman's *Loss and Gain;* "those were the times! Everything went on quietly then". "I value the Prayerbook", she said to her Tractarian daughter, "as you cannot do, my love, for I have known what it is to one in deep affliction . . . If affliction comes on you, depend on it, all these new fancies and fashions will vanish from you like the wind, and the good old Prayer-book alone will stand you in any stead."

Mrs Bolton had no objection to reading desks and pews, and her Churchmanship was none the worse for that. But what suited her would not suit the younger Churchmen. (It is interesting to notice that this is happening over again. Parish Communions and whitewashed walls are all very well; but Mrs Bolton says, "Give me good old Edward the Seventh, and Mattins at 11".)

THE RECASTING OF EIGHTEENTH-CENTURY CHURCHES

What ought a good ecclesiologist to do with a Georgian, or Georgianized church? In the early days of the revival, the tendency was to leave it alone, except, perhaps, for some touching up at the east end. A complete restoration could be looked forward to, or a complete rebuilding in a better style, but meanwhile the best thing to do would be to build another church, correctly arranged, in which services could be conducted in the proper way, and the poor could have free seats. In many small towns the parish church continued in the old ways, dominated by churchwardens and vestry, and the worship was still more or less Georgian: it seemed to keen Churchmen to be quite out of touch with the realities of the nineteenth century. The new church was the place where you would find things done properly.

But as the parish churches, one by one, were restored, and adopted the new ways of worship, people tended to go back to them, and some of the new churches became rather useless. St Saviour's, Tetbury, was built in 1846–8 from plans by S. W. Dawkes, only a short distance from the parish church. It is hard to imagine that there was ever a time when there was a serious lack of accommodation in the parish church. There is certainly none now, and St Saviour's has been demoted to the status of a cemetery chapel. (This has at any rate preserved it from twentieth-century embellishments, and it is worth visiting as an unaltered Victorian church, with the peculiar atmosphere that comes from being used for funerals only.)

In some places the new church continues to be used, but it does not flourish very much: the old church has the attraction of old associations, and is usually much better placed for the casual dropper-in. There are no places now where the parish church is entirely in the hands of pew-owners, and the only place in which free seats and a bright service can be found is the Gothic Revival church half a mile away. But there were many in the 1840s and '50s.

However, the restoration of the parish churches was tackled everywhere sooner or later; and the question of what to do with eighteenth-century work had to come up. If it was in an old church, the answer was simple: Get rid of all of it. If the whole church was eighteenth-century, the answer was, Rebuild it all if possible: if it is not possible, remodel it: and if that is not possible do what you can to rearrange it.

This is how St Peter's chapel, Pimlico, was treated (Charlotte chapel, built in 1766). The *Ecclesiologist* admitted that it was a proprietary chapel, not a church, but it said that it was to be consecrated as soon as possible.

> . . . Now happily all is changed, and the furniture of the chapel is as seemly as perhaps at present practicable. The pews bereft of doors have been cut down to a convenient height: a chorus cantorum, whence the prayers are intoned, has been formed by a double row of raised longitudinal benches and desks, on either side of the approach to the altar; but it is not fenced in by either rood-screen or parclose. The altar-precinct is furnished with wooden sedilia and credence table, and its floor has been raised on steps, and a foot-pace added: the altar itself is duly vested, supports a super-altar, and is decked with a cross and lights; a velvet hanging constitutes the only reredos. The cornices and cieling about this portion of the chapel have been decorated with colour; the pulpit has of course been removed to a lateral position; a choir has been formed, whose members are attired in surplices, and the entire service is choral. Alms-boxes have been placed at the entrance, and daily matins and evensong commenced . . .[1]

Margaret chapel was given an altar of old-fashioned High Church type, copied from that of Littlemore, in 1839. This was superseded, in the second half of the '40s, by an ecclesiological altar, with frontal, super-frontal, gradine, and reredos.

There is no modern church so unsatisfactory in its style and arrangements that it cannot, in the hands of a Catholic-minded incumbent, be very con-

[1] *Ecclesiologist*, No. LXXIX, Aug. 1850, p. 146.

siderably ameliorated, and rendered not altogether unsuitable for the performance of Catholic worship. Such a task will, we doubt not, be often a very difficult one, and still more often a very distasteful employment of time and thought . . . Still however this undertaking may be in reality more truly meritorious than the very attractive one of rendering beauty still more beautiful. It may be a real and unadulterated act of love, a more entire offering DEO et Ecclesiae, than the former, where aesthetical feeling, the desire of the gratification of one's own sense of beauty, may have mixed itself up (who can tell how far?) with our wish of doing our duty to The Giver of all good things, and may therefore bring down greater blessings on those by whom it has been undertaken.[1]

But it was, of course, better to recast a church than simply to rearrange it.

Wasperton church, near Warwick, was rebuilt in brick in the eighteenth century: the old, low chancel was kept. The Reverend Thomas Leveson, vicar for forty-eight years, who died in 1883, spent his time and his means—as his memorial says—in repairing, enlarging, and beautifying the church. Scott was his architect. The chancel was lengthened, and an organ chamber was added; south aisle and porch were added to the nave; new roofs were erected, a turret was built, the walls were cased with stone, and new windows were inserted. The result is a delightful Camdenian village church. Scott, here, looks more like Carpenter. The roof has far more character than most roofs of the period. It is of tie beam and king post construction, with embattled wall plates and beams. The screen is a real rood screen; not, of course, with a crucifix—but it has a cross with decorated ends; it is inscribed *Non nobis*, etc., 1845. The altar is adorned—unusually—with diaper tiles by Minton; the east window, by Hardman, was designed by Pugin. The whole church is so pleasing that, for once, we approve of a nineteenth-century Gothic recasting of an eighteenth-century church. But in this case the recasting has been done so thoroughly that the eighteenth-century work has entirely disappeared. Only the ironwork altar rails remain, and it would be possible to visit the church without realizing that it had ever been eighteenth-century.

The eighteenth-century church of Birdingbury, War., was given a Gothic chancel and apsidal sanctuary in 1876. The effect is rather good—with windows by Clayton and Bell (and one by Hardman), elaborate tiles, and painted wooden vault; and if the rector, and John Cundall the architect, had been willing to stop there, we should have

[1] Ibid., No. LIV, Dec. 1846, pp. 204-5.

approved. As a matter of fact, the fittings of the nave were left—box pews, pulpit, west gallery, and font; but the windows were gothicized, and the roof was raised to a Gothic pitch. The west end, with its Doric pilasters, pediment, and octagonal turret and dome, was left; but the steep pitch of the roof behind it looks extremely odd and awkward.

Chalfont St Peter, Bucks., was gothicized by Street, and a chancel was added. Buckingham was gothicized by Scott from 1862, and the work was continued by J. O. Scott. A chancel was added, and the nave was converted into E.E. The two tiers of windows were kept, though the galleries were removed.

Stony Stratford, which was rebuilt in 1776–7 by Francis Hiorn, was Gothic already, but various unsuccessful efforts were made to improve it. A faculty for reseating was given in 1864. New galleries were erected in 1876, a chancel was formed, and the windows were given plate tracery: Street was responsible for this. New vestries by E. Swinfen Harris in 1892; decoration and screen by Bodley in 1905.

A late example of gothicizing is St Mary's, Monmouth. The vestry decided in 1879 that the eighteenth-century church needed to be reseated, repaired, and improved. Street made plans for a complete rebuilding in fourteenth-century style, but he was forced to alter his plans owing to lack of funds. So St Mary's was remodelled by the insertion of Gothic arcades and lancet windows, and an extension eastwards. The remodelled church is a failure. The proportions are obviously those of the eighteenth-century church, and the high walls with their pairs of long lancets have an 1840-ish look.

The church was reopened on 2 November 1882, and the local paper gave the usual kind of report.

> Very few shops were opened in the morning, the day being pretty generally observed as a holiday throughout the town. The streets of the Borough were gaily decked with bunting in honour of the occasion, the flags having been hired for the purpose with money raised by subscription. Several private houses also exhibited flags, and the general effect was very pleasing. In the afternoon the band of the Royal Monmouthshire Engineer Militia played a selection of music in Agincourt-square, considerably enlivening the neighbourhood.

The Bishop of Llandaff preached at Mattins at 11.30, taking as his text "There were some that had indignation within themselves, and said, Why is this waste of the ointment made?"

Afterwards there was a luncheon of a *recherché* description at the Beaufort Arms. The vicar proposed the toast of the Church and the Queen, and Mr Rolls proposed the health of the Bishop and Clergy. The bishop, replying, congratulated the vicar and people of Monmouth:

> During the 33 years which he had been in the episcopacy he had looked over and over again at the condition of Monmouth Church—its badly constructed pillars, its miserable chancel and high pews, and heartily longed to see it—he would not say destroyed, because so long as they had nothing else it was better to have it than nothing, but to have it restored if possible to something like its primitive state. (*Hear, hear.*) It had, however, always been in his mind the wish rather than the expectation, for he felt that the cost of defraying the expenses of such a work was so great that there hardly seemed to him any possibility of doing it. But happily times had altered, there was a better feeling in the country with regard to Church work, and what was once beyond all expectation of fulfilment had now been accomplished, and in such a way as to give them all entire satisfaction. (*Applause.*)

The Reverend D. G. Davies proposed the health of the Restoration Committee. Mr Griffin replied:

> He ventured to hope they thought the committee had not carried out the work so very badly. The result they had before them in the newly restored edifice, and he believed they would all agree that the church was now a fair and goodly one, handsome with a plain dignity of its own ... One objection, that the old church was good enough, had been fully answered in the Bishop's sermon that morning ...

Mr Cordes proposed the toast of the Mayor and Corporation, who had given their best cooperation and hearty assistance. The mayor replied. The Reverend Sidney Phillips, the late vicar, proposed the health of the churchwardens, and the churchwardens replied. There were two more speeches, and "the proceedings then terminated".[1]

The other point of view was expressed to me in 1936 by an old lady who remembered Smith of Warwick's church of 1736. She said, "It was a beautiful old church. Why couldn't they leave it alone?"

It became easier to deal with eighteenth-century churches when it was admitted that foreign styles might be used. There was Italian Gothic that was hardly Gothic at all—more Romanesque than Gothic: it was not at all pure, but it might be used for the purpose. Byzantine, too, was just legitimate—or a mixture that can only be called

[1] *Monmouthshire Beacon*, 4 Nov. 1882.

Victorian. S. S. Teulon was responsible for several remodellings of this kind.

Sunbury church, Middlesex, was recast by Teulon in 1856 and onwards: "one of the cleverest transformations of a 'Churchwarden' structure into a Byzantine church to be seen in the kingdom". He added an apse and chancel aisles "in a kind of Italianizing Romanesque style". Banded colouring in brickwork was added outside, and two circular staircase turrets were built on to the tower. The seating was remodelled, and the galleries were given open iron fronts. A belfry was designed for the tower, adorned with pierced tracery and the four Evangelists standing at the corners; a square spire with an open niche at the top and circular spired tourelles at the angles. But this was not carried out.[1] The interior was dark, barbaric, and not unimpressive; but it was too strong for twentieth-century taste, and it has recently been re-whitened and purified.

St Mary's, Ealing, was reconstructed by Teulon in 1866–72. The first part of the work was the building of a chancel with aisles, and the alteration of the walls "into a series of semi-circular arches, surmounted by a clerestory of Byzantine windows", the building of an ambulatory on either side of the nave, the addition of an organ chamber and baptistery, and the erection of a pointed open roof. This was completed in 1867. The completion of the main part of the work was commemorated by a series of services on New Year's day 1873. The recasting and heightening of the tower was not finished until 1874. There are metal pillars supporting horseshoe arches. Bishop Tait spoke of the "conversion of a Georgian monstrosity into the semblance of a Constantinopolitan basilica". The account in the *Builder* called the style "a mixture of Byzantine and Louis Quatorze".

Holy Trinity, Leicester, a plain chapel built in 1838, was remodelled in the same style.

St George's, Queen Square, Holborn, was erected by a committee —Sir Streynsham Master, and fourteen other gentlemen, including Robert Nelson—who in 1705 agreed with Arthur Tooley to build a chapel and two houses for £3500. It was bought by the commissioners for building the Fifty New Churches, repaired and beautified, and consecrated in 1723. In 1867 Teulon set to work on it. A new chancel was formed on the south side, the pews and all but one of the galleries were removed, a light screen of pitch pine was put up between the body

---

[1] *Ecclesiologist*, No. CXII, Feb. 1856, pp. 77–8, and No. CXLIV, June 1861, pp. 205–6.

of the church and the chancel; new pulpit, lectern, and reredos were erected, and the roof and pillars were decorated. The windows were enlarged and given tracery, and a spire was built.

Christchurch, Blackfriars, was given a Romanesque apse, of brick with coloured ornamentation.[1]

St Peter at Arches, Lincoln, was reseated, and given a new pulpit; the galleries were provided with open ironwork fronts.[2]

St Martin's, Worcester, was given a new east window by Hopkins "a kind of broad late Pointed, with tracery round a central wheel"— with glass by Hardman.[3] The sanctuary arch was raised, the west galleries were taken down, and the pews and pulpit lowered, and the east bay was arranged as a chancel.

Wilsthorpe, Lincs., an interesting church of 1715, was maltreated by James Fowler in 1862. The windows were filled with coarse tracery, and the tower was crowned with a silly slate spire. All the fittings, except the font, were turned out.

Wolverton, Hants., a very striking church of 1717, was altered by C. Smith of Reading in 1872. The windows were given tracery, the iron chancel gates were turned out, and a Gothic font was set up. Dr Cox in the Little Guide to Hampshire is justifiably cross about this restoration.

Abbots Ann, in the same county, remains much as it was, but the windows in the chancel, and two in the nave, have been filled with tracery—enough to spoil the inside.

St Lawrence's, Brentford, was recast by B. and E. B. Ferrey in 1875. The galleries were removed, high wooden arcades were inserted, and the windows were filled with tracery.

St Thomas's, Clapton, was remodelled in a basilican style. It was built as a proprietary chapel about 1774[4] and enlarged by Joseph Gwilt in 1827. In 1861 the Reverend F. W. Kingsford became incumbent, and in 1864 altered the east end, inserting choir stalls, etc. In 1873 William Burges was called in to make plans for remodelling the whole church. The pews and galleries were to be cleared out, and the lower windows blocked. An ornamental ceiling was to be constructed. For the chancel, he "endeavoured to adopt the time-honoured arrangement existing at St Clemente at Rome, adapting it to our own ritual".[5]

---

[1] Ibid., No. CXXIII, Dec. 1857, p. 396.

[2] Ibid., No. CXII, Feb. 1856, p. 78; plan in the Lincoln diocesan records.

[3] Ibid., No. CXIV, June 1856, p. 234.   [4] See p. 197.

[5] H. S. Kingsford, *A Short Account of St Thomas's Church, Stamford Hill*, 1913, p. 50.

This was carried out, except for the baldachino that Burges proposed; the walls were painted, and much glass, chiefly by Powell, was inserted.

Later in the century, some architects began to realize that, if classical churches were to be altered or embellished, their style should be respected.

Sir A. W. Blomfield—who certainly could not always be trusted to deal with eighteenth-century churches—added a decent enough chancel to St Mary Magdalene's, Bridgnorth, in 1876. In 1888 he enlarged Holy Trinity, Guildford, with an apse.

J. A. Chatwin's additions to the east end of St Philip's, Birmingham (1883–4), are, on the whole, such as an eighteenth-century architect might have designed.

A chancel was added to Blandford church, Dorset, in 1896 by C. Hunt, a local architect. It was designed on the model of the rest of the church, and the apse was moved to the east of it. The church looks all of a piece, and the extension has decidedly improved it.

All Saints', Wandsworth, was given a classical chancel by E. W. Mountford in 1899.

In 1903–5 a classical chancel was added to St John's, Wakefield, by Micklethwaite and Somers Clarke; it had been designed some years before, in 1881.

THE REPLACEMENT OF EIGHTEENTH-CENTURY CHURCHES

In many parishes a completely new church took the place of the eighteenth-century one. (A list of some of them is given in the appendix.[1])

This was sometimes due to a genuine need for more accommodation. Obviously something more was needed for the churchgoers at Swinton, Lancs., than the small chapel of 1791; and the opportunity was taken of building a really fine new church, from plans by Street. Sometimes the motive was purely ecclesiological—the desire to build a noble, beautiful, and expensive church in place of one that was said to be—and probably was—humble and utilitarian. Toddington, Glos., had an old church, the body of which was rebuilt in 1723 by the Rt. Hon[ble] Thomas Charles Lord Viscount Tracy. This was superseded by the present magnificent church, designed by Street, which was

[1] See pp. 232–7 below.

begun in 1869, and not completely finished for ten years: the cost was
£44,000. In building a church like this, there was, obviously, no
calculation of the number of sittings needed, and of the cost per sitting:
the population of Toddington is now given as 359. The idea was
simply to build as good a church as possible. It was, of course, assumed
that the Family would always be there, and could be relied on to pay
for the upkeep. It is sad to see the Hanbury–Tracy pew at Toddington
deserted, and it is difficult to see how churches like this are to be maintained in the future. But we are glad that they exist, and we can
forgive the sacrifice of their eighteenth-century predecessors. In other
cases, forgiveness is more difficult—when quite a distinguished
Georgian church disappeared to make room for a rather ordinary
Gothic Revival one—as at Shalford, Surrey, or Hints, Staffs. But
there is nothing that can be done about it, and we must accept the
Victorian substitutes, which are already beginning to acquire a historical value of their own.

A list is also given in the appendix[1] of some of the places in which,
when a new church was built, the eighteenth-century one was left
standing. Most of these survivals are now in a derelict state, and it is
hard to see any future for them.

THE DEMOLITION OF EIGHTEENTH-CENTURY
CHURCHES

For many years before the end of the century, the move outwards
to new suburbs had been going on, and the streets from which the
Georgian town churches had drawn their congregations were becoming commercial, seedy, or really slummy. Many churches were pulled
down, and the sites were sold; new churches were, of course, built
elsewhere with the money.

In the City of London, St James's, Duke Place, and St Martin
Outwich were taken down in 1874. Liverpool lost St George's in 1897,
and St John's and St Paul's in 1898. In Manchester, St Clement's, St
Thomas's, St John's, St Mary's, and St Paul's were demolished. And
the massacre has continued in this century. St Peter le Poer disappeared
from the City in 1907; and St Alphage's, London Wall, followed in
1923, and St Catherine Coleman in 1925.

In 1900 Charles Booth visited St Olave's, Southwark. He wrote:

[1] See pp. 238–9 below.

St Olave's is a stately old-fashioned Georgian building, with great fluted columns carrying roof and galleries. It is fitted with pews even in the galleries. Below they are very high, and some are of the old-fashioned square pattern. The centre aisle is wide and was set out with benches. It was a chilly Sunday morning in February, and no one had yet come. The gas was burning to warm the air. Later, I found a congregation of six adults, with some charity children, seated in the aisle.[1]

The church lingered on, always locked, until 1926, when it was pulled down.

St Peter's, Liverpool, was taken down when it was no longer needed as a pro-cathedral, and St Peter's, Manchester, came down in 1907.

St Mary's, Birmingham, was demolished in 1925. St Bartholomew's was closed in 1935, and later destroyed in a raid. St John's, Deritend, after a period of degradation as a manufacturer's store, was also pulled down.

St Paul's, Leeds, went in 1905. St James's was taken down after the Second World War; and Holy Trinity has been threatened.

St Paul's, Sheffield, a very handsome eighteenth-century church, would have made as good a cathedral as St Philip's, Birmingham; but the diocese has preferred to spend thousands of pounds on enlarging the less convenient St Peter's; and St Paul's was removed in 1939. St James's was bombed, and has been taken down.

What is to be done with down-town churches? There is room in every large town for at least one church with a non-parochial congregation, and special services on weekdays; but not for several. To pull down the unwanted buildings, and to sell the sites for large sums, is obviously tempting. But it is sad to see the centre of so many towns becoming almost churchless, and there can be little doubt that too many churches have been sacrificed. The almost casual way in which so many churches have been taken down contrasts oddly with the care that has been taken to preserve and catalogue their parish books in the local record offices.

And, from the point of view of church study, it leaves a serious gap. It is difficult to appreciate the church building achievements of a particular period if the churches are no longer there. Even their furniture has been dispersed: there may be a pulpit in one suburban church, and an organ case in another; but no attempt has generally been made to keep the furnishings together. And the absence of eighteenth-century churches in so many places gives encouragement to those who still

[1] Charles Booth, op. cit., Vol. IV, 1902, pp. 171-2.

believe that Georgian Churchmen were lazy, and did nothing much in the way of building. It may be an effort to look at the shopping centre of Anytown, and to remember that here were once houses where families lived, and that where Woolworth's or Marks and Spencer's now stands there was a church, with pews and galleries that were filled by the families Sunday after Sunday. But so it was; and the enlightened Churchman should try not to forget it.

APPENDIX I

THE ALLOTMENT OF SEATING

West Woodhay, Berks., may serve as an example. After the church had been rebuilt, the seats were allotted, and the arrangement is given in a petition to the Archdeacon of Berkshire, dated February 1717–18.[1]

Imprimis   ON THE NORTH SIDE OF THE SAID CHURCH

William Sloper's Servants   Numb: 1
Henry Durnford, for the Farm   Numb: 2

Widow Wats
William Stockdale   for their
William Ryman   Lease &   } Numb: 3
Cottagers   Copy-holds

ON THE SOUTH SIDE OF THE SAID CHURCH

The Rector   for the Parsonage
Laurence Green   Hatch House Farm   } Numb: 1
—Fairchild   & Knights Copyhold

Thomas Mundy   for Blandys &
Andrew Twitchin   the Malthouse Farms   } Numb: 2

Cartwright Prosser   for their
John Rawlins   Copy Holds   } Numb: 3

Henry Osborne
Edwd. Noyes   for their Copy
Thomas Thatcher   & Lease Holds   } Numb: 4
John Harvy

THE SERVANTS OF THE SAID PARISH:

The Men on the Benches on the north side of the Tower—
The Maid Servants on the Benches on the South Side of the Tower.
The Male Children of those who pay no Scot or Lot in the said parish with the Men Servants.

[1] Oxford archdeaconry papers in the Bodleian, c. 161, f. 402.

The female Children of those who pay no Scot or Lot, with the Maid Servants of the sd Parish.

Dan: Bevan Rector ibidem
Henry Durnford ⎫
Cartwright Prosser ⎬ Churchwardens
John Rawlins ⎭
Edward Fairchild
Laurence Green

APPENDIX II

ACTS OF PARLIAMENT CONCERNED WITH
CHURCH BUILDING

The following is a list of 18th-century Acts connected with Church building.

Stat. 9. Annae, c. 22, 1710. An Act for granting to Her Majesty several Duties upon Coals, for building fifty new Churches in and about the Cities of London and Westminster, and other Purposes therein mentioned.

Stat. 10. Annae, c. 11, 1711. An Act for enlarging the Time given to the Commissioners appointed by Her Majesty, pursuant to an Act granting to Her Majesty [as before] . . . and also for giving the said Commissioners further Powers for better effecting the same; and for appointing Moneys for rebuilding the Parish Church of St Mary Woolnoth in the City of London.

Stat. 12. Annae, St. I, c. 17, 1713. An Act to vest in the Commissioners for building Fifty new Churches . . . as much of the street near the May Pole in the Strand in the County of Middlesex as shall be sufficient to build one of the said Churches upon . . .

Stat. 1. Georgii I, St. II, c. 23, 1714. An Act for making Provision for the Ministers of the Fifty new Churches . . . ; and for rebuilding and finishing the Parish Church of St Mary Woolnoth, in the said City of London.

Stat. 4. Georgii I, c. 5, 1717. An Act for finishing the Tower of the Parish Church of St Michael, Cornhill, London, out of the Duties arising pursuant to the Act of the ninth year of the late Queen, for building Fifty new Churches . . .

Stat. 4. Georgii I, c. 14, 1717. An Act to empower the Commissioners . . . to direct the Parish Church of St Giles in the Fields, in the County of Middlesex, to be rebuilt, instead of one of the said Fifty new Churches.

Stat. 5. Georgii I, c. 9, 1718. An Act . . . for establishing certain Funds to raise Money, to proceed in the building of new Churches . . .

Stat. 13. Georgii I, c. 35, 1726. An Act for establishing a certain Provision for maintaining the Curate of the Parish of St Catharine Cree Church, alias Christ Church, London, and for repairing and supporting the Chancel of the said Parish Church.

Stat. 2. Georgii II, c. 16, 1729. An Act to make the Chapel of Ease of the Holy and Undivided Trinity in the Town of Leeds, in the County of York, a perpetual Cure and Benefice; and for defraying some Expenses in finishing the said Chapel, yet remaining unpaid.

Stat. 3. Georgii II, c. 19, 1730. An Act for providing a Maintenance for the Minister of the new Church near Bloomsbury Market, in the County of Middlesex; and for making more effectual an Act passed in the fourth year of His late Majesty's Reign, for empowering the Commissioners for building the fifty new Churches, to direct the Parish Church of St Giles in the Fields, in the said County, to be rebuilt, instead of one of the said fifty new Churches.

Stat. 4. Georgii II, c. 20, 1731. An Act for rebuilding the Parish Church of Gravesend in the County of Kent, as one of the fifty new Churches . . .

Stat. 5. Georgii II, c. 4, 1732. An Act for rebuilding the Parish Church of Woolwich in the County of Kent as one of the fifty new Churches . . .

Stat. 6. Georgii II, c. 8, 1733. An Act for rebuilding the Parish Church of Saint George the Martyr in the Borough of Southwark, in the County of Surrey, as one of the fifty new Churches . . .

Stat. 8. Georgii II, c. 27, 1735. An Act for rebuilding the Parish Church of Saint Leonard, Shoreditch, in the County of Middlesex.

Stat. 9. Georgii II, c. 22, 1736. An Act for rebuilding the Parish Church of Gainsburgh in the County of Lincoln.

Stat. 11. Georgii II, c. 5, 1738. An Act for taking down and rebuilding the Church of the Parish of All Saints in the City of Worcester.

Stat. 11. Georgii II, c. 21, 1738. An Act to empower the present Trustees under the last Will and Testament of John Marshall, Gentleman, deceased, to lay out a certain Sum of Money, now in their Hands, for pulling down and rebuilding the Parish Church of Christ Church in the County of Surrey . . .

Stat. 11. Georgii II, c. 23, 1738. An Act to explain and amend an Act passed in the eighth year of His present Majesty's Reign, intituled, "An Act for rebuilding the Parish Church of St Leonard, Shoreditch, in the County of Middlesex".

Stat. 12. Georgii II, c. 4, 1739. An Act to enable the Inhabitants of the Parish of St Nicholas, in the City of Worcester, to raise Money for discharging the Debts they have contracted in rebuilding their Parish Church.

Stat. 12. Georgii II, c. 7, 1739. An Act to enable the Parishioners of the Parish of Ealing, in the County of Middlesex, to raise Money by Rates upon themselves for finishing the Church of the said Parish.

Stat. 12. Georgii II, c. 9, 1739. An Act for applying a Sum of Money given by the Will of Daniel Wiseman, Esquire, deceased, for finishing the new Church at Woolwich, in the County of Kent . . .

Stat. 12. Georgii II, c. 17, 1739. An Act to enable the Parishioners of the Parish of St Catharine Coleman, in Fenchurch Street, in the City of London, to rebuild the Church of the said Parish.

Stat. 14. Georgii II, c. 5, 1741. An Act for making the Chapelry of Nether

Knutsford, in the Parish of Rosthern and County of Chester, a separate and distinct Parish, and for erecting a Parish Church therein . . .

Stat. 14. Georgii II, c. 15, 1741. An Act for finishing and completing the Parish Church of Gainsborough in the County of Lincoln.

Stat. 14. Georgii II, c. 27, 1741. An Act to enable the Parishioners of the Parish of Saint Botolph, without Aldgate, in the City of London and County of Middlesex, to rebuild the Church of the said Parish.

Stat. 15. Georgii II, c. 12, 1742. An Act to explain and amend an Act passed in the twelfth year of His present Majesty's Reign, intituled, "An Act to enable the Parishioners of Saint Catharine Coleman, in Fenchurch Street, in the City of London, to rebuild the Church of the said Parish . . ."

Stat. 16. Georgii II, c. 28, 1743. An Act to make the Hamlet of Bethnal Green in the Parish of St Dunstan, Stepney, in the County of Middlesex, a separate and distinct Parish, and for erecting a Parish Church therein.

Stat. 18. Georgii II, c. 3, 1745. An Act to enable the Parishioners of the Parish of Saint Margaret, within the Borough of King's Lynn, in the County of Norfolk, to raise Money by Rates upon themselves, for finishing the Church of the said Parish.

Stat. 19. Georgii II, c. 15, 1746. An Act for enabling the Inhabitants of the Hamlet of Bethnal Green, in the County of Middlesex, to complete their Church . . .

Stat. 20. Georgii II, c. 27, 1747. An Act for founding and building a Chapel in Wednesfield, in the Parish of Wolverhampton, in the County of Stafford.

Stat. 21. Georgii II, c. 24, 1748. An Act for building a Church in the Town of Liverpool, in the County Palatine of Lancaster . . .

Stat. 24. Georgii II, c. 15, 1751. An Act to enable the Parishioners of the Parish of St Mary, Islington, in the County of Middlesex, to rebuild the Church of the said Parish.

Stat. 24. Georgii II, c. 37, 1751. An Act for dividing the Parish of Saint Philip and Jacob in the County of Gloucester and in the City and County of Bristol; and for erecting a Church in the new intended Parish.

Stat. 26. Georgii II, c. 38, 1753. An Act to enable the Parishioners of the Parish of Stone, in the County of Stafford, to rebuild the Church of the said Parish.

Stat. 26. Georgii II, c. 45, 1753. An Act for building a new Church within the Town of Manchester, in the County Palatine of Lancaster.

Stat. 26. Georgii II, c. 58, 1753. An Act for building a Chapel on the Common, in the Parish of Portsea, in the County of Southampton . . .

Stat. 26. Georgii II, c. 94, 1753. An Act to enable the Owners of Houses and Lands in the Parish of Saint Botolph Without, Aldersgate, and the Inhabitants thereof, to repair the Church and Steeple belonging to the said Parish.

Stat. 28. Georgii II, c. 34, 1755. An Act for erecting and building a new Chapel in the Town of Wolverhampton in the County of Stafford.

Stat. 29. Georgii II, c. 75, 1756. An Act for completing and finishing a new Church and laying out and inclosing a Cemetery thereto, in the Island of Portland.

Stat. 29. Georgii II, c. 89, 1756. An Act for rebuilding the Parish Church, and enlarging the Churchyard, of Saint John of Wapping, in the County of Middlesex.

Stat. 1. Georgii III, c. 38, 1760. An Act for repairing the Parish Church of Croydon, in the County of Surrey.

Stat. 3. Georgii III, c. 49, 1762. An Act for taking down the Parish Church of Saint Andrew, in the City of Canterbury; and for building a new Church in a more convenient place.

Stat. 5. Georgii III, c. 65, 1765. An Act for rebuilding the Parish Church of Allhallows on the Wall, in the City of London , , ,

Stat. 6. Georgii III, c. 63, 1766. An Act for the Support and Preservation of the Parish Church of Folkestone, and the lower part of the Town of Folkestone, in the County of Kent.

Stat. 6. Georgii III, c. 75, 1766. An Act to render more effectual an Act passed in the last Session of Parliament, for rebuilding the Parish Church of Allhallows on the Wall, in the City of London . . .

Stat. 7. Georgii III, c. 69, 1767. An Act for rebuilding the Parish Church of Saint Martin, within the City of Worcester.

Stat. 7. Georgii III, c. 74, 1767. An Act for enlarging the Term and Powers granted by two Acts of Parliament of the third of King George the First, and the eleventh of His late Majesty, for enabling the Parishioners of Saint Mary, Rotherhithe, in the County of Surrey, by certain Funeral Rates therein mentioned, to finish the said Parish Church . . .

Stat. 7. Georgii III, c. 80, 1767. An Act for enlarging the Term and Powers granted by an Act of the second year of the reign of His present Majesty, for erecting and building two new churches, and providing Burial Places, in the Town and Parish of Liverpool, in the County Palatine of Lancaster.

Stat. 9. Georgii III, Sess. 2, c. 60, 1769. An Act to enable Edward Byrom, Esquire, to complete a Building intended for a new Church, in the Town of Manchester . . .

Stat. 9. Georgii III, Sess. 2, c. 61, 1769. An Act for raising Money to discharge Debts contracted for rebuilding the Parish Church and Tower of Saint Nicholas, in the City of Bristol; and to rebuild the Spire; and for other purposes.

Stat. 9. Georgii III, Sess. 2, c. 85, 1769. An Act for building a Chapel at Plymouth Dock, in the Parish of Stoke Damerell, in the County of Devon.

Stat. 10. Georgii III, c. 112, 1770. An Act for building a new Parish Church, and declaring the present Parish Church a Chapel; for making a Cemetery or Churchyard; and for building an House for the use of the Minister of the Parish of Saint Mary le Bone, in the County of Middlesex.

Stat. 12. Georgii III, c. 36, 1772. An Act for completing a Building intended for a new Church or Chapel at Richmond, near Everton, in the County Palatine of Lancaster, and for other purposes.

Stat. 12. Georgii III, c. 40, 1772. An Act for amending and rendering more effectual an Act, made in the tenth year of His Majesty's Reign, intituled, An Act for building a new Parish Church [in St Mary le Bone].

Stat. 12. Georgii III, c. 64, 1772. An Act for building two new Chapels, and providing Burial Places thereto, within the Town of Birmingham, in the County of Warwick.

Stat. 14. Georgii III, c. 12, 1774. An Act for vesting a piece of waste Ground within, and parcel of, the Manor of Clapham, in the County of Surrey, in Trustees, and for enabling them to build a new Parish Church thereon.

Stat. 14. Georgii III, c. 93, 1774. An Act for rebuilding the Church of the Parish of Lewisham, in the County of Kent.

Stat. 14. Georgii III, c. 94, 1774. An Act for establishing a new Church or Chapel erecting at Toxteth Park, in the Parish of Walton, near Liverpool, in the County Palatine of Lancaster.

Stat. 14. Georgii III, c. 95, 1774. An Act for rebuilding the Parish Church of Battersea, in the County of Surrey . . .

Stat. 15. Georgii III, c. 49, 1775. An Act for taking down the Church of All Saints, in the Town of Fulbourne and County of Cambridge, and for the better repairing and keeping in Repair the Church of Saint Vigors in the said Town.

Stat. 17. Georgii III, c. 32, 1777. An Act for building a new Church within the Town and Parish of Buckingham.

Stat. 18. Georgii III, c. 9, 1778. An Act for taking down the Parish Church of Lilford, being a Vicarage united to the Rectory of Achurch, in the County of Northampton, and for repairing the Parish Church of Achurch afore-said . . .

Stat. 20. Georgii III, c. 15, 1780. [An Act repealing part of the Act for St Marylebone.]

Stat. 21. Georgii III, c. 76, 1781. An Act for building a new Church and Rectory House within the Parish of Escrick, in the County of York . . .

Stat. 25. Georgii III, c. 94, 1785. An Act for repairing, new pewing, seating, and erecting Galleries, and making other Alterations and Additions in and to the Parish Church of Kidderminster, in the County of Worcester.

Stat. 25. Georgii III, c. 95, 1785. An Act for rebuilding the Parish Church of Christ Church, otherwise the Holy Trinity, within the City of Bristol . . .

Stat. 26. Georgii III, c. 54, 1786. An Act for enabling the Right Honourable Edmund Earl of Cork and Orrery, in the Kingdom of Ireland, and Baron Boyle of Marston, in England, to pull down the present Parish Church of Marston Biggott, otherwise Marston Bygood, in the County of Somerset, and for building a new Parish Church there.

Stat. 26. Georgii III, c. 117, 1786. An Act for pulling down and rebuilding the Church of All Saints, in the Town of Newcastle upon Tyne . . .

Stat. 27. Georgii III, c. 17, 1787. An Act for rebuilding the Chapel of East Stonehouse, in the County of Devon.

Stat. 27. Georgii III, c. 49, 1787. An Act for dividing the Parish of Saint James, in the City and County of Bristol, and County of Gloucester, and for building a Church . . .

Stat. 27. Georgii III, c. 62, 1787. An Act for taking down and rebuilding the Chapel of Hanley, in the County of Stafford . . .

Stat. 27. Georgii III, c. 63, 1787. An Act for rebuilding the Church of the Parish of Saint Mary Wanstede, alias Wanstead, in the County of Essex.

Stat. 27. Georgii III, c. 64, 1787. An Act for building a new Chapel upon Portsmouth Common, in the Parish of Portsea, in the County of Southampton.

Stat. 28. Georgii III, c. 10, 1788. An Act for pulling down the Church of Saint James at Clerkenwell, in the County of Middlesex, and for building a new Church . . .

Stat. 28. Georgii III, c. 62, 1788. An Act for pulling down and rebuilding the Parish Church of Saint Peter le Poor, within the City of London . . .

Stat. 28. Georgii III, c. 74, 1788. An Act for rebuilding the Parish Church of Paddington, in the County of Middlesex . . .

Stat. 28. Georgii III, c. 83, 1788. An Act for repairing the Church of the Parish of Saint Paul, Covent Garden, in the County of Middlesex.

Stat. 29. Georgii III, c. 11, 1789. An Act to enable Mary Alsager, Margaret Alsager, and Judith Alsager, to finish and complete a new Church or Chapel, in the Parish of Barthomley, in the County of Chester, and to endow the same.

Stat. 29. Georgii III, c. 14, 1789. An Act for amending an Act of the twenty-seventh year of His present Majesty [for rebuilding Wanstead church].

Stat. 29. Georgii III, c. 30, 1789. An Act to amend and enlarge the Powers of an Act, passed in the last Session of Parliament [for repairing St Paul's, Covent Garden].

Stat. 29. Georgii 3, c. 31, 1789. An Act for rebuilding the Parish Church of Saint Chad, in the Town of Shrewsbury, and County of Salop . . .

Stat. 29. Georgii III, c. 47, 1789. An Act for providing an additional Burial Ground for the Parish of Saint James, Westminster, and erecting a Chapel adjoining thereto . . .

Stat. 30. Georgii III, c. 20, 1790. An Act for rebuilding the Parish Church and Tower of Saint Thomas within the City of Bristol.

Stat. 30. Georgii III, c. 64, 1790. An Act for establishing a Chapel at Ramsgate, in the Parish of Saint Lawrence, in the Isle of Thanet, in the County of Kent, as a Chapel of Ease to the Church of the same Parish.

Stat. 30. Georgii III, c. 69, 1790. An Act for amending and enlarging the Powers of, and rendering more effectual, an Act made in the twenty-eighth year of the Reign of His present Majesty [for rebuilding Clerkenwell church]; and for purchasing Pentonville Chapel, and making the same a Chapel of Ease to the said Church.

Stat. 30. Georgii III, c. 70, 1790. An Act to amend an Act of the last Session of Parliament [for the burial ground and chapel for St James's, Westminster].

Stat. 30. Georgii III, c. 71 (1), 1790. An Act for taking down the Church and Tower belonging to the Parish of St John at Hackney, in the County of Middlesex, and for building another Church and Tower . . .

Stat. 30. Georgii III, c. 72, 1790. An Act for taking down the Church, Chancel, and Tower belonging to the Parish of Banbury, in the County of Oxford, and for rebuilding the same.

Stat. 30. Georgii III, c. 79, 1790. An Act for rebuilding the Parish Church of East Grinstead in the County of Sussex.

Stat. 31. Georgii III, c. 71, 1791. An Act for taking down and rebuilding the Parish Church of All Saints, within the Town and County of the Town of Southampton . . .

Stat. 31. Georgii III, c. 73, 1791. An Act for repairing the Parish Church of Saffron Walden, in the County of Essex.

Stat. 31. Georgii III, c. 74, 1791. An Act for building a new Church in the Town of Wakefield, in the West Riding of the County of York . . .

Stat. 31. Georgii III, c. 75, 1791. An Act for enlarging the Powers of an Act, passed in the twenty-ninth year of the Reign of His present Majesty [for rebuilding St Chad's, Shrewsbury].

Stat. 32. Georgii III, c. 30, 1792. An Act for taking down the Church, Chancel, and Tower belonging to the Parish of Saint Mary Magdalen, in Bridgnorth, in the County of Salop, and for rebuilding the same . . .

Stat. 32. Georgii III, c. 39, 1792. An Act to enable the Inhabitants of the Parish of Saint Botolph Without, Aldersgate, in the City of London, to raise Money for paying and discharging the Debts that have been contracted in repairing their Parish Church . . .

Stat. 32. Georgii III, c. 64, 1792. An Act for repairing, altering, and improving the Parish Church of Saint Bridget, otherwise Saint Bride, in the City of London . . .

Stat. 32. Georgii III, c. 76, 1792. An Act for building a new Church or Chapel within the Town and Parish of Liverpool, in the County Palatine of Lancaster.

Stat. 32. Georgii III, c. 87, 1792. An Act to enable the Dean and Chapter of Hereford to rebuild the west end of the Cathedral Church of Hereford, and to repair other parts thereof.

Stat. 32. Georgii III, c. 88, 1792. An Act for rebuilding the Chapel, and enlarging the Chapel-yard, of Lane End, within the Parish of Stoke-upon-Trent, in the County of Stafford.

Stat. 32. Georgii III, c. 89, 1792. An Act for building a new Church or Chapel in the Town of Leeds, in the West Riding of the County of York.

Stat. 33. Georgii III, c. 43, 1793. An Act for enlarging the Powers of, and rendering more effectual, an Act made in the twenty-eighth year of the Reign of His present Majesty [for rebuilding Paddington church].

Stat. 33. Georgii III, c. 45, 1793. An Act for taking down and rebuilding the Tower of the Parish Church of Hanbury, in the County of Worcester, and for repairing the said Church, and rendering the same more commodious for the Parishioners.

Stat. 33. Georgii III, c. 101, 1793. An Act for amending and enlarging the Powers of an Act, made in the thirty-first year of the reign of His present Majesty [for rebuilding All Saints', Southampton].

Stat. 34. Georgii III, c. 88, 1794. An Act for taking down and rebuilding the Parish Church of Tipton, otherwise Tibbington, in the County of Stafford . . .

Stat. 35. Georgii III, c, 47, 1795. An Act for taking down the Chapel of the Chapelry of Haydon, in the Parish of Warden, in the County of Northumberland, and for building a new Chapel, in a convenient situation within the said Chapelry.

Stat. 35. Georgii III, c. 70, 1795. An Act for amending an Act passed in the thirtieth year of the Reign of His present Majesty [for rebuilding Hackney church].

Stat. 35. Georgii III, c. 71, 1795. An Act for building a new Church or Chapel in the Town of Halifax, in the West Riding of the County of York.

Stat. 35. Georgii III, c. 73, 1795. An Act for dividing and inclosing the open common Fields within the Hamlets of Upper Eatington, and Fulready, in the Parish of Lower Eatington, in the County of Warwick, and for taking down and rebuilding the Church of the said Parish.

Stat. 36. Georgii III, c. 35, 1796. An Act to enable the Trustees for executing an Act passed in the thirty-second year of the Reign of His present Majesty [for repairing St Bride's] to raise a further sum of Money for completing the Purposes of the said Act.

Stat. 36. Georgii III, c. 65, 1796. An Act for rebuilding the Parish Church of Saint Paul, Covent Garden, within the Liberty of Westminster, in the County of Middlesex ...

Stat. 36. Georgii III, c. 103, 1796. An Act for rebuilding the Parish Church of Saint Martin Outwich, in Threadneedle Street within the City of London.

Stat. 37. Georgii III, c. 43, 1797. An Act for building a new Chapel at Plymouth Dock, in the Parish of Stoke Damarel, in the County of Devon.

Stat. 37. Georgii III, c. 55, 1797. An Act for taking down and rebuilding the Parish Church of Milbrooke, in the County of Southampton ...

Stat. 38. Georgii III, c. 35, 1798. An Act to alter and enlarge the Powers of an Act passed in the twenty-seventh year of the Reign of His present Majesty [for building a new church in the parish of St James, Bristol].

APPENDIX III

SOME EXAMPLES OF BRIEFS

(1) Shropshire was a county in which there was a good deal of repairing and rebuilding in the eighteenth century, and the Quarter Sessions records (in the County Record Office) contain many accounts of petitions for briefs. Here are some examples.

In July 1709 it was "Ordered that a Certificate be drawn & delivered to the Lord Chancellor under the hands of the Justices of the Peace for the County for the Repaireing & Rebuilding of Adderley Steeple in this County and it is hereby Ordered accordingly". The tower was rebuilt in 1712–13.

In April 1714 George Grice, mason, Thomas Adams, carpenter, John Wynn, smith, and John Holland, plumber and glazier, gave their evidence about Hinstock church. It appeared that it was ruinous and out of repair, and that the parishioners were unable to rebuild it, and it was ordered that a certificate for a brief be granted.

January 1721–2: £535 had been spent in the last eleven years on Newport church: the cost of rebuilding would be £2000—on the oath of George Gryce and Edward Hodson, masons, and Mathias Sherman and Thomas Cooper, carpenters.

April 1731: Abdon church was very ruinous in the roof, walls, and steeple, and must be taken down and rebuilt. The charge, on the oath of William Poyner and Richard Poyner, carpenters, and Richard Lawley and Thomas Burgesse, masons, would by a moderate computation be £503 15s.

July 1731: Beckbury church must be rebuilt, "the Charge whereof upon the Examination upon Oath of Stephen Powell mason and James Wedge carpenter by a moderate computation is £500:14:9:".

January 1733–4: Eyton church must be rebuilt. The estimate was £587, sworn to by Edward Hodson and William Parsons, masons, and Francis Hamersley, John Shelton, and Thomas Davies, carpenters.

The same workmen gave evidence about Longdon upon Tern church. A further brief was granted in 1738–9, and the church was rebuilt in 1743.

April 1742: a brief was sought for rebuilding Battlefield church: no details are given.

January 1782: a petition stated that "The Parish Church of Drayton in Hales in this County is a very ancient Structure and greatly decayed in many Parts thereof . . . The Truth of the Premises hath been made appear to us this day in open Court not only by the said Inhabitants of the Parish of Drayton in Hales aforesaid but also upon the Oath of Richard Baker an able and experienced

Architect who has carefully viewed the said Church and made an Estimate of taking down repairing and rebuilding the same which upon a moderate Computation amounts to the Sum of two thousand one hundred and sixty four Pounds and upwards exclusive of the old Materials." A further brief was asked for in July 1786. The north wing had been taken down and rebuilt; the south wing had been taken down and must be rebuilt; and the whole body of the church and the galleries must be new pewed before divine worship could with safety be performed therein. There remained a deficiency of £1667 to complete the work. The truth was made to appear on the oath of Thomas Harding.

July 1784: Lee Brockhurst church needed to be rebuilt. The estimate was stated to be £634 14s, on the oath of Richard Baker of High Fields in the parish of Audlem in the County of Chester. The brief was issued next year.

April 1786: Stapleton church was out of repair and must be rebuilt. The truth of the premises was made to appear by John Carline and William Harris; their estimate was £1300.

July 1789: Madeley church must be rebuilt. Jonathan Scoltock gave evidence.

October 1789: the chapel of Weston must be rebuilt, and Jonathan Scoltock had made an estimate of £1000. The brief had little result, and the cost of rebuilding in 1791 was met chiefly by Sir Richard Hill.

St Mary Magdalene, Bridgnorth, needed rebuilding in January 1790. John Asprey had estimated the charge at £5735 13s 9d. In 1795 a further brief was applied for, as £5455 16s 1¼d was still needed.

A further petition for Adderley was presented in January 1793. The walls on each side were more than 15 in. out of the perpendicular, and the roof was so weak that it would not bear to be covered with slate or tile. The church was ruinous and decayed in every part, except for the tower. It must be rebuilt: Richard Baker's estimate was £1248 18s 6d, exclusive of old materials.

The brief brought in only £114 11s 8¼d, and a further brief was granted in January 1795. In October 1799 another one was granted, as the previous collection only amounted to £127 2s 11d. The rebuilding of the body of the church began in 1801, and a further petition for a brief was presented in July 1802. In October 1809, when another was asked for, it was stated that the estimate could not be produced owing to the death of Mr Baker the architect.

April 1793: Joseph Bromfield estimated the cost of rebuilding Church Aston at £1469, exclusive of old materials. A further brief in 1799.

January 1799: Cheswardine church needed rebuilding. "Also the roof and floor of the tower are so ruinous that they must be made new, and the parapet Wall must be taken down and rebuilt, being now in a dangerous state." The truth was made to appear by Richard Baker, whose estimate was £1155 17s 6d, exclusive of the old materials, which were of little or no value. There were further briefs in 1804, 1809, and 1813.

October 1800: Child's Ercall was in decay: it must be rebuilt and the tower repaired. Richard Baker estimated the cost at £875 15s. Further briefs were granted in 1806 and 1811.

(2) Here are some from Leicestershire: the sessions records are in the County Record Office.

1758: a petition from Lutterworth. The walls and roof were much out of repair, and the steeple must be rebuilt. The charge would be £1162. The estimate survives among the Sessions records in the County Record Office. It is dated 3 October 1758, and signed by John Wagstaff and Robert Sanders.

July 1759: "It appearing to this Court that the Parish Church of ffrowlesworth in this County is by Length of time brought into a ruinous Condition the Tower thereof being on three sides cracked from Top to Bottom one of the Buttresses So Mouldered and Decayed that it is in Great part tumbled down and the Inhabitants considered it absolutely necessary to take down the Bells Sometime ago and that the parishioners cannot Assemble therein to perform Divine Service Without Manifest Danger of their Lives So that the Tower together With the Spire can no longer be Supported but must be wholly taken down and rebuilt which upon a Moderate Computation will amount to the Sum of one Thousand one hundred and Eighty three pounds ten Shillings . . .", what else could the Court do but request a brief?

Carlton and Packington were dealt with in January 1761. Carlton was a very ancient structure, and the roof and greatest part of the walls of the chancel were fallen down; the foundation, walls, and roof of the body of the church were ruinous, and so was the steeple. The brief, for £1102 17s 3d, was issued at Michaelmas. The Packington brief was issued at the same time—for £1013 to enable the roof and parts of the walls to be taken down and rebuilt.

April 1763: Foston was in danger of falling, and divers able and experienced workmen estimated the cost of rebuilding at £1150.

July: Divers able and experienced workmen had estimated the cost of unspecified work at Ratby at £1886 14s 6d.

October: Shackerstone was in a ruinous condition, and part of the steeple, and the whole of the north and south aisles, must be taken down and rebuilt; and there must be an entire new roof. The estimate was £1274 18s 8d.

There were three cases in May 1764. At Claybrook "The North and South Isles the Roof and Coping of the Middle Isle and the Roof and Coping of the Tower thereof with other parts of the said Middle Isle and Tower and the Arch between the Tower and Church are greatly decayed". A brief for £1119 2s 6d was granted (but only £165 was raised).

The body of Croft church must be taken down and rebuilt, and the steeple was very much out of repair. The estimate for rebuilding the body and repairing the steeple was stated to be £1102 13s 2d—on the oath of Noble Reeve, architect and master builder, and Richard Biddle and John Swinton, plumbers and glaziers. The brief was issued at Michaelmas 1765.

Kilby had been surveyed by John Westley, master builder, and other able and experienced workmen, who had made an estimate of £1070 19s 4d for rebuilding. The brief was issued at Easter 1766.

In October 1766 Market Bosworth presented their petition. The greatest part of the steeple, and a great part of the walls of the body of the church, must be rebuilt; the middle and south aisles must be entirely new roofed, and the rest must be considerably repaired. This was stated on the oath of John Wyatt, John Balm, Thomas Underwood, John Simpson, and John Yeomans, whose estimate was £1076 12s 2d.

April 1767: Great Sheepy: the roof, the parapet wall round the whole body of the church, and the south aisle, must be taken down and rebuilt, and the other parts repaired. William Parker, Joseph Baker, and Benjamin Harris made an estimate of £1108 8s 8d; but the brief (Michaelmas 1768) was for £1048 8s 8d.

A year later, George Rawlinson and John Wyatt gave evidence that Shenton must be rebuilt at a cost of £1010 19s 8½d.

John Wyatt also gave evidence, with John Mills, in January 1768 that Hugglescote church needed rebuilding: their estimate was £1027 18s 7d.

October 1770: Broughton Astley: the steeple must be taken down and rebuilt, the body of the church wanted new roofing, and the walls were greatly out of repair. The estimate was £1009 15s—by Samuel Cooper, mason, William Taylor, plumber, and John Bray, carpenter.

There were four in 1771. January: Ibstock: it appeared "That the North Isle of the said Church must be entirely taken down and rebuilt the Middle Isle thereof entirely new roofed and that several Other parts of the Body of the said Church and also several parts of the Steeple are greatly out of Repair." John Wyatt and John Mills, master builders, had made an estimate of £1021 5s 6d. The brief was issued at Easter 1772.

April: Kincote: a large part of the steeple had fallen down, and damaged the west end of the church. John Wooton and Benjamin Button, master builders estimated the cost of repair at £1092 13s 6d.

July: Leir steeple was very much out of repair, and the walls and roof of the body must be rebuilt. Samuel Cooper, mason, John Bray, carpenter, and William Taylor, plumber, had made an estimate of £1013 2s 8d.

October: The roof, part of the north and south walls, and the steeple of Sharnford must be rebuilt. The estimate of £1033 8s 11d was made by William Cotton, Gabriel Nixon, and Thomas Bray.

October 1775: Earl Shilton needed largely rebuilding at a cost of £1019 17s 8¾d.

Thurlaston gave more details in April 1776. The outward wall of the south aisle, the southward wall, pillars and arches of the middle aisle, and the battlement walls round the body and the tower, required to be rebuilt. The whole of the body needed reroofing; and the outward wall of the north aisle was to be raised 6 ft. or more, "to render the roof thereof durable and lasting". A new staircase to the tower was needed, and so were many other considerable repairs. The estimate was £1061 10s 8d.

In April 1777 Benjamin Harris gave an estimate for rebuilding Higham on the Hill (£1034 3s 4d).

(3) A petition for a brief for Alcester was presented at Quarter Sessions at Warwick at Easter 1727. The church must be rebuilt, at an estimated cost of £460 and upward. The estimate was made by Samuel and John Rogers and Thomas Hunt, carpenters, Anthony Smith, Samuel Fenimore, and John ?Ryan, masons, the old Benjamin Smith, Benjamin Smith the younger, and Joseph Smith, plumbers and glaziers, and Jos. Hall, joiner.

Quarter Sessions, Trinity 1720, issued "A Lycense for the Inhabitants of the parish of Barston in the County of Warwick" (in margin, "to continue one year") "to request the Inhabitants of this County for the repaires of the parish Church of Barston the roof thereof being fallen & the Inhabitants thereof not being able to repaire the same and the charges thereof amounting to 300^l & upwards & that there has been 12^d in the pound levy received for repaire of the s^d Church, notwithstanding the same hath fallen & hath cost yearly great sume of money towards repairs of the same this appeares upon the oath of Tho ffisher of Barston." A further appeal was made in 1721.

A petition for a brief was made at Quarter Sessions on 14 January 1734. It stated that "Saint John's Chappell in Deritend in the parish of Aston juxta Birmingham in the County of Warwick being a very antient building is become ruinous and decayed and great part thereof is fallen down and the remainder must be entirely taken down and rebuilt . . . The charge of which amount unto the sume of 1643:12:6 . . . by the Oaths of Jonathan Johnsons and Samuel Rowe Carpenters and Samuel Avery and John Willinger Bricklayers able and experienced workmen who have Carefully and Dilligently examined the truth of the premises and made estimates of the Charges of rebuilding the same . . .".

On 15 April 1735, Nuneaton was shown to be an ancient and large fabric supposed to have been built at least 500 years. It needed to be repaired and partly rebuilt. The cost "as appears from the Estimate and by the Oaths of Thomas Baxter Edward Kingston John Chaplin William Robinson and William Hewson able and Experienced Workemen who have Carefully View'd and Examined the said Church" would amount to £1050 and upwards.

The case of Polesworth came up at Epiphany 1737. The church must be rebuilt: the cost—£1063 and upwards—was estimated by Thomas Moore and John Banks, carpenters, Henry Baker and Thomas Austin, masons, and William Hewson, plumber.

APPENDIX IV

NINETEENTH-CENTURY TREATMENT OF
EIGHTEENTH-CENTURY CHURCHES

In Oxfordshire, to take a typical county, Chislehampton and Wheatfield were left alone, and a new church was built to take the place of Nuneham Courtenay. Hailey, St Peter le Bailey, Oxford, Shifford, and Wheatley disappeared. The rest were restored as follows.

Ardley: the nave, rebuilt in 1791–2 by the Duchess of Marlborough, was reseated in 1865. "The little Church quite pretty now", wrote Bishop Wilberforce.

Baldon Marsh: the eighteenth-century north aisle was rebuilt when the church was restored by Somers Clarke in 1890.

Banbury: S. P. Cockerell's church, consecrated on 5 September 1797, was not appreciated by the ecclesiologists. Parker wrote, "Such a building may have been well-enough adapted for the exhibitions of gladiators or of wild beasts in ancient Rome, but it is totally unfit for a Christian Church." It was restored by Blomfield. 1863, nave decorated (Heaton, Butler, and Bayne), pews lowered, and pulpit moved. 1873, chancel arch removed, internal apse built, and roof raised to the level of the nave. Choir formed, organ moved, and floor of the chancel raised. Walls decorated, new font. New pulpit 1885.

Bladon: rebuilt in 1802–4 by the Duke of Marlborough. Entirely remodelled by Blomfield in 1891–2.

Cuxham: a countrified church, rebuilt of old materials early in the eighteenth century. It was restored by C. C. Rolfe in 1895, and a chancel was added.

Godington was rebuilt in as plain a manner as possible in 1792. The rector had a design made for a new E.E. church by J. C. Sharpe, but was unable to raise enough money. In 1852 he abandoned the plan, and spent about £100 in altering the eighteenth-century church. The windows were altered to lancets, and the interior was refitted.

Hampton Gay, a tiny and remote church, was rebuilt in 1767. It was gothicized, apart from the tower, in 1859. The plans were made by the incumbent, the Reverend F. C. Hingeston, and carried out by George Wyatt of Oxford.

Upper Heyford: partly rebuilt in 1769, and entirely rebuilt by T. T. Bury in 1866–7.

North Leigh: the aisle built by James Perrott was left. The chancel, "modernised in the Italian style", was de-Italianized when Street restored the church in 1864–5.

Mongewell: Morris and Stallwood restored the church in 1880–1. Bishop Barrington's Gothic extension at the west was left, but his other work was removed, and the chancel was restored to a Norman appearance. (The church fell into ruin in this century: the chancel has been recently repaired, and the monuments have been moved into it.)

Oxford, All Saints': the interior was refitted by T. G. Jackson in 1896.

Sarsden: 1740, attached to the house; enlarged by George Repton in 1823. Restored in 1899 by W. E. Mills of Banbury: two galleries removed; new paving, seating, and pulpit.

Shenington: the north walls of the nave and chancel, and the east wall of the chancel, which had been rebuilt in the eighteenth century, were again rebuilt when Pearson restored the church in 1879.

Souldern: chancel rebuilt 1773, and again by Bucknall and Comper in 1896.

Spelsbury was partly rebuilt in 1774. Restored in 1886. Most of the eighteenth-century work has been removed, but the transepts and aisles have ends of this date. The chancel was gothicized.

Stoke Talmage was rebuilt in 1758. It was mostly rebuilt by Scott in 1860: aisle, vestry, porch, and buttresses were added, the ceiling was removed, and the interior was restored and refitted.

Waterstock: mostly rebuilt in 1792, and completely restored by Street in 1858.

Wendlebury: poorly rebuilt in 1761–2. Reseated in the nineteenth century, and restored by J. O. Scott in 1902.

Weston on the Green: 1743; restored in 1885, when the windows were given tracery.

Woodstock: the north aisle, rebuilt from plans by John Yenn in 1783, was rebuilt by Blomfield in 1878. Teulon's more exciting scheme for restoring the church did not come off. Stephen Townsend's tower was left. Alfred Rimmer, in *Pleasant Spots round Oxford*, protested against the restoration and the removal of the box pews.

APPENDIX V

NINETEENTH-CENTURY REPLACEMENTS OF EIGHTEENTH-CENTURY CHURCHES

In many parishes a completely new church took the place of the eighteenth-century one. The following list gives a few examples.

BEDFORDSHIRE

Souldrop: a very good church by Henry Clutton, taking the place of one that was rebuilt in 1800.

BERKSHIRE

Midgham: 1869, by John Johnson, in place of the church of 1714.

Twyford: 1846–7, by Benjamin Ferrey, on a different site from that of the old chapel opened in 1728. This was taken down in the '80s, and a school built on the site.

West Woodhay: a new church by Blomfield 1882–3 on a new site: the church of 1716 was pulled down.

BRISTOL

Bristol, St Andrew the Less: (Dowry Chapel) 1746, by George Tully; new church by J. Neale 1873.

  St George's: 1752, by Samuel Glascodine; new church by Philip E. Masey opened 8 May 1880.

BUCKINGHAMSHIRE

Colnbrook chapel was consecrated in 1794; new church by Ferrey 1852.

Eton: 1769, rebuilt 1819–20. It was superseded by the church designed by Ferrey and built in 1852–4.

Kingsey: 1780–2, was superseded in 1892–3 by a church "more substantial in its structure and more ecclesiastical in its appearance", designed by H. W. Moore of Oxford.

CAMBRIDGESHIRE

Knapwell: 1866, by W. M. Fawcett, in place of a church rebuilt in 1785.

Wendy: 1735; new church 1867 by R. R. Rowe.

CHESHIRE

Wallasey: rebuilt in the eighteenth century (brief 15 February 1757). A new church was built on a different part of the same churchyard; consecrated 28 July 1859.

CUMBERLAND

Alston: rebuilt 1768, and again in 1869–70.

Cockermouth: rebuilt 1711, and enlarged later; burned, and a new church built by J. Clarke: consecrated 1852.

Workington: rebuilt in 1772; rebuilt after a fire in 1887.

Wreay: 1739; new church 1842, designed by Sarah Lash of Woodside.

DERBYSHIRE

Atlow: new church by I. H. Stevens 1874, on a different site from the eighteenth-century one, which was taken down.

Derwent: the church of 1757 was removed, and a new church built in 1867 by W. White. (It is now submerged in the Ladybower Reservoir.)

DEVONSHIRE

Ivybridge: 1799; foundation stone of a new church on a different site 8 June 1881; architects Hine and Odgers.

Withycombe Raleigh: the old chapel was taken down in 1745 and rebuilt; new church by E. Ashworth 1863, and the chapel demolished in 1865.

DURHAM

Bishop Auckland, St Anne's chapel: 1781; demolished 1847; new church by A. Salvin.

Wolviston: 1759; demolished; new church on a different site by Austin and Johnson, 1876.

ESSEX

Canvey Island: consecrated 9 November 1875, in place of a church rebuilt in 1745.

Pleshey: the eighteenth-century church was rebuilt in 1868 by F. Chancellor.

GLOUCESTERSHIRE

Toddington: 1723; new church by G. E. Street begun 1869–71, completed 1879.

HAMPSHIRE

Hursley: the church of 1752–3 gave way in 1866 to a new one by J. P. Harrison.

Southampton, St Mary: nave rebuilt in 1711, chancel in 1723; new Church by Street 1879–84.

HERTFORDSHIRE

Ayot St Peter: 1751; demolished 1862: new church built. Struck by lightning in 1874, and a new church on a different site by J. P. Seddon.

HUNTINGDONSHIRE

Waresley: rebuilt 1728 "in humble imitation of the Chapel at Pembroke College". A new church by Butterfield was built on a different site in 1856.

KENT

Shipbourne: 1722, by J. Gibbs; new church 1881 by Mann and Saunders.

LANCASHIRE

Altcar: consecrated 1747; new church 1879 by J. Douglas.

Bolton, All Saints: 1726, consecrated 1743; new church by Street 1871.

Bradshaw: rebuilt 1775; rebuilt 1872 by E. G. Paley.

Crompton (Holy Trinity, Shaw): rebuilt 1739, and 1870 (R. W. Drew).

Great Crosby: rebuilt 1774; new church of St Luke 1854. The eighteenth-century church was demolished in 1864, though the tower stood until 1880.

West Derby: rebuilt in the eighteenth century; new church by Scott 1853–6.

Field Broughton: consecrated 30 June 1745; rebuilt 1893–4 by Paley and Austin.

Finsthwaite: 1724; rebuilt by Paley and Austin in 1874.

Flookburgh: 1777–8; new church by Paley and Austin 1897–1900.

Garston: rebuilt 1715–16: new church by J. L. Pearson 1876–7.

Gorton, St James: rebuilt 1755; and 1871 by G. and R. Shaw.

Grimsargh: 1726; rebuilt 1868 by Paley and Austin.

Hollinwood, St Mary: consecrated 8 July 1769: rebuilt 1879 by R. Knill Freeman.

Liverpool, St Anne: under an improvement act of 1867, the church of 1772 was demolished, and a new one built east of the old site from designs by Robson, architect and surveyor to the Corporation.

Longton: rebuilt 1770, and again in 1887: architect J. E. K. Cutts.

Manchester, St Clement: 1793; St Clement's, Greenheys, by H. R. Price, takes its place.

    St George: opened 1798. Rebuilt on a different site (in the Oldham Road) in 1877.

    St Paul: consecrated July 1785. Rebuilt in 1878 at New Cross by J. O. Scott; part of the materials was used.

Milnrow: 1798; new church by G. E. Street 1869.

Mossley, St George: 1757. Rebuilt in 1882 by A. H. Davies-Colley.

Oldham, St Peter: begun in 1765, consecrated 2 June 1768. Rebuilt in 1901—architects Wild, Collins, and Wild.

Padiham: rebuilt 1766. Rebuilt again by William Waddington in 1869.

Pilling: a new church by Paley and Austin, 1883, took the place of the eighteenth-century church.

Swinton: consecrated 23 July 1791; new church by G. E. Street consecrated 2 October 1869; the eighteenth-century church was taken down in 1870.

LINCOLNSHIRE

Flixborough: 1789; rebuilt 1886 by C. Hodgson Fowler.

Fosdyke: rebuilt 1756, and again in 1870–2.

Lincoln, St Mark, rebuilt 1788; new church by W. Watkins 1871–2.

St Martin: 1739–40; a new church on a different site 1876, by Beckett of Nottingham.

St Michael on the Mount: rebuilt 1744; new Church by S. S. Teulon 1854.

St Paul in the Bail: foundation stone of the rebuilt church—by John Barnard—30 January 1786; new church by Sir A. W. Blomfield 1877–9.

St Peter in Eastgate: rebuilt 1778–81; new church by Blomfield 1869–70.

St Swithin: 1801–2 by Hayward; new church by Fowler of Louth 1871 and subsequent years.

Nocton: 1775; new church by Scott 1862.

Revesby: rebuilt 1739; new church by C. Hodgson Fowler 1891.

Spridlington: by Fowler, consecrated 1875, in place of the eighteenth-century church.

High Toynton: rebuilt 1772, and 1872—by Ewan Christian.

Woolsthorpe: 1791–2; new church 1845–7 by G. G. Place of Nottingham.

LONDON, SOUTH

Newington: the new church, by Fowler of Louth, was finished in 1875 on a new site. The eighteenth-century church was pulled down, but a chapel of ease—St Gabriel's, by Cutts—was afterwards built on the site.

MIDDLESEX

Ashford: by Butterfield, 1858, in place of the eighteenth-century church.

Hanwell, St Mary: 1841, by Scott and Moffatt, in place of the eighteenth-century church.

OXFORDSHIRE

Hailey: a new church was built in 1868 (C. C. Rolfe architect), and the church of 1761 was pulled down except for a fragment of the west end.

Oxford, St Peter le Bailey: new church by Basil Champneys, begun in 1872, eighteenth-century church demolished in 1874.

Shifford: rebuilt 1780; new church by J. Clarke 1863.

Wheatley: consecrated in 1795. A new church, on another site, by G. E. Street, was consecrated in 1857.

SHROPSHIRE

Meole Brace: new church 1867–9 by Edward Haycock.

SOMERSET

Bath, St Michael: the eighteenth-century church was superseded by a new one, designed by G. P. Manners, in 1835–7.

STAFFORDSHIRE

Great Barr: a new church by Griffin of Wolverhampton took the place of the eighteenth-century church in 1860.

Lichfield, St Mary: tower and spire were rebuilt by G. E. Street in 1852, and the church in 1868–79 by J. Fowler.

Mucklestone: 1883, by Lynam and Rickman, in place of the eighteenth-century church.

Newcastle-under-Lyme: rebuilt by William Smith in 1720; new church by Scott 1873–6.

SURREY

Cheam: it was decided to build a new church in 1862: the architect was F. H. Pownall. The eighteenth-century church was taken down: the Lumley Chapel, which had not been rebuilt in the eighteenth century, was left.

Felbridge: a new church by William White, 1864–5, took the place of the one built in 1787.

Roehampton: the chapel was rebuilt in 1777; new church by Ferrey. This was disused when the new church by Fellowes Prynne was built; it was finished in 1898.

Shalford: the church of 1788–90 (a "great domed hideousness", according to the *Ecclesiologist*) was demolished, and a new church built from plans by Ferrey in 1847.

Titsey: 1776; Pearson's church—1861—took its place.

WARWICKSHIRE

Sherbourne: the fine church by Scott was built in 1862–4. The old church, rebuilt in 1747, with chancel of 1802, was demolished.

YORKSHIRE, EAST RIDING

Escrick: 1781; new church by F. C. Penrose 1856-7.

YORKSHIRE, NORTH RIDING

Bagby: 1751; new church by E. B. Lamb opened 1 June 1862.

Thirkleby: another church by Lamb in place of an eighteenth-century predecessor.

YORKSHIRE, WEST RIDING

Bishopsthorpe: rebuilt in 1768, and again by C. Hodgson Fowler in 1900.

Bramley: rebuilt 1732; new church by Perkin and Backhouse opened 1863.

Chapel Allerton: "a neat structure in the Corinthian style"; demolished; new church by Bodley 1897-1900 on a different site.

Dean Head (Scammonden): brief 1799: the rebuilding was accomplished in 1805; new church 1865 by E. W. Tarn.

Drighlington. c. 1783; new church 1876-8.

Farnley: 1761; new church, by Chorley and Connon, 1885.

Gildersome: the former church was consecrated on 29 August 1787. It was burned down in 1873; new church by Adams and Kelly.

Horsforth: 1720-1; new church by J. L. Pearson begun on a different site in 1877; faculty for demolition of the eighteenth-century church 1884.

Hunslet, St Mary: much enlarged in 1744; new church, partly on the same site, by Perkin and Backhouse, 1862-4.

Marsden: rebuilt 1758; new church on a different site by C. Hodgson Fowler 1896.

Wortley, St John: 1787; new church 1896-8 by T. H. Farrar.

This list is far from complete; but it may help to explain why the church-building accomplishments of the eighteenth-century are so easily forgotten.

APPENDIX VI

SOME ABANDONED EIGHTEENTH-CENTURY CHURCHES

In some parishes a new church was built, but the eighteenth-century church was left.

BEDFORDSHIRE

Segenhoe: the mainly eighteenth-century church is now in a state of dereliction. A new church was built at Ridgmont, from designs by Scott, in 1854-5.

ESSEX

Kelvedon Hatch: rebuilt 1750-1. A new church 1895, by J. T. Newman, but the older one remains.

Mistley, by Wadmore and Baker 1871. Adam's two towers remain from the eighteenth-century church.

HAMPSHIRE

Blendworth: the faculty for building a new church was given on 23 March 1759. This curious little building was left when the new church was built in 1850-1 by W. G. and E. Habershon.

Dogmersfield: the rebuilding of the old church was suggested in 1800, and it was finished in 1804. It remains, quite dismantled. New church by Ferrey, some distance away, 1843.

Emsworth: 1840, by Elliott of Chichester. The chapel of 1790 was kept, though desecrated.

Kingsley keeps its attractive old church, mainly rebuilt in brick in 1778. A new church was built in the village in 1875-6.

South Tidworth: 1784; a new church was built in 1880, and the former was turned into a mortuary chapel. It was pulled down later—in 1892.

LANCASHIRE

Tarleton: 1719; new church 1886 by W. Bassett Smith.

OXFORDSHIRE

Nuneham Courtenay: a faculty was given in 1872 for demolishing the church of 1764 and building a new one on a different site. The new church was built; but the eighteenth century one kept as a private chapel.

SHROPSHIRE

Bicton: new church 1886 by A. E. Lloyd Oswell. The former church was disused.

Jackfield: the church of 1759 is derelict; new church 1863, by Blomfield.

SOMERSET

Bath, St Andrew's, by Scott, was built to take the place of Margaret chapel, which was sold by auction in 1871, and used for various purposes.

SURREY

Long Ditton: Street's church of 1880 stands beside the remains of Sir Robert Taylor's church of 1776—which has mostly been removed, but the floor and part of the walls remain: enough to remind one of what it was like.

WARWICKSHIRE

Alveston: a new church was consecrated in 1839. The 18th-century chancel has been left standing.

WORCESTERSHIRE

Finstall: a new church was built in 1883, and the humble brick church rebuilt in 1773, near the railway, has been left to decay.

Lower Mitton: the old church, enlarged in 1790, is disused; a new church (J. O. Scott, architect)—"a building in every way fitted for the worship of God"—was built in 1881.

Upton on Severn: rebuilt in 1756–7 by John Willoughby of Upton, under Richard Squire of Worcester. The tower was given a cupola by Anthony Keck in 1770. A big, dull church by Blomfield was built in 1878–9, and the eighteenth-century church gradually fell into ruin. At last it was demolished down to the cills of the lower windows, and filled up to make a garden—fit to be illustrated on a Calendar of Great Thoughts. The tower and cupola are standing.

YORKSHIRE, NORTH RIDING

Aislaby: rebuilt 1732; new church 1897. The old building was converted into a parish hall in 1915.

Brotton in Cleveland: a new church in 1888–91 by W. S. Hicks. The church of 1778 was allowed to survive.

High Worsall: rebuilt *c.* 1710. A new church was built in 1894, and the old used as a mortuary chapel.

YORKSHIRE, WEST RIDING

Lightcliffe: was rebuilt in 1775; new church 1873–5 by W. Swinden Barber.

INDEX OF PERSONS

1. GENERAL

2. ARCHITECTS, ARTISTS, CRAFTSMEN AND WORKMEN

INDEX OF PLACES AND PARISHES